Ben E. Swearingen is a colle  War II memorabilia. A middl cipal he lives with his family n. Lewisville, Texas.

The Mystery of
HERMANN GOERING'S SUICIDE

Ben E. Swearingen

ROBERT HALE · LONDON

Robert Hale Limited
Clerkenwell House
Clerkenwell Green
London EC1R 0HT

ISBN 0-7090-4244-2

Printed in Great Britain by
St Edmundsbury Press Limited, Bury St Edmunds, Suffolk
and bound by WBC Bookbinders Limited

To Gloria, Sharon, and Stephen,
in the hope that they will forgive
the "too busy" husband and father

CONTENTS

ILLUSTRATIONS

DRAMATIS PERSONAE

Col. Burton C. Andrus: commandant of the Nuremberg prison. Though he was absolved of negligence by the army's investigation of Goering's suicide in 1946, Andrus was personally attacked by some segments of the press. He went to his grave believing himself responsible for Goering's escape from the gallows.

Erich von dem Bach-Zelewski: SS general. Bach-Zelewski testified for the prosecution during the trials. In 1951 he told U.S. Army authorities that he had given the poison to Goering.

Dr. Werner Bross: an associate of Dr. Stahmer, Goering's defense counsel. Bross believed he knew who gave Goering the poison; however, he said nothing until many years later.

Maj. Gen. William ("Wild Bill") Donovan: wartime chief of the Office of Strategic Services (OSS), the forerunner of the CIA. He made a "deal" with Goering in order to induce him to testify against Hitler at the trials.

Chaplain Henry Gerecke: Lutheran minister from Missouri, chaplain to Goering and the other Protestant defendants during the trials. The Russians suspected him of giving Goering the poison.

Dr. Gustave M. Gilbert: prison psychologist. Although Goering and Gilbert hated each other, Colonel Andrus harbored dark suspicions about the psychologist's role in Goering's suicide.

Emmy Goering: Hermann Goering's second wife. Many thought she had transferred the poison to her husband during a last kiss. However, she had her own idea of how he got the poison.

Hermann Goering: Nazi Reichsmarschall, commander in chief of the Luftwaffe, and Hitler's designated successor. His suicide, less than two hours before he was scheduled to hang, created an international furor and all but wiped out the hoped-for psychological effect of the trials.

Col. B. F. Hurless: officer, Third Army Headquarters. He was sent to Nuremberg to witness the executions. After Goering's suicide, Colonel Hurless was appointed chairman of the three-man Board of Officers that investigated Goering's death.

Justice Robert H. Jackson: chief prosecutor for the United States during the trials. He came off a poor second best during his verbal duels with Goering.

Dr. Douglas M. Kelley: psychiatrist during the early months of the trials. His admiration for Goering, coupled with his own strange death some years later, made many believe he had given the poison to Goering.

Gen. Georgi Malkov: Soviet member of the Quadripartite Commission, the four-power commission responsible for the detainment of the major war criminals. He was skeptical of the claim that no one had secretly given Goering the poison after he was imprisoned.

Gen. Pierre Morel: French member of the Quadripartite Commission. He praised Colonel Andrus's security regulations and accepted the Board of Officers' finding that Goering had always had the poison.

Franz von Papen: defendant at Nuremberg Trials. Acquitted. He later claimed that an American guard had offered him poison.

Brig. Edmund Paton-Walsh: British member of the Quadripartite Commission. He strongly supported the Board of Officers' conclusion that no one had smuggled Goering the poison.

Dr. Ludwig Pfluecker: German POW officer and doctor in the Nuremberg prison. He regularly saw Goering and the other defendants and was the last to visit Goering's cell before the suicide.

Brig. Gen. Roy V. Rickard: American member of the Quadripartite Commission. He appointed the officers of the board and ordered them to "affix responsibility" for Goering's suicide.

Maj. Stanley T. Rosenthal: member of the Board of Officers. He belonged to the 6850th Internal Security Detachment under the command of Colonel Andrus.

Lt. Charles J. Roska: U.S. Army officer and doctor in the Nuremberg prison. He examined Goering's corpse. The Board of Officers ignored his statement that Goering could not have hidden the poison in his navel.

Dr. Otto Stahmer: Goering's defense counsel. Despite being widely suspected of giving Goering the poison, he was never questioned by the Board of Officers.

Capt. Robert Starnes: chief prison officer. He told the Board of Officers that Goering's cell toilet was inspected on a regular basis. Despite Starnes's testimony, the board concluded that the poison had been hidden in the toilet.

Maj. Frederic C. Teich: prison operations officer. Only shortly before Goering's death, Teich told reporters that suicide precaution in the prison was "so good that it could not be improved upon."

Col. William H. Tweedy: member of the Board of Officers. He belonged to the 6850th Internal Security Detachment. Many years later, he refused to discuss Goering's suicide with me.

Lt. Jack G. "Tex" Wheelis: prison officer and "good friend" of Colonel Andrus's. Throughout much of the trial, Wheelis wore a wristwatch that had belonged to Goering and bragged of his friendship with the Nazi Reichsmarschall.

Lt. Jean Paul Willis: officer of the guard on the night that Goering killed himself. He never forgot the sight of a Russian general slapping the dead Goering in the face. Thirty-five years later, Willis still insisted Goering never put his hands beneath the blankets on the night of his death.

Lt. Gerald R. Wilson: an officer of the 26th Infantry, the regiment from which much of the guard personnel was drawn. Wilson believed he knew who gave Goering the poison but was told by one of the prison officers that he should keep silent.

PREFACE

On the morning of July 7, 1981, I stepped into the Nuremberg prison cell where former Nazi Reichsmarschall Hermann Goering committed suicide nearly thirty-five years before. Less than two hours before he was scheduled to hang as a convicted war criminal, Goering crushed a tiny vial of hydrocyanic acid between his teeth as a U.S. Army guard helplessly looked on through an aperture in the cell door. Goering died almost immediately. His final and dramatic act of defiance elated many Germans and all but erased the psychological effect the Allies had hoped for in executing Hitler's top henchmen. Goering's suicide also placed the United States Army in a highly embarrassing situation. Despite its best efforts, it had allowed Goering to make good his prediction that he would never hang.

The cell was extremely small. As I walked through the door, my shoulders nearly brushed the frame. The massive Goering, I thought, must have had to turn sideways every time he entered or left his cell. The tiny cubicle looked much the same as it had in 1946. Immediately inside and in a recessed alcove to the right was a toilet. It was not the toilet Goering had used but a more modern replacement. A small wooden table stood against the right wall. Above the table, the present occupant of Goering's cell had pasted *Playboy* centerfolds, the only jarring contrast to the cell's former appearance. There was a window in the end wall but so high and recessed that one would have to stand on a chair to look out. Along the left wall and bolted to the floor was a simple metal cot. It was the same cot on which Goering died. It was, the prison director told me, the only thing in the cell that had been there in 1946.

The director was wrong. Unknown to him, in my pocket was the metal container that had held the poison vial Goering used to kill himself. It had been found in an envelope clutched in his lifeless hand. Now, after nearly thirty-five years, it was once again in the death cell.

How, after so many years, had the metal container come into my possession? Why had I brought it back to the scene of Goering's suicide? The answers to these questions are the latest links in the fascinating chain of its history.

In April 1977 I was contacted by an individual who had read in the newspapers about my purchase of a silver vase that had belonged to Goering. This gentleman wrote that he owned the metal container that held the poison vial with which Goering had killed himself. Further, he said he also had the glass vial from the backup capsule Goering had hidden in a jar of skin cream. Though I knew such items had been found after Goering's death, I was, at first, skeptical of these claims. Nevertheless, I answered his letter, asking for details.

Further correspondence revealed that this individual's father, a former U.S. Army officer, deceased for some years, had indeed been in the right place at the right time to have procured the souvenirs. The documentation provided to me left no doubt in my mind; my correspondent did have the metal capsule and the glass vial. After much time and the exchange of many letters and telephone calls, the two items came into my possession.

At first I was content to accept the brass container for what it was: an object of some historical interest. Then I began wanting to know more of its history. I found out that these self-destruction devices had been developed and manufactured on orders from SS *Gruppenfuehrer* Arthur Nebe and were originally intended for issue to German secret agents. In 1944 approximately 950 of these devices were sent to Hitler's Berlin headquarters for distribution to senior state and party officials who might prefer suicide to capture. Goering undoubtedly procured his capsules at this time.

Each glass vial contained 1 cc of hydrocyanic acid. The diameter of the vial was approximately 9 mm, and the length about 35 mm. Spent rifle shells had been fashioned into protective casings resembling small lipstick tubes. Modified cartridge casings had also been used for the 9-mm-long caps that were designed to be pushed down over the lower cases. An expansion groove was cut into the caps to provide for a snug fit. These suicide devices were manufactured in the notorious Sachsenhausen concentration camp under the supervision of trusted

SS officers. The hydrocyanic acid that killed Goering was itself synthesized by a concentration camp inmate, a Dr. Kramer.

I learned all this, but such meager information was no longer sufficient. I also realized I was not the first to be curious about the history of the brass cartridge in my possession. The Board of Officers that had investigated Goering's suicide had an equal curiosity, though inspired by a different motive. I decided to acquire from the National Archives a copy of the formerly classified "Report of Board of Proceedings in Case of Hermann Goering (Suicide) October 1946." Soon I had the full and official transcript of the 1946 U.S. Army inquiry into the suicide of Goering.

Initially, I looked through the report for specific information on the brass cartridge and the glass vial from the backup capsule, but my interest was soon drawn to other aspects of it. I found myself flipping back and forth through the pages, making notes, and checking the sworn testimony of one witness against that of another. Gradually, I began to realize that the army's explanation of how Goering managed to kill himself was not nearly as convincing as I had previously believed and that I had long accepted certain misconceptions as the truth. Slowly but surely, as I read the report questions arose, questions that the board had not answered. It was then I decided to put my thoughts on paper. Little did I realize I was beginning a project that would take years to complete and that would result in a book challenging the conclusions the United States Army had reached in 1946.

It is not the purpose of this book to cast gratuitous aspersions on the United States Army and those officers who conducted the investigation into Goering's suicide. Indeed, it was with great reluctance that I was finally forced to conclude that the army, subject to both internal and external pressures and considerations, had refused to consider the possibility that Goering had been given the poison by someone within the prison shortly before his death. The army's reasons for not doing so may have had some validity in 1946. However, there is no reason now why the full truth about Goering's suicide cannot be told. This I have attempted to do.

Hermann Goering is long dead. Why resurrect the almost forgotten subject of his suicide? Does the method by which he procured the poison really matter any longer? I fully realize that to many it makes no difference at all. But it was not for them that this book was written. It was written for those whose curiosity continues to be intrigued by the unexplained mysteries of history. If those readers find in the pages of this book the answer to the riddle of Goering's suicide, that is for me enough reason for having written it.

THE MYSTERY OF
HERMANN GOERING'S SUICIDE

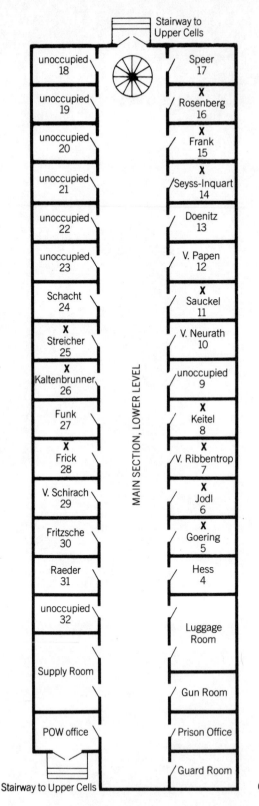

Stairway to
Upper Cells

unoccupied 18		Speer 17
unoccupied 19		**X** Rosenberg 16
unoccupied 20		**X** Frank 15
unoccupied 21		**X** Seyss-Inquart 14
unoccupied 22		Doenitz 13
unoccupied 23		V. Papen 12
Schacht 24		**X** Sauckel 11
X Streicher 25		V. Neurath 10
X Kaltenbrunner 26		unoccupied 9
Funk 27		**X** Keitel 8
X Frick 28		**X** V. Ribbentrop 7
V. Schirach 29		**X** Jodl 6
Fritzsche 30		**X** Goering 5
Raeder 31		Hess 4
unoccupied 32		Luggage Room
Supply Room		Gun Room
POW office		Prison Office
		Guard Room

MAIN SECTION, LOWER LEVEL

Stairway to Upper Cells

Bottom floor of the prison wing in Nuremberg jail where Goering and the other defendants were held. After sentences were pronounced on October 1, 1946, those not sentenced to death were moved to the second floor. The condemned (in cells marked **X**) remained in the cells they had occupied throughout the trial.

Feet
0   5   10

1

Visits with a Dead Man

The prison cell was too small to allow its occupant the luxury of pacing back and forth, so Hermann Goering sat on the edge of his metal-frame bunk, nervously drumming his fingers on his thighs and tapping the toes of his riding boots on the stone floor. He glanced up at the American soldier peering at him through the aperture in the heavy wooden door and smiled sheepishly. The cell guard returned the smile. He knew this September day of 1946 was a special one for the man he kept under constant observation. After a separation of seventeen months, Goering was again to see his wife.

Finally, heavy footsteps were heard in the long corridor outside the row of cells. Goering's escort guard had come to take him to the visitation room where Emmy Goering was already waiting. He arose from his bunk, smoothed the folds in his now baggy and faded uniform, and automatically extended his right arm so that he might be hand-cuffed to the guard's left wrist. Once out of the cell, Goering all but dragged his escort down the hall in his eagerness to reach the visitation room. "See," he quipped to the guard, "I am still a leader." The guard laughed, as he often did in response to one of Goering's jokes, and quickened his own step.

Entering the room where he was to meet with his wife, Goering was steered to one of the small partitioned cubicles that had been used by the defendants to consult with their lawyers. He took his seat next

1

to that of the escort guard and through a divider of wire mesh and glass saw his wife sitting on the other side. Emmy Goering, too, was flanked by an American GI, and behind her stood one of the American prison chaplains. Knowing that any attempt on his part to make physical contact with his wife—even placing his open hand against hers on the screen—was forbidden and would cause the immediate termination of the visit, Goering resisted his natural impulse. Instead, he sat looking at his wife for a moment.

The once-heavy and always stylishly dressed Emmy Goering had changed drastically since the last time he had seen her. Though she had taken great pains to look her best for the meeting, the many months of her own imprisonment and deprivation had taken their toll; she looked tired and thin. Goering did not know that the dress and pair of shoes his wife was wearing were the only ones she possessed, nor did he know that she and their young daughter had no home of their own and were often cold and hungry. Emmy Goering had deliberately withheld any distressing news from the letters she had been permitted to write him, and it was her intention to do the same during the visits.

Goering was overjoyed to see his wife again. Not wishing to waste even a minute of the time allowed them in the coming weeks, he immediately advised her: "Write down everything you wish to ask and tell me. I will do the same. Otherwise, one will forget too much of importance in such a short time." Frau Goering, still overcome with emotion, nodded her head.

It was not easy for Emmy Goering to speak; the presence of the American guards at first inhibited her. But her husband was bursting with questions about friends and relatives. The first person he asked about was Edda, their eight-year-old daughter. In his cell was a treasured photograph of her, on the back of which she had written in her childish hand: "Dear Daddy, come back to me again soon. I have such longing for you. Many thousand kisses from your Edda!!!" He was assured that all was well with his daughter but that she still missed him terribly. Frau Goering told her husband of the many funny things that Edda had done and said, and he laughed heartily as each incident was recounted. Goering then asked his wife about her own welfare, and she evasively told him she was being looked after by "friends." The truth would have surprised Goering. Few of their former friends were in a position to help anyone, and many now treated her as a pariah. Most of the help she received came from friendly Americans and those émigré Germans—many of whom were Jewish—who had returned to Germany, often in the uniform of the United States Army, to prepare the trials of those who had persecuted them.

The thirty-minute visit concluded all too swiftly, and Frau Goering watched helplessly as her husband was led back to his cell by the guard. The ordeal of the visit had totally exhausted her, but she was happy believing her efforts had given her husband some respite from his own misery.

They met again several times over the next few weeks, and Edda was once permitted to see her father. Preparing the little girl for the visit, her mother had warned her, "Edda, don't say anything sad and don't cry when you see Daddy. You must remember, that when we leave Daddy we can discuss everything sad, but Daddy will be alone and he has no one with whom he can talk." Edda promised to obey, but when Goering saw his daughter, he broke down in tears. Edda quickly put him in good spirits by asking, "Daddy, when you come home, will you please wear your medals in the bath—like people say you do? I've never seen them all covered with soap. Do they tickle?" Goering laughingly promised he would, and there was much more happy laughter and conversation between father and daughter. Before the visit ended, Frau Goering remembered a request made by Robert Kropp, her husband's longtime and faithful valet: would the Reichsmarschall please write a statement to the effect that his valet had never been a member of the Nazi party? Goering did so without demur, and it may have caused him some amusement to realize that the word of a man in his position was considered by the Allies proof of Kropp's good character. Previously, they had accepted his word on very little else.

The next meeting between Goering and his wife took place on September 29, only shortly before the verdicts were to be announced. Goering had been indicted on four counts: crimes against peace, war crimes, crimes against humanity, and participation in a common conspiracy to commit these crimes. Yet Frau Goering, even at this late date, still had hope. "Don't you believe, Hermann," she asked, "that we three will again be together in freedom?"

Knowing his fate had been decided long before—even if the verdicts had yet to be delivered—Goering shared no such illusions. The smile left his face as he told his wife the harsh truth: "You don't seem to realize that we here have been tried under English justice, and that a new law was coined that applies only to us." Drawing an analogy from history, he quoted Mary, Queen of Scots, who had been tried and condemned to death for sedition in 1587: "Woe to the poor victim, when the same mouth that gave the law also pronounces the judgment." Emmy Goering was still resisting what her husband was trying to tell her. Seeing this, Goering spoke bluntly: "Emmy, I beg you fervently; give up all hope." Finally, she realized that her husband was going to die.

Utterly crushed, Emmy Goering left the prison. During the next few days, she anxiously awaited news of her husband's fate. On October 1 the verdict was delivered and sentence pronounced: Goering was found guilty on all four counts of the indictment and sentenced to hang.

Frau Goering's first duty was to inform her daughter. She took her for a walk in the woods and there told her the terrible news. Edda refused to believe her father really was going to die. "Perhaps a miracle will happen," she suggested. Unwilling to crush the little girl's hopes, Emmy knelt with her daughter in prayer, beseeching God for the miracle that would spare Hermann Goering.

But there was no heavenly intercession, and Frau Goering and Edda spent the next few days psychologically preparing themselves for the worst. Edda sought consolation by imagining that her father, "if he really has to die," would then see in heaven all those departed persons he had loved on earth. "Oh, Mommy, don't be so terribly sad," she said. "Maybe we won't have to live much longer, and then we will soon be with Daddy; and there won't be screen and glass between us up there." Emmy Goering, realizing little Edda was trying to comfort her as much as herself, hugged the child and wept.

Word came to Frau Goering that her husband had asked to see her a final time. "He knows that it will be grievous for himself and his wife," wrote the German prison doctor in his memoirs, "but is prepared to put up with anything if he can see her once more."

On October 7 Emmy went again to Nuremberg, where she stayed in the home of her husband's lawyer. He gave her Goering's wedding ring, which had been entrusted to him at the time of their last meeting. With her husband's ring in her hand, Emmy Goering fought an emotional breakdown. "It was exactly as if I had a remembrance of a man already dead in my hand." But the two had one final hour of life to share.

Goering saw his wife on the afternoon of October 7. The first questions he asked were about his daughter: "How has Edda taken the sentence? Does she know what is going to happen to me?" Frau Goering said the little girl knew her father had to die. When Goering was told of his daughter's wish that she, too, might not live much longer, he replied, "My little Edda, hopefully life will not be too hard on her." Goering told his wife he was not afraid to die. "My God, what a deliverance death would be for me if I only knew that you both were protected. Perhaps I can help you more from the other side than from a cell."

After a moment of silence, Goering asked his wife if she wished him to appeal for mercy. "No, Hermann," she answered. "You may die in peace and with pure conscience. You have done here in Nuremberg all that you can for your comrades and for Germany." Emmy Goering told her husband it had always been her wish to die with him, but she could not now bring herself to leave their daughter alone in the world. "I will do everything to make Edda's life tolerable. Everything! That I promise you. I would otherwise be ashamed before every woman who had lost her husband in the war, yet bravely went on living for the sake of their children." She would always be convinced, she said, that her husband, like other soldiers fallen in battle, had died for Germany.

All the torment left Goering's face as his wife spoke. "I thank you for these words," he said. "You have no idea how much you have helped me with them."

His thoughts again turned to his own fate, and he told his wife that there were, for him, worse things than death. With eyes blazing, Goering said, "I'll tell you what for me was the most terrible thing on the day of sentencing. As we who had been sentenced returned to our cells, I saw before the cells of Schacht, Papen, and Fritzsche, the three who were released by the Allies, German police! German police!! Emmy, imagine that I had been released, and then German police would have come to arrest me. That I could not bear. Believe me, I feel as if delivered that I am permitted to die."

Having accepted the death penalty, Goering spoke bitterly of the court that had decreed it. He angrily told his wife, "These foreigners can murder me, but they have no right to judge me. That I deny them." It was the same sentiment he had expressed throughout the trial.

The strain was growing intolerable, and Frau Goering asked if it would be better if she were to go. "No," Goering answered, "if you can, remain a while longer." They then spoke of their marriage, their child, and of happier times.

The final hour came to an end. As Goering rose from his seat, he raised his left hand. "I bless you and our child. I bless our beloved Fatherland, and I bless everyone who does good to you and our child." In a moment he was gone forever from Emmy Goering's sight.

But he was never gone from her thoughts during those terrible days to come. Over and over, she must have thought of a question she had asked during one of the visits. She had looked at her husband, hand-cuffed like a common criminal and sitting beside the impassive and gum-chewing American GI, and recalled their years together, when he was Germany's popular Reichsmarschall, respected and honored both at home and abroad, wealthy and powerful, a devoted husband and proud father. Her head swam. Uncomprehendingly, she had asked, "Hermann, how has it come to this?"

Goering had opened his mouth as if to answer, but no words came out. Finally, he shook his head. If there had been any one thing in his past that had impelled him down the road to the Nuremberg gallows, it escaped him. Bewildered, he could only shake his head.

2

The Road to Nuremberg

Hermann Wilhelm Goering was born in Rosenheim, Bavaria, on January 12, 1893, the fourth child of Heinrich and Franziska Goering. His mother, who had left her husband at his diplomatic post in Haiti, named her son in honor of Hermann von Epenstein, his godfather, and Kaiser Wilhelm II, the German emperor. But Franziska Goering returned to her husband and three older children in Haiti when her son was ten weeks old, leaving him in the care of family friends. Hermann was not to be reunited with his own family until he was three years old. It was the opinion of biographer Willi Frischauer that Goering, in later life, "was always trying to recapture the mother love which he had missed in his infancy."

Heinrich Ernst Goering, Hermann's father, retired from diplomatic service in 1898 at the relatively youthful age of fifty-six. With little else to do, he began to drink heavily, and slowly his relationship with his wife and family started to disintegrate. However, von Epenstein, who was a wealthy bachelor, moved into the vacuum Heinrich left and invited the Goerings to make their home at Burg Veldenstein, a fortress-castle he owned near Nuremberg. They accepted von Epenstein's offer, and a new and grand life began for Hermann Goering, exploring the battlements of the castle and playing the military games he adored.

Sadly for Hermann, the day came when he was forced to leave his

7

castle behind. He was six years old and had to go to school in Fürth, near Nuremberg. He hated the school immediately. One day, over-come by homesickness, he refused to get out of bed, claiming to be ill. To pass the time—he remained in bed for over four weeks—he played with his toy soldiers. A visitor to his room noted with surprise that Hermann had set up two large mirrors in his bed, one on each side of his soldiers, and asked the reason. Contemptuously, Goering answered, "In this way, I can triple my army. It is obvious that you will never become a general."

During one summer vacation, Goering traveled with his family to Austria, where they stayed with von Epenstein at his home, Mau-terndorf Castle. While there, Heinrich Goering resided in one of the lodges on the grounds, and Frau Goering lived in the main house, acting as hostess at von Epenstein's dinner parties. "In Mauterndorf," wrote Erich Gritzbach, "a new world opened itself to the young Her-mann Goering." He was deeply impressed, not only by the magnif-icence of the castle but even more by his godfather and the grand style in which he lived. Hermann Goering had found his first hero. But his hero was not without flaws. It was common knowledge among visitors to Veldenstein and Mauterndorf that Franziska Goering was von Epenstein's mistress (the Goerings' fifth child, a boy born some seven years after Hermann, was the image of von Epenstein, if reports are to be believed). Despite this relationship, however, Goering never rejected von Epenstein. "Once he had chosen his hero," said someone who knew Goering as a young man, "he would stand by him through thick and thin."

When vacation was over, Goering had to return to school. "If only Fürth would burn down," he wailed and hopefully offered his parents the alternative that he might now "become a soldier." But Goering was once again packed off to Fürth and continued there until he was eleven years old. However, he did so poorly in his studies and rebelled so strongly against authority that he was finally sent to a much stricter school at Ansbach. He hated this school even more than Fürth and ran away after learning from the headmaster—and being ridiculed by the other boys—that his beloved godfather von Epenstein was a Jew.

Goering's departure from Ansbach brought about the fulfillment of his dearest wish: he would attend military school. At twelve he enrolled in the military academy at Karlsruhe, and immediately his problems ceased. He graduated from the academy at sixteen, his final report a glowing one that said he should go far in life because he was "not afraid to take a risk."

From Karlsruhe Goering went to the officer training school at Lichterfelde, near Berlin. He completed his training at nineteen and received a commission in the Prinz Wilhelm Regiment. He told his family and friends, "If war breaks out, you can be sure I'll give a good account of myself and live up to the name of Goering."

Two years later, at twenty-one, Goering welcomed the outbreak of what was to become World War I. In it he proved to be a courageous, capable officer. After concocting a daring scheme to kidnap a French general—though the plan miscarried—Goering was cited in regimental dispatches and awarded the Iron Cross, Second Class, the first of many medals he promised himself he would win. However, he developed rheumatoid arthritis in 1915, and his life in the trenches was over. While recuperating in a hospital, he decided to transfer to the newly formed air force and wrote his commanding officer, asking for an official transfer. After two weeks, having received no answer, he checked himself out of the hospital and made his way—without orders—to Ostend, Belgium, where he became an observer in a plane piloted by his good friend Bruno Loerzer. In June 1915 Goering was sent to the fighter-pilot school at Freiburg and earned an excellent record there. On completing his training, he was assigned to *Jagdstaffel* (fighter squadron) No. 5, a unit operating on the western front. But in spite of his fine training record, Goering quickly became a victim of in-experience: he allowed himself to be ambushed by British fighters as he was intently attacking a slow-flying bomber. Wounded in the thigh and his plane shot-up, Goering managed to crash-land near a German field hospital. Had it not been for this piece of luck, he might have bled to death from his injury.

Goering eventually became a skilled and experienced fighter pilot and by 1917 had seventeen "kills" to his credit. He could have had more, but he never allowed his thirst for glory and medals to give way to senseless hatred for those whom it was his duty to shoot out of the sky. Goering once deliberately spared the life of an enemy pilot whose machine gun jammed in the middle of an encounter. Seeing his opponent helpless, Goering circled close to the enemy aircraft, put his hand to his cap in salute, and broke off the engagement. By May 1918 Goering had downed twenty enemy planes, for which he was awarded the highest decoration a grateful fatherland could bestow, the Ordre Pour le Mérite. Goering's reputation as a flier and leader had so impressed his superiors that they appointed him commander of *Jagdgeschwader* No. 1, as von Richthofen's celebrated Flying Circus was named after the death of its legendary commander. Goering led the squadron well, but the war had already taken a heavy toll of Germany's men and resources. The end was near, both for Germany and the von Richthofen squadron. When the war ended in November 1918 in revolution and turmoil within Germany's borders, the armistice came as a shock and outrage to Goering and his officers, none of whom was ready to give up the fight. Goering was ordered to surrender his squadron to the nearest Allies, but he refused to do so, choosing to fly the planes back to Germany.

Goering and his officers reported to Aschaffenburg, near Frankfurt. There the squadron officially disbanded. But Goering and many of his pilots remained in the city, gathering often in a restaurant where they relived the days of glory and comradeship. Former squadron adjutant Karl Bodenschatz wrote, "In this new, strange, dreadful and defeated Germany, we all felt like aliens and like aliens we clung together. The restaurant was our ghetto, and most of us left it as little as possible." Outside, the officers were set upon by revolutionaries intent on stripping them of their badges of rank and medals. Goering himself had to fight to keep his Pour le Mérite from being snatched off his collar and hurled into the dirt.

Goering eventually left Aschaffenburg and went to Berlin. There, in front of a mass meeting of German officers, he insulted Gen. Hans-Georg Reinhardt, the republic's new minister of war, excoriating him for his support of the revolutionary decrees ordering officers to remove their traditional symbols and rank and replace them with blue stripes on their sleeves. His speech was a tremendous success, but it made Goering a marked man, wiping out any chance he might have had of becoming an officer in the new German army. On that day Goering had cast his lot with those dedicated to the destruction of the German republic.

Disgusted with the situation in Germany, Goering went into self-imposed exile in the Scandinavian countries, where he promoted Anthony Fokker's commercial planes, flying barnstorming tours in Denmark and Sweden. He also ran an air-taxi service using a borrowed plane. In the winter of 1920, during a severe storm, he flew Eric von Rosen from Stockholm to von Rosen's castle at Rockelstadt in central Sweden. At the castle Goering met Carin von Kantzow, his future wife. The two were attracted to each other, and soon Carin, who lived in Stockholm, deserted her husband and moved into an apartment with Goering. The following year Goering left Sweden because of the scandal his alliance with Carin had caused, his lack of a career, and notification from his mother that he had been accepted at the University of Munich. (Carin would soon follow Goering to Germany and live with his mother, then return to Sweden to get her divorce. In 1923 Hermann and Carin married in Munich.)

Goering began his work at the university in 1921, studying history and political science. But he had little in common with the younger students—Goering was then twenty-eight—and spent much of his time attending meetings of the various nationalistic groups that had sprung up in Munich after the war. At one of these meetings, in 1922, the crowd called for Adolf Hitler to speak. But Hitler refused to do so. "It was pure coincidence," Goering said, "that I stood near by and heard the reasons for his refusal. He considered it senseless to launch protests that had no weight behind them. This made a deep impression on me. I was of the same opinion."

A few days later, Goering attended one of Hitler's own meetings and found himself in complete agreement with what Hitler said. "The conviction was spoken word for word as if from my own soul," Goering recalled. It was not Hitler's oratory that won him over but that the

Nazi party was "the only one that had the guts to say 'To hell with Versailles!' while the others were crawling and appeasing." The muddled racial philosophy of the Nazis did not hold much appeal for Goering. "I joined the Party," he said, "precisely because it was revolutionary, not because of the ideological stuff." Goering introduced himself to Hitler after the meeting. The two men were in immediate accord, and Goering told Hitler that he and all he possessed "were completely at his disposal." Later Goering took Hitler's hand and solemnly told him: "I unite my faith with yours. I dedicate myself to you in good times and in bad, even unto death." Hermann Goering had found his second hero.

The timing of the meeting between Hitler and Goering was most fortuitous because Hitler had been looking for a new commander of his Storm Troopers (*Sturmabteilungen,* or SA), the private army of the Nazi party. The Storm Troopers were then a ragtag collection of ex-soldiers and officers, students and young idealists, the unemployed (and many others of less-than-savory reputation), all of whom badly needed organization, discipline, and purpose. Goering was the perfect choice to achieve these goals, and within a short time he whipped the Storm Troopers into a powerful force for Hitler to use.

Emboldened by the strength of the Storm Troopers and encouraged by deteriorating conditions in Germany, Hitler attempted a putsch in Munich on the night of November 8, 1923. A large detachment of Storm Troopers surrounded and occupied the Bürgerbräukeller, a beer hall where the leading members of the Bavarian state government were holding a mass meeting. Hitler forced the officials into negotiations at gunpoint in a back room, while Goering took charge of the meeting, alternately threatening and cajoling the captive audience. Before the mood in the hall turned completely sour, Hitler reappeared and told the crowd that the Bavarian officials had agreed to cooperate in forming a revolutionary government headed by himself. The Nazis agreed to release the Bavarian state ministers, but they arrested and kept as hostages the mayor of Munich, the Socialist town councillors, and other city officials. However, the plan began to fall apart as soon as the trusting Nazis released the Bavarian ministers. Once free, they repudiated their agreement with Hitler and organized an active resistance to the Nazi revolution. On the morning of November 9, Hitler and Goering with their followers began a march into the heart of Munich, hoping to drum up popular support for their revolution. When a cordon of police halted the marchers, Goering sprang forward, threatening that all hostages would be killed if the Nazis were not allowed to pass. The police gave way, unaware that Goering's threat was an empty one—the remaining hostages had been left at the Bürgerbräukeller.

The marchers reached the Odeonsplatz in the center of the city, but there was no time to bluff the police who blocked entry to the square. A shot was fired—it was never determined by whom—and the police opened fire on the Nazis with machine guns and rifles. Goering was severely wounded as a bullet, glancing off the pavement, struck his groin. Some Storm Troopers carried him to the nearby residence of a furniture dealer. There he was cared for by Frau Ilse Ballin and her sister until he could be taken to a hospital the next day. "We shall never forget what you have done for Hermann," a grateful Carin told the sisters. Many years later, Goering arranged for the Ballins, who were Jewish, to leave Germany with all their capital.

Over the next few days Hitler and the other surviving leaders of the putsch were arrested. Goering was captured at the Austrian border and taken to a hospital in Garmisch-Partenkirchen. He was in such intense pain that he had to be given morphine daily. Goering was not guarded, having given the police his word of honor he would not attempt an escape. But he broke his word—with a guilty conscience—after Carin pointed out that the members of the Bavarian government had already broken their word to Hitler. Goering accepted this dubious rationalization and allowed himself to be smuggled across the Austrian border to Innsbruck, where he entered a Catholic hospital. He remained there, taking increasingly larger doses of morphine until his release on Christmas Eve, 1923. Goering went from the hospital to a guesthouse owned by an Austrian Nazi. According to a letter written by Carin Goering, her husband was "sick, lost and white as snow."

Goering's health soon improved enough for him to receive visits from other Nazis, German exiles like himself, and make a series of speeches. But when he began to associate openly with Austrian Nazis, government authorities pressured him to leave the country. Goering had nowhere to go. He wrote his mother-in-law that he wanted to return to a Nationalist Germany but "not to this Jew republic." Moreover, a return to Germany was out of the question—he was subject to arrest.

Goering and his wife left Austria for Italy, where Mussolini and his Fascist party were consolidating power as the Nazis had hoped to do in Germany. But Goering spent a discouraging year in Italy. He lacked money and suffered from morphine addiction. He tried, pathetically, to ingratiate himself with the Fascists, offering his services as "a simple Fascist awaiting orders." The Fascists, however, had no use for Goering, and in May 1925 he and his wife moved to Sweden, Carin's homeland. The following September, as a result of his morphine addiction, Hermann Goering was taken to the Langboro Asylum for the Insane. The doctor who treated him concluded that his patient was "a sentimentalist lacking in basic moral courage." Goering was cured of his addiction, but for the rest of his life he lived under the stigma of having been (and many thought he always was) a "dope addict."

Goering returned to Germany in 1927 after a general political amnesty was declared, leaving his wife, who was then ill, in Sweden. He immediately contacted Hitler, whose party was on the rise, but the Fuehrer had no use for the unemployed and penniless ex–war hero. Instead of engaging in politics, Goering took a job in Berlin as the representative of the Bavarian Motor Works. He lived alone in a hotel room and missed dreadfully his wife's companionship. Carin finally joined him in the spring of 1928.

Goering prospered selling aviation products and making many influential contacts in the business world. Thinking that Goering might now be useful, Hitler visited him in Berlin and offered him a Reichstag candidacy on the Nazi slate. Goering accepted the offer and was elected to the German parliament in May 1928 as one of twelve Nazi deputies. Suddenly, Hermann Goering was once again a leading figure in the

Hitler movement, one who could give the party an element of re-
spectability it had hitherto lacked. Among those who sent telegrams
of congratulations was Crown Prince Wilhelm, the oldest son of the
exiled kaiser.

During the next few years, Goering was an indefatigable champion
of Hitler's cause and became a highly effective—if unorthodox—speaker.
During one of his speeches, he exhorted the crowd to urge everyone
they knew to vote for the Nazi party, including "your illegitimate
children, if they are old enough." Although some were shocked by
Goering's often-coarse humor, the majority roared with laughter. Certainly the tactics he and Hitler used were effective. The Nazis captured
6½ million votes and 107 Reichstag seats in the 1930 elections—a
landslide victory. Clearly the Nazis had gained considerable power,
and it became Goering's special task to win support from the rich
industrialists and assure them that Hitler represented no threat to private property. Goering, with his "respectable" background, was perfect
for this job, and large amounts of money flowed into the party coffers.

His wife, Carin, was the only person to whom Goering was more
devoted than he was to Hitler. He was never unfaithful to her, but
politics occupied more and more of his time. Her death in Sweden
in 1931 was no doubt a blow to Goering—who had left her bedside
to answer an urgent summons from Hitler to return to Germany. Later
Goering would bring her body to Germany, entombing it with great
pomp and ceremony on the grounds of Carinhall, the manor named
in her honor. It may well be that guilt feelings were part of his lifelong,
ostentatious veneration of her memory.

Carin no longer in his life, Goering devoted all of his energies to
politics, using his considerable influence with those around von Hindenburg in a behind-the-scenes attempt to negotiate power for Hitler.
By 1932 von Hindenburg was willing to make Hitler vice-chancellor
and Goering Prussian minister of the interior. But Goering indignantly
refused the offer: "The Fuehrer has never been *vice* to anyone." Goering knew time was on the side of the Nazis. Adolf Hitler was named
chancellor of Germany on January 30, 1933. That night Goering stood
beside Hitler as the two watched from a balcony the thousands of

Storm Troopers who paraded through the streets of Berlin in a torch-light victory celebration. Hitler rewarded him with three offices: min-ister without portfolio in the cabinet, Reich minister for aviation, and Prussian minister of the interior. For the time being this last position was the most important, as it gave Goering control over the police in Prussia, the seat of the capital.

If it was Hitler who initiated the orders to suppress all opposition to the National Socialist state, it was Goering who put them into effect. To his critics, Goering replied that he could not allow himself "to be crippled by any legal considerations." He was not, he freely admitted, concerned with "justice." "My mission," he declared, "is only to destroy and exterminate, nothing more." Hermann Goering had seem-ingly changed from the days his older sister characterized the young man at Veldenstein as a *Gerechtigkeitsfanatiker*, a "fanatic for justice." However, as was often the case, Goering's actions did not measure up to his bluster. Though he compared the harsh treatment meted out to foes of National Socialism to splinters that naturally result when a piece of wood is planed, he was distressed when cases of unnecessary brutality were reported to him. When he learned that Ernst Thael-mann, the German Communist leader, had been maltreated in a concentration camp, Goering had the man brought to him. He apol-ogized to Thaelmann for the beatings and promised to punish anyone who ill-treated him in the future. However, he added, "My dear Thaelmann, I know that if you had come to power I would not have been beaten up, but you would have chopped off my head pronto."

The threat of internal Communism was broken, but Hitler found himself faced with a revolt within his own ranks. Ernst Roehm, the Storm Troop commander, was not satisfied with the status of the revolution Hitler had brought to Germany. Roehm believed that he and the other Storm Troop leaders, who had served Hitler so faithfully during the years of struggle, should form the nucleus of a "People's Army," which would be imbued with their radical spirit of National Socialism and opposed to the conservative outlook of the *Reichswehr*, the regular German army. The thought of accepting Roehm and his homosexual clique as any sort of equals was repugnant to the aristocrats of the General Staff, and Hitler realized a hard choice had to be made. Early on the morning of June 30, 1934, Hitler and a detachment of SS troops arrested Roehm and numerous other Storm Troop leaders at a hotel in Bad Wiessee, in southern Bavaria. They were taken to Stadelheim prison in Munich where many were summarily executed by a firing squad; Roehm was shot to death in his cell after refusing to commit suicide. On July 1 it became obvious to Goering that the purge was getting out of hand and innocent people were being killed as a result of personal vendettas. He telephoned Hitler asking that the bloodletting be stopped. With the high command of the Storm Troopers decimated, there was no longer any danger—real or imaginary— to the National Socialist revolution; therefore, Hitler ordered the murders to cease. Over 150 people died before the carnage ended.

The foreign press excoriated Hitler and Goering for their roles in the purge. But in Germany, with its controlled press, the reaction was much different. Indeed, Goering was cheered in the streets whenever he appeared, and the president of the republic sent a congratulatory telegram: "Accept my approval and gratitude for your successful action in suppressing the high treason. Hindenburg." But the accolade of which Goering was most proud was his Fuehrer's praise. All else was secondary.

But now Hitler was no longer the only important person in Goering's life. He had fallen in love with Emmy Sonnemann, an actress at the National Theater in Weimar. It was impossible to keep the relationship secret, and Goering made little attempt to do so. One night he slipped into his theater box just as Emmy delivered the lines "Ah, I ask myself only if he loves me—and is there any question that he loves me?" Tittering swept the audience, and all eyes turned toward Goering, who joined in the good-humored laughter and beamed at Emmy. It was obvious that he did love her. Goering and Emmy Sonnemann were married April 10, 1935, in Berlin's Protestant cathedral. Adolf Hitler was Goering's best man. After the ceremony Goering and his wife went to the steps of the church so that the crowds might see them. Though the marriage was Emmy's second, she wore a traditional white gown. But her husband, who wore a self-designed air force general's uniform with all his medals and a sword, far outshone her. Goering's choice of uniform—he had many from which he could have picked—demonstrated the importance he then placed upon his title of air minister. The title had appeared to carry little weight in 1933 when the Nazis came to power, since Germany was forbidden by the Treaty of Versailles to have an air force. But Goering was determined to build a strong air arm, and if it was necessary, would train his pilots in secrecy under the guise of having them belong to flying "sports clubs."

Almost immediately Goering began assembling from among his World War comrades the nucleus of the Luftwaffe leadership. Karl Bodenschatz became Goering's personal adjutant. Bruno Loerzer, with whom Goering had first flown, headed the Air Sports Clubs, which provided glider training for future pilots. Both came willingly at Goering's call. But the director of Lufthansa, the German civilian airline, Erhard Milch, whom Goering wanted as state secretary at the Air Ministry—a position that would control the development of the Luftwaffe—proved more difficult to recruit. Milch's reluctance to associate with the Nazis may have been based, primarily, on his unwillingness to lose his generous Lufthansa salary—but there may have been another reason. Erhard Milch had a Jewish father, a fact known to Goering but evidently of little importance to him. His attitude toward Milch's Jewishness was similar to what he expressed when asked if he would use a Jewish invention in an airplane. Goering laughingly replied, "I certainly would. For me, engines have no Jewish grandmothers." But he worried how Hitler might react if he discovered Milch was half-Jewish. Goering resolved to use a subterfuge to settle the matter. He arranged for Milch's mother to sign a document stating her son was the illegitimate child of another, whose Aryan pedigree was without blemish. This formality observed, Goering was satisfied. Indeed, when Hitler learned of Milch's reluctance in accepting Goering's offer, he himself appealed to his sense of patriotism. Unable to refuse the Fuehrer, Milch finally accepted and became state secretary at the Air Ministry.

In 1935 Goering asked for money to build a stronger air force.

Hjalmar Schacht, the minister of economics, told him no more was available because the German people had already sacrificed to the limit. Goering decided to take matters into his own hands.

For weeks he worked on a speech that he intended to deliver in Hamburg. There, in front of an audience of party supporters, Goering played his trump. He told his audience that rearmament was imperative for Germany. "What is the use of being in the concert of nations," he asked, "if Germany is only allowed to play on a comb?" After the applause subsided, Goering went on: "We have no butter, comrades, but I ask you: would you rather have butter or guns?" To drive home his point, Goering patted his huge stomach and said, "Butter only makes us fat!" The resulting gales of laughter showed that the German people were willing to make even greater sacrifices if *der Dicke* (the "Fat One") asked them to do so. Of all the Nazi leaders, only Goering could have asked the German people to make further sacrifices and have received such cheerful compliance: his love for uniforms and medals, considered ludicrous in much of the world, made him the most popular and human figure at home.

Jokes at Goering's expense abounded. But he took delight in them, saying, "If they make jokes about me, it only proves how popular I am!" Only in one instance did Goering indicate his displeasure over a cabaret witticism at his expense. After Emmy Goering's pregnancy was announced, Werner Finck asked his audience if they knew what name Goering would give his firstborn if it were a boy. Then Finck said the name "Hamlet" and recited the famous lines "To be or not to be, that is the question." In German the lines also mean "His or not his, that is the question." Goering was not in the least amused at this slur on his manhood, and Finck was advised to drop the joke from future performances. But behind Goering's bonhomie, there lay extreme vanity and overweening ambition. During the first years of the Third Reich, he collected offices and titles as he did uniforms and medals. In addition to being Reich minister of aviation and Prussian minister of the interior, Goering became creator and head of the Gestapo, the dreaded secret state police; Reich forestry commissioner and master of the hunt; commander in chief of the Luftwaffe; and commissioner of the Four-Year Plan, by which Germany was to secure the money needed for rearmament. Curiously, Goering held no official position in the Nazi party. Despite this, he was pathologically jealous of his special position with Hitler and declared in a speech, "I have received many titles and honours, and yet no title and no decoration has made me so proud as the name which the German people has given me—'The most faithful Paladin of his Führer!' "

Goering's devotion to Hitler manifested itself in word and deed, and in neither did he wish to appear second to any. To Hitler, Goering attributed "an overwhelming greatness of character and genius." When Hitler distributed to "the faithful" his signed portrait in a silver frame, Goering was not satisfied with the one given him. He had the photo greatly enlarged and commissioned Zeitner, his favorite jeweler, to design a special silver frame for it. Publicly Goering was always careful to parade his loyalty to Hitler. Privately he often disregarded some aspects of the philosophy his Fuehrer championed. The official Nazi policy toward the churches was one of open harassment and persecution, but Goering refused to boycott those ceremonies they traditionally conducted. He was married in the Church, and when his daughter was born in 1938, he took part in her christening ceremony. He intended, he said, to show "weak-willed persons . . . that, if the second man in the State goes to Church . . . they can do the same."

Goering had a much more ambivalent attitude toward the persecution of Germany's Jews. There is little doubt that he developed very strong anti-Semitic prejudices in the years following World War I. He regarded with suspicion and alarm the number of Jews who played leading roles in the economic and cultural life of the republic, believing them to represent "a serious danger for the German nation." After the Nazis came to power, the Jews were pressured to leave Germany. "We even encouraged their emigration to Palestine, and helped them leave Germany," Goering said. In answer to those Jews who insisted that Germany, not Palestine, was their rightful home, the Nazis passed the Nuremberg Laws in 1935, depriving Jews—irrespective of how long they and their families had lived in Germany—of German citizenship and the rights thereof. As president of the Reichstag, Goering signed these laws without demur. But he was not an anti-Semite on a personal basis. In his private dealings with Jews, he was quite prepared to make exceptions as he had done with Erhard Milch. He could later claim quite truthfully, "I can name many people I have helped, even . . . Jews."

Many of those Goering helped were Emmy's friends from the theater. After it became known that she was willing to intercede with her husband on behalf of Jewish friends, Goering was deluged with appeals for assistance. "We had better put up a sign," he jokingly told Emmy, "that my office will help all Jews." Only half-jokingly he added, "You are going to get Himmler after me!" The SS chief was not yet powerful enough to attack Goering personally, but he complained to Hitler about the intercessions concerning Emmy's friends and others. Hitler immediately ordered Goering to cease interfering with Himmler's work. "Now you see," a worried Goering told his wife, "you are even turning the Fuehrer against me." Goering was afraid of Hitler's disapproval and increasingly looked the other way as Jews disappeared into concentration camps. He ignored his conscience not only because he feared losing Hitler's confidence; he undoubtedly also feared losing the power, wealth, and comfort he had acquired since 1933. Hitler's mastery of Germany and success in acquiring territory through a series of bloodless coups had also caused Goering's power and wealth to increase, and he had no desire to lose both by offending his benefactor.

Shortly after the Nazis seized power, Goering had acquired a vast hunting reserve near Berlin. On this land he built Carinhall, the magnificent manor named in honor of his first wife. It was to Carinhall (which was continually being enlarged) that Goering went more and more to enjoy himself among the valuable paintings and other art treasures he had collected from all over the world. At Carinhall Goering also felt most free to indulge in those eccentricities of dress and behavior for which he was to become famous. Few visitors came away from Carinhall without stories of their host's bizarre behavior. Staid members of foreign diplomatic corps were shocked when Goering treated them to the spectacle of two bison mating. A guest had her dress ruined when one of Goering's pet lion cubs, who roamed the rooms freely, urinated on it. The duchess of Windsor never forgot the comical sight of a completely serious Goering, in full dress uniform and with medals clinking, forcing his corpulent body between the rollers of an Elizabeth Arden reducing machine to demonstrate how it worked. The duke, however, was fascinated by Goering's electric trains, and the two spent hours happily playing with them. Goering was aware of the strange impression he was creating, but he did not let it bother him, for it seemed to increase his popularity at home and abroad. Sir Nevile Henderson, the British ambassador, wrote, "Of all the big Nazi leaders, Hermann Goering was for me by far the most sympathetic." But Sir Nevile added that Goering "in any crisis, as in war, would be quite ruthless."

By August 1939 the possibility of war was very real. Hitler was demanding the return of the Polish Corridor, that strip of land separating East Prussia from the rest of Germany ceded to Poland by the Treaty of Versailles. Poland, backed by treaty assurances from England and France, refused to give in to Hitler's demands and threats. War seemed inevitable.

Hermann Goering did not want war. For quite some time, behind the back of Foreign Minister Joachim von Ribbentrop—whom he despised—Goering had been trying to avoid war through his own brand of inept but sincere personal diplomacy, utilizing Birger Dahlerus, a Swedish national, as a conduit to the British. Before any real plans could be put into action, von Ribbentrop concluded a treaty with Soviet Russia, hitherto considered National Socialist Germany's greatest enemy. With Germany protected in the East, Hitler was no longer interested in a diplomatic solution to the matter of the Polish Corridor, believing that England would never go to war for the sake of Poland. On the morning of September 1, 1939, Poland was simultaneously invaded by German and Russian troops. England and France, much to Hitler's surprise and dismay, met their treaty obligations by declaring war on Germany. When Goering heard this news, he could only murmur, "If we lose this war, then God have mercy on us!"

The war proceeded much better than Goering had thought. With the French and British in no position to intervene, the campaign in Poland was over in a few weeks. Goering's Luftwaffe played a key role in sapping the Poles' will and ability to resist, and Hitler was full of praise for the air force and its commander in chief. By July 1940 the French had surrendered and the British had retreated via Dunkirk from the Continent. It appeared as if Germany had won the war. Special honors were in store for Goering. Having already appointed Goering his successor should something happen to him, a grateful Fuehrer promoted "his most faithful Paladin" to the unique rank of Reichsmarschall and awarded him an equally unique medal, the Grand Cross of the Iron Cross. Hitler handed Goering a box containing his new insignia, which Goering took with "boyish pride and satisfaction" that was, according to eyewitness William L. Shirer, "almost touching." Unable to contain his curiosity, Goering "could not deny himself a sneaking glance under the cover of the lid." Later Hitler would give Goering a magnificent ivory baton studded with diamonds, the symbol of his authority as Germany's Reichsmarschall. Though he did not realize it then, Goering had reached the zenith of his career. The months and years following his promotion to Reichsmarschall would bring setbacks for the Luftwaffe and humiliation for its commander.

Despite Dunkirk, the British did not respond to Hitler's peace overtures, and a German invasion of England appeared imminent. Goering assigned the Luftwaffe the task of destroying the British fleet and air force. He felt that his air force alone could never bring Britain to her knees, although it could disrupt, interfere with, and destroy defenses, thus weakening the country for the invasion. "The Luftwaffe cannot occupy," Goering warned Hitler, who continued to postpone giving orders for the invasion to begin. The invasion never came, and it was left to the Luftwaffe to subdue the British. Goering's plan involved concentrated bombing of airfields, factories, and harbors. The plan might have worked. Then the British bombed Berlin. The actual damage was negligible, but Hitler's wounded pride and the outcry from the bombed citizens of the capital forced Goering to change his strategy. He told Emmy, "The Berliners have yelled at me on the streets, asking what was wrong, and why London was not being bombed."

Despite his better judgment—Goering said later that he had "considered the attacks on London useless"—the Reichsmarschall did as Hitler wished and diverted the Luftwaffe from strictly military targets to indiscriminate attacks on London. As a result the stubborn British, though their capital was being bombed to rubble, retained the ability to fight on and hope that a miracle would save them. Hitler provided that miracle when he ordered the invasion of Russia on June 22, 1941. Hitler's plans shocked Goering, who told him that the proposed attack was contrary to what the Fuehrer had written in *Mein Kampf*. It was, Goering maintained, "economically mistaken, politically mistaken and militarily mistaken." But once again, the Fuehrer's will prevailed. Worse yet was Hitler's decision to divert much of the Luftwaffe from the western to the eastern front. Again, against his better judgment, Goering followed the orders of his Fuehrer. The inevitable result was that the German air force was unable to win a decisive victory on either front. Goering later blamed Hitler for this lack of success. "I had definite plans," he said, "but in 1940 Hitler began to interfere, taking air fleets away from our planned operations. I was forced by Hitler to divert air forces to the East, which I always opposed." It was Hitler's interference, Goering claimed, that "was the beginning of the breakdown of Luftwaffe efficiency" and "only the diversion of the Luftwaffe to the Russian front saved England."

With reduced opposition in the skies, the British took the offensive, bombing German cities daily, almost unopposed by the Luftwaffe. The raids made a mockery of Goering's famous boast—if any enemy bombers crossed Germany's borders, "then my name is not Hermann Goering, but Meier!" Thousands of postcards and letters, all addressed to "Herr Meier," began to arrive at the Air Ministry. Worse yet for Goering was Hitler's constant criticism of him in the presence of others. Humiliated, he ceased attending Hitler's military conferences, sending the loyal Bodenschatz in his stead so that he bore the brunt of Hitler's scathing comments about Goering. "Where is *Der Eisener* ['the Iron Man'] today?" Hitler would ask. "Shooting defenseless deer again instead of British aircraft, I suppose."

The devastating raid on Cologne in May 1942 finally ruptured the special relationship between Hitler and Goering. After receiving initial reports, Hitler berated General Jeschonnek, Luftwaffe chief of staff, screaming that the general's estimate of two hundred attacking bombers was a lie. Exhausting his fury on Jeschonnek, Hitler then caustically observed, pointedly omitting Goering's title in a deliberate insult, "Herr Goering, of course, is not here." Bodenschatz, who heard Hitler's remarks, telephoned Goering, advising him that trouble was brewing and that he should present himself at Hitler's headquarters at once. When the Reichsmarschall arrived, Hitler deliberately ignored his outstretched hand. Hitler's humiliation of Goering in front of junior officers clearly signaled to all that the Reichsmarschall no longer enjoyed the Fuehrer's confidence and friendship. The effect upon Goering, Bodenschatz recalled, "was pitiable." The relationship between Hitler and Goering worsened after the Americans and British bombed Hamburg in July 1943, creating a fire storm that killed thousands and destroyed most of the city. The disaster was of such magnitude that Goering decided the Luftwaffe should go on the defensive, its chief task protecting German cities. But when he presented his plan to Hitler, the Fuehrer screamed that Goering and his pilots were cowards, afraid to face the British planes and antiaircraft batteries protecting England. The Luftwaffe had disappointed him once too often, Hitler raged. Abruptly and without ceremony, Hitler ordered Goering out of his presence. In the anteroom to Hitler's office, Goering broke down in despair.

As Germany's collapse accelerated, Goering took less and less part in the conduct of the war, leaving his subordinates to preside over the death of the Luftwaffe. For months on end, he absented himself from his office and Hitler's conferences, going to Carinhall to enjoy the works of art plundered from conquered territories. Only there, insulated from the insults and reproaches Hitler and others heaped upon him and dosing himself with the paracodeine pills that he had been taking since 1938, could Goering forget the war, preferring the splendid solitude of Carinhall to the harsh realities fast overtaking him and all of Germany. Goering did realize, eventually, that the war was lost and that he had no influence with Hitler; but he never disassociated himself from the Nazis' lost cause. He briefly thought of suicide and asked Emmy if she would go with him. But he then rejected the idea as "cowardly." He toyed with the idea of resigning but never went through with it. Though he later gave a number of reasons why he did not resign, perhaps the truth is that he did not want to give up the wealth and privileges he still enjoyed as Reichsmarschall and Hitler's successor.

There may have been another reason why Goering clung to the sinking ship of Nazism. As Goebbels noted in his diary, "Goering perfectly realizes what is in store for all of us if we show any weakness in this war. On the Jewish question, especially, we have taken a position from which there is no escape." Goebbels well knew that it was Goering who, on July 31, 1941, issued the order—on Hitler's directive—for "a final solution of the Jewish question." Perhaps the eventual "Final Solution" was not the one originally envisioned by Goering, but there can be little doubt that he, despite his later disclaimers, learned what was taking place in the extermination camps.

On April 20, 1945, Goering went to Hitler's headquarters in Berlin, ostensibly to offer the Fuehrer congratulations on his fifty-sixth (and last) birthday. Goering also intended to persuade Hitler to move his headquarters to the safety of Berchtesgaden. But Hitler refused to leave besieged Berlin, insisting that the Russians would meet their bloodiest defeat in the German capital. At this point Goering asked permission to depart for Berchtesgaden in order to attend to "urgent tasks." Permission was granted. The leave-taking between Hitler and Goering was cold, and there were no words of thanks to the Reichsmarschall for his past services. Perhaps Hitler was thinking of the time that Goering had pledged fidelity to his Fuehrer, "in good times and in bad, even unto death."

On April 23 Goering learned that the Fuehrer considered the situation in Berlin hopeless. He sent Hitler a telegram, asking if he should "assume immediately the total leadership of the Reich with complete freedom of action at home and abroad." If he received no answer by the end of a specified time, Goering said, he would assume that Hitler had lost his freedom of action and would then take over the leadership of the nation. When Goering's telegram arrived, Martin

Bormann, Goering's longtime enemy and rival for power, emphasized to Hitler the time limit Goering had set and insisted it was "an ultimatum." Persuaded by Bormann, Hitler radioed Goering: "Decree of June 29, 1941, rescinded by my special instruction. My freedom of action undisputed. I forbid any move by you in the direction indicated." With this message Goering suddenly found himself removed from his position as Hitler's successor. A short while later, Hitler also learned that Goering had sent telegrams to leading members of the Reich government, ordering them to report to him at Berchtesgaden. Hitler was now convinced that the Reichsmarschall was attempting to seize power. He sent Goering another message, accusing him of high treason. Despite this treason, Hitler said, he would not insist upon the death penalty if Goering would immediately resign all his offices.

Bormann, however, ignored Hitler's decision to spare Goering's life and sent a telegram of his own, ordering the SS at Berchtesgaden to arrest Goering and shoot him when the situation in Berlin became untenable. The SS arrested Goering and his family, keeping them under guard at his mountain home at Berchtesgaden. An air raid destroyed the house on April 29, and Goering persuaded the SS to permit a move to Mauterndorf (which he had inherited). There Goering heard the news of Hitler's death. Distraught, he said to Emmy, "Now I can no longer vindicate myself. I can never look him in the face and tell him that he wronged me, that I remained loyal to him." With Hitler dead and the war lost, the SS had little desire to shoot Goering, and loyal Luftwaffe troops eventually freed him from captivity. "It was one of the most beautiful moments of my life," Goering said, "to stand there again in front of my troops and see them present arms to their Commander-in-Chief."

Goering and his family set out to find the advancing Americans, hoping to surrender and place themselves under their protection. The Goerings finally made contact, and on a traffic-jammed road, the Nazi Reichsmarschall surrendered to the first American he met—1st Lt. Jerome N. Shapiro, a Jewish officer from New York. Goering's captors at first accorded him preferential treatment, and he assumed he was slated to meet with General Eisenhower on a "marshal to marshal" basis. However, some days later reporters, who were allowed to interview Goering, revealed to him his true situation. As the obviously ill and profusely sweating Reichsmarschall sat answering the routine questions he had expected, one reporter asked if he were aware that his name headed "the list of war criminals." The fixed smile on Goering's face faded. "No," he answered. "That surprises me very much, for I cannot imagine why." Even after the trial, unable to answer his wife's question concerning what had happened, Goering still could not understand what he had done that had brought him to Nuremberg and the brink of execution—having convinced himself that the trial was politically motivated and the outcome a foregone conclusion. Some days before he died, however, he may have finally understood the fatal flaw in his character that had placed him in the Nuremberg dock.

A few days after the verdicts were announced, Goering asked the prison psychologist what the inkblot tests he had taken revealed about him. The psychologist reminded him of a specific card that had a red spot and said that "morbid neurotics often hesitate over that card and then say there's blood on it." Goering, too, had hesitated upon seeing the red spot, but he did not call it blood. The doctor reminded Goering, "*You tried to flick it off with your finger,* as though you thought you could wipe away the blood with a little gesture." Goering sat silently listening, and the doctor continued, "And you did the same thing during the war too, drugging the atrocities out of your mind. You didn't have the courage to face it. That is your guilt. You are a moral coward."

It is impossible to say what effect the psychologist's words had upon Goering. A few days later, Germany's Reichsmarschall was dead, a suicide in his cell. The psychologist wrote what he thought was a proper epitaph: "Goering died as he had lived, a psychopath trying to make a mockery of all human values and to distract attention from his guilt by a dramatic gesture."

It might have surprised the doctor to have learned that not all those who had been with Goering during the months of his imprisonment and trial shared his opinion of the Reichsmarschall and the manner of his death. One of them had furnished Goering with the poison he used to kill himself.

3

Nuremberg

Hermann Goering made his way to Nuremberg prison via a circuitous route and only after the elapse of much time. The interval between his surrender and being brought to Nuremberg to stand trial was one of the most traumatic periods in his life.

When Goering was handed over to Brig. Gen. Robert I. Stack of the 36th Division, he was still under the impression that the Americans were prepared to accept him as a suitable representative of the post-Hitler German government. He believed himself to be particularly popular with the Americans, and nothing in his meeting with General Stack changed this delusion.

Emmy Goering, who was present at the meeting, remembered General Stack as a very tactful man who treated her husband with great consideration and respect. Though Goering spoke English, Stack had an interpreter translate every word that passed between them. According to Frau Goering, Stack said that he had been in touch with General Eisenhower by telephone and that the general had agreed to meet with Goering the next day. In the meantime, the Goerings were to go to Schloss Fischhorn at Zell-am-See, until it could be determined if Burg Veldenstein was still habitable. Eisenhower had pledged his word of honor, Emmy Goering quoted Stack as saying, that her husband would have complete freedom to come and go as he wished and that the Reichsmarschall and his family were under his personal protection.

Goering and his family were taken to Schloss Fischhorn, where he believed he was the temporary guest of General Stack. They were given comfortable rooms on the second floor of the castle, and Goering was invited to supper with the general and his staff. He returned to his room late that night and told his wife that he was going to have breakfast with Stack and then be gone for a few days. When Frau Goering appeared apprehensive, her husband reassured her, "Look, General Eisenhower through General Stack has given me his word of honor that I will have complete freedom of movement." The next morning, Goering left for 36th Division Headquarters at Kitzbühel. He was not to see his wife again until September 1946, after the trial.

Before leaving Zell-am-See, Goering told Robert Kropp, "Everything is fine, Robert. I am going to a conference with General Eisenhower." Goering personally organized the party to accompany him to Kitzbühel. He traveled in an American car but had his own supercharged Mercedes 200 follow behind. He was, according to Kropp, in "high spirits."

At 36th Division Headquarters, Goering was received and entertained by high-ranking American officers, and he still felt no reason for concern. Champagne was served, and the American officers allowed themselves to be photographed in close and friendly conversation with Goering. Luftwaffe Gen. Karl Koller was relieved to hear that "Goering had been seen on the balcony of the hotel headquarters, laughing, surrounded by high ranking American officers, a glass of champagne in his hand." The scene was reminiscent of one that might have taken place during World War I when victorious fliers toasted opposing comrades-in-arms who had not been so lucky. But, as Goering and his hosts were soon to find out, times had changed.

Correspondents reported in an extremely negative manner the champagne party and friendly treatment accorded Goering by the Americans. Upon reading these reports in the newspapers, General Eisenhower ordered that Goering henceforth be treated as an ordinary prisoner of war and be sent as soon as possible to Seventh Army

Interrogation Center at Augsburg. If Eisenhower had ever agreed to a "marshal to marshal" meeting with Goering, the idea was quickly dropped after the hostile press reports.

Kropp received orders to take charge of Goering's luggage and meet his master at the Kitzbühel airport. Upon his arrival at the airport, Goering immediately sensed that something was amiss. "There is something wrong," he said to Kropp, "no American escort, no officer to accompany me?"

Goering's reception at the interrogation center was very different from the ones he had hitherto enjoyed, and there could no longer have remained in his mind any doubt as to his true status. Rather than being met by high-ranking officers, he was coolly received by Maj. Paul Kubala and his staff. "He was processed in accordance with the then standing regulations of the Interrogation Center," said Col. William W. Quinn, G-2 (intelligence) officer for Seventh Army. "The processing entailed the disarmament, the search for hidden arms, weapons, poisons, the removal of jewelry, cash, possessions and practically everything that did not constitute toilet articles or necessary clothing." First to go was Goering's Reichsmarschall's baton, which he was carrying in its gray leather case. Later he was relieved of his medals and the hunting dagger given to him by Count von Rosen, his Swedish brother-in-law.

Photographers were called in to witness Goering's humiliation. Sitting in a small office, facing an American officer, and wearing a drooping white armband on his left sleeve, Goering was photographed reaching under his uniform jacket to unfasten the hunting dagger. He appeared to be clearly exasperated. Standing behind him, Col. Berndt von Brauchitsch, his adjutant, stared morosely at the floor. It is clear from the picture that both had realized the Reichsmarschall was no "guest" of the Americans and that there would be no meeting with Eisenhower.

After processing, Goering was taken to a block of primitive apartments on the outskirts of Augsburg, where he was assigned quarters by Lt. Rolf Wartenberg, a former Berliner who had fled the Nazis and subsequently joined the United States Army. Goering was even further depressed by the shabbiness of his accommodations, and Colonel von Brauchitsch burst into tears because of what he believed to be a deliberate insult to his chief. When Kropp finally arrived with Goering's luggage, he noticed immediately that his master's attitude had undergone a drastic change since his arrival in Augsburg. Goering, stripped of his medals and signs of authority, was in a state of "utter dejection."

When Wartenberg arrived at Goering's quarters the next day, the Reichsmarschall anxiously quizzed him about the fate of his personal possessions. Upon being assured by Wartenberg that they were safe, Goering glumly shook his head and said, "The way things are going, I fear that from now on you are going to take the pants off me." His spirits improved when Wartenberg told him that he was invited that night for cocktails with the camp commandant.

It had not been forgotten that Eisenhower had ordered Goering to be treated as "an ordinary prisoner of war," but it was thought that the fastest way to get information from him was to alternate the stick and the carrot. The method worked, and Goering returned from the party at 2:00 A.M., "a little flushed, still lively and talkative." He told Kropp that he and the Americans had been discussing "the war." This was exactly what his interrogators wanted, and the evening cocktail parties continued.

Gradually, Goering began to relax, seeing himself as the "host" of these nightly get-togethers. The atmosphere was informal, and Goering joined in the singing of popular American and German songs, clapping his hands during the chorus of "Deep in the Heart of Texas." The music was supplied by Goering's own accordion, but he himself did not play it. "He was too fat to get it over his stomach," Wartenberg recalled. (The accordion was later presented to Wartenberg by Goering as a farewell gift; the former Berliner still has it.)

Another of Goering's gifts caused a problem for the American recipient. At one of the nightly parties, Goering said to an officer, "Let me send Robert to get a few more clothes—and one or two other things! I may have a surprise for you!" When Robert returned with a large package, Goering unwrapped a valuable painting. Turning to the officer, he said, "Here, my friend—with the compliments of the

Marshal of the German Reich!" The next day, Kropp recalled, the officer was arrested for accepting presents from his prisoner.

After Goering was drained of information, the interrogations came to an end, and a report was sent to headquarters. The agent wrote:

> *Reichsmarschall* Hermann Goering is by no means the comical figure he has been depicted so many times in newspaper reports. He is neither stupid nor a fool in the Shakespearean sense, but generally cool and calculating. He is able to grasp the fundamental issues under discussion immediately. He is certainly not a man to be underrated. Although he tried to soft-pedal many of the most outrageous crimes committed by Germany, he said enough to show that he is as much responsible for the policies within Germany and for the war itself, as anyone in Germany.

Perceptively, the agent concluded that "Goering is at all times an actor who does not disappoint his audience."

Far from disappointing his audiences, Goering was delighting them— too much so. From Supreme Allied Headquarters came the urgent request that Goering be immediately sent to the American internment center at Mondorf-les-Bains, Luxemburg. Further, it was ordered that no more interviews by the press should be allowed. The first stage of Goering's imprisonment was at an end.

On May 20, 1945, Goering was flown to Mondorf, where the top Nazis were being assembled for further interrogation. The Palace Hotel at Mondorf, code-named Ashcan, was another unpleasant experience for Goering. The once-luxurious hotel had been turned into a prison. K. Robert Wilheim, one of the interrogators assigned to Ashcan, remembered that "the hotel grounds were surrounded by two ten-foot-high barbed-wire fences, with an elevated guardhouse, equipped with floodlights for the nights, in each corner." Inside the inner barbed-wire fence was a low, double-strand fence, about two feet high, that, Wilheim and the prisoners were told, was "constantly charged." All in all, the Palace Hotel had become a foreboding structure.

On the main floor of the hotel were all the administrative offices and guardrooms. Interrogations were held in various rooms on the same floor. Goering and the others were housed in single rooms, from which every vestige of luxury had been stripped, on the upper floors. "All of these rooms," said Wilheim, "had, for security reasons, the windows removed and a heavy-gauge mesh installed in their place. Each room had an army cot, a little table, and one or two small chairs." Security was aimed at preventing suicides, and "all internees had to turn in their trouser belts, even shoelaces. All POWs were allowed to use eyeglasses on the main floor only but before going upstairs to their rooms had to deposit them in a specially built rack."

Still, the Nazis were allowed a greater freedom at Mondorf than they were ever to experience again at the hands of their captors. They were allowed to wear their uniforms, converse with each other, play chess and other games, and walk together in the gardens. The only interruptions in this routine were the interrogations to which they were subjected time after time. Sgt. Richard Raabe, who was later to go with the defendants to Nuremberg, recalled that "Mondorf was an open thing, just like a big open house, and Goering and the others had an opportunity to walk around and talk with each other. There were uniformed persons without firearms on two levels of the hotel. I was on the first level. Basically, we were there to make sure the prisoners did not get in a squabble with each other. It was very low-key, because we had interrogations going on, and we were really piecing history together."

Wilheim said that the interrogations at Ashcan were "a lot easier" than those he had previously conducted with prisoners of war. "The war was lost and most of the men I had occasion to talk to only tried to whitewash themselves." The questions that Wilheim and the other interrogators asked had been prepared in Washington for the purpose of preparing "grounds for the later trials and to elaborate on the relations, good or bad, between the inmates."

Wilheim, though he did not personally interrogate Goering, made a point of conversing with him for a half hour or so. "He was wearing a silk robe and got up from his cot when I entered the room. He evidently was not feeling well." Despite Goering's illness, Wilheim gained the impression that "he was one of the most intelligent of the lot."

Wilheim found Goering to be of special interest: "I recall one late afternoon during my time at Ashcan, when all the internees had been assembled in a large room. They were shown the film depicting the concentration camp horrors, a film lasting about 20–30 minutes. I did not watch the film as much as I did the faces of our inmates. Most of them watched with bored expressions and later refused to comment on what they thought was propaganda. But I remember Goering sitting on one side of the hall with a handkerchief in his hands and nervously wiping his face." It was hot in the hall, Wilheim said, "but not that hot!"

The months that Wilheim spent in the Ashcan were interesting ones, but he felt that none of the interrogators "was really qualified for the job. It should have been done by men with legal background—but that is the way the army works!"

The man in charge of the internment center at Mondorf was Col. Burton C. Andrus, a career officer who had joined the army in 1917. Andrus was five feet ten inches tall and weighed only 160 pounds, but his tight-fitting uniform jacket, under which he carried a pistol, made him look heavier. His steel-rimmed glasses and carefully trimmed mustache gave him a stern appearance. As did a few of his Nazi charges during their heyday, Andrus carried a short riding crop, using it to point out various prisoners to visiting dignitaries. Andrus wore a highly shellacked helmet to top off his sartorial splendor. An officer who served under Andrus described him as "a typical cavalry officer, a dying breed, who exhibited extreme pride in his crossed-sabre lapel insignia." He likened Andrus in manner and dress to Gen. George S. Patton, the flamboyant tank commander whose personality left none indifferent to him.

Goering and Andrus took an immediate dislike to each other. "He was brought into my office," said Andrus, "perspiring profusely." When he weighed in, Goering tipped the scales at 264 pounds. He was, Andrus said, "rude, bombastic and annoyed," and the Reichsmarschall was hastily sent to his room. Andrus was convinced that Goering was going to be trouble for him.

The problems began sooner than expected. Shortly after Goering had been removed from Andrus's office, an American officer came in to see the commandant. "I felt you should see this, sir," said the officer, who was carrying one of Goering's sixteen suitcases. Looking into the bag, Andrus saw "the biggest collection of pills I had ever seen in my life." The tablets were the paracodeine pills that Goering had been taking for years.

Andrus immediately notified his superiors that "Prisoner Goering brought with him enormous quantities of paracodeine. He is taking twenty times the normal dosage." Andrus expressed his fear that "if we suddenly remove this from him, he will become totally demented." The commandant suggested that it would be best if Goering were gradually weaned from the dosage to which he had been accustomed. He was not sure if Goering was totally rational but was convinced that "certainly his perversions have brought him to a state of emotional instability."

The officer to whom Andrus wrote expressed his complete approval of the manner in which Goering's drug-addiction problem was being handled. He told Andrus, "We are concerned with his state of health insofar as he remains reasonably coherent for some time yet. There are a number of things which we wish to ask him before we finally lose interest in what happens to him."

Every third day, the dosage was reduced by one tablet. Because he usually swallowed the pills by the handful, Goering did not at first notice the reduction, but later he complained of headaches and sleepiness. By August 12 Goering was completely free of his addiction and enjoying a vitality he had not experienced for years. "When Goering came to me at Mondorf," said Colonel Andrus, "he was a simpering slob with two suitcases full of paracodeine. I thought he was a drug salesman. But we took him off his dope and made a man of him." Andrus did not yet realize that it would have been better for him had Goering remained a "simpering slob."

While Goering was having his addiction to the paracodeine tablets broken, his health remained poor. Laboring under the strain of his immense weight, Goering's heart gave him—and Andrus as well—problems.

One night Andrus was awakened by a telephone call informing him that "Goering has had a heart attack!" When examined, it was determined that he had had only a palpitation. But the rumor got out that Goering had suffered a heart attack because Andrus had cut off his drug supply and that the Reichsmarschall might not live to stand trial.

Andrus took Goering to the Mondorf hospital for a thorough examination. The cardiograph showed that his heart was sound. "You see, Goering," Andrus said, "there is nothing at all wrong with your heart. If there was—the doctors say—you could not have carried your tremendous obesity for so long." Goering's smile faded after Andrus told him that his heart palpitations were caused by "nothing but fear."

Andrus might have been correct, but Goering's heart problems continued throughout his imprisonment. On August 22 Dr. Clint L. Miller informed the commandant that Goering was again having palpitations. He had been taken from his cell, walked fifty yards, and forced to climb three flights of stairs to an interrogation room. In the room he was discharged from the German Army. It was Dr. Miller's opinion that "this heart attack was produced by the physical exertion of walking up and down three flights of stairs, combined with the mental duress associated with his discharge from the German Army, and all the implications there-with." Dr. Miller recommended that Goering's exercise period be extended to thirty minutes a day "to increase his physical stamina and help prevent future recurrence of heart attacks." Andrus reluctantly concurred with the doctor's suggestion.

All the while, the interrogations continued. "Goering knows that we are trying to convict him of something," wrote one of the interrogating officers, "but he is not quite sure what that is and is continually fishing for news which might give him a 'lead.' " Though Goering spoke volubly on any subject, "he frequently reverts to falsehoods and apparently has the happy faculty of believing his own fabrications which upon repetition become more and more plausible to him."

When the interrogations of Goering and the others came to an end, they were transferred on August 12, 1945, to Nuremberg prison.

By this time Goering knew what was in store for him, and as the plane taking them to Nuremberg passed over the Rhine, he told his fellow defendants: "Take a good look at it. That's the last you may ever see of it."

Nuremberg is located in the southern part of Germany, approximately ninety-two miles northwest of Munich. It was originally a royal fortress and later became a junction of medieval trade routes between the Italian states and northern Europe. It developed into one of the most beautiful of all German cities and could boast of its cultural and intellectual achievements as well as its having been the home of some who bore the most famous names in German history. In the 1930s Nuremberg became known to the world for another reason. It was the site chosen by Adolf Hitler for the annual Nazi party rallies—extravaganzas unequaled in ceremony, pomp, and mysticism. Other than Munich, Nuremberg was the city most firmly linked to Hitler and Nazism. After World War II ended and most of the ancient city lay in ruins from Allied bombs, Nuremberg was selected as the site of the war crimes trials of Hitler's defeated henchmen. It is probably with this historic event that the name of the city is most closely associated today. Few are unfamiliar with what has come to be known as the Nuremberg Trials.

It was no easy matter to find a suitable location for the trials, because few of the city's buildings were intact. However, the Palace of Justice complex, located on Fürth Strasse approximately three miles from the heart of the city, was eventually decided upon. The buildings had suffered minimal damage and were quickly repaired by German POWs. The largest of the twenty courtrooms housed in the Palace of Justice, the court of assizes, was selected for the trials and was made even larger by knocking out a wall and combining two rooms. To the left and rear of the Palace of Justice was a huge prison, capable of holding over a thousand prisoners. It was divided into several three-tiered wings radiating from a central block. One of these wings was selected to hold the surviving members of Hitler's hierarchy who were to go on trial for their lives, while another was chosen to house the witnesses who were to be used against them. Adjacent to the prison was a large exercise yard, and between the prisoners' and witnesses' wings was a small gymnasium. A wooden walkway was constructed from the prisoners' wing directly to the entry of the Palace of Justice so that the defendants could be escorted to and from the courtroom without outside observance or interference. From the very beginning, the United States Army was determined that it was not going to lose one of its Nazi prisoners at the hands of someone seeking personal vengeance or, more likely, through suicide. Prison officials were to boast that security was so tight as to make suicide "impossible" for the defendants.

Once at Nuremberg, the prisoners lost whatever freedom they had experienced at Mondorf. Arriving at the prison, Goering was taken to a holding cell. Sergeant Raabe went into the cell with him. "My responsibility," he said, "was to go in with the medical people who would do the examining. I would take away Goering's clothes and make sure that the garments were placed in the prison baggage room." In the presence of Sergeant Raabe, the doctors, and prison officials, Goering was forced to strip for a physical examination. His only comment during this humiliating experience was an embarrassed confession of what was all too obvious to those who saw him. "I am too heavy," Goering said.

After the physical examination, Raabe gathered up all the clothes that Goering had been wearing and took them out of the cell. In return, he brought him cast-off GI uniforms, stripped of all insignia. "He didn't have one piece of his own clothing when I walked out of that cell! He didn't have one thing—shoes, boots, anything."

Before placing Goering's uniform in the prison baggage room, Raabe carefully stripped it of all insignia. No military insignia could be worn, nor was German military rank recognized by the Allies; otherwise it would have been necessary to follow the Geneva Convention regulations on the treatment of prisoners of war, who, under it, could not be held in solitary confinement. As Goering learned that night, he was to be held in isolation for the remainder of his life.

While Goering slept fitfully in the holding cell, his permanent cell was being gone over with a fine-tooth comb. "We took everything out that was in that cell," Raabe recalled. "For the first two times, we used GIs who went over every inch of the cell with their hands. The walls were gone over, the floor, the bunk—everything that could not be removed." After the GIs searched the cell, teams of German POWs were used for a double check. "I don't remember who it was, but one of the Germans brought us a nail which we must have missed." When the cell was considered ready for occupancy, a mattress that had been thoroughly inspected was brought in. "We checked that mattress immediately to see if any holes had been pushed into it." No holes were found. Only then was Goering, clad in his GI clothing, brought into the cell that was to be his for the remainder of his life.

When he was placed in Cell #5, prison authorities were satisfied that Goering carried no contraband with him. He was "clean."

Cell #5 was typical of those used to confine all of the accused during the trial. The only furniture in the tiny (4.05 meters by 2.34 meters) cubicle was a metal bunk bolted to the floor and covered by a mattress, a flimsy table designed to break under the weight of a man, and a chair that remained in the cell only during the day. A primitive toilet without a seat was in a recessed alcove to the right of the door. To reduce the possibility of suicide, the cell had been drastically modified by the removal of all electrical wiring, all metal projections from the wall, and the replacement of the glass in the one high window with Plexiglas. The cell had not been properly maintained for years; the whitewashed walls were filthy, and large patches of plaster had fallen away. The large wooden door had a portal through which the prisoners could be observed by a sentinel outside the cell. Throughout the night a light was fixed to shine through this aperture, making sleep all but impossible for Goering, who was not allowed to turn away from the glare or put his head beneath the covers.

The next task of the prison officials was to ensure that Goering remained "clean" and that he was afforded no opportunity to commit suicide. Colonel Andrus, now the prison commandant, initiated the strictest of regulations—rules designed to control the actions of the prisoners from the time they woke up in the morning to the time they went to bed at night. Colonel Andrus later said, "We allowed the prisoners to have no weapons whatever, nor any article that we believed could possibly be used for offense against themselves or anyone else. Their rooms were thoroughly searched when they went to court. When they went to court, they were accompanied by an escort guard. Their clothes were brought to them for court after they had passed examination. Their cells were subjected to search and besides there were periodic shake-downs, when their cells and they were searched together. They were thoroughly searched when they bathed, which was twice a week."

Despite these security regulations, one of the prisoners killed himself before the trial started. On the night of October 24, 1945, Robert Ley, head of the German Labor Front, choked himself to death while sitting on the toilet, the only spot in the cell where he was not in full view of the cell guard. Ley had torn the edge off a towel and tied the end around the pipe that brought water into the toilet. After stuffing rags in his mouth to muffle any noise, he had leaned against the noose he had fashioned at the other end of the towel until he was dead. By the time the guard was aware of what had happened, it was too late.

The flaw in the system that had allowed Ley to kill himself was that a single guard was expected to observe for a period of two hours the activities in four cells. Sergeant Raabe remembered the problems this caused: "When our guards first came to the prison, they were on duty for two hours and then off for four. Now, you visualize yourself standing in front of the doors and looking into those cells for two hours. If one of the prisoners gets up and goes to the toilet, whether it is for two minutes, three minutes, or five minutes, and you are into that second hour, you lose track of time. It's a fatiguing type of thing. And that's how the guard lost Ley."

The result of Ley's suicide was that a guard was placed at each cell door, and only for an hour at a time. Colonel Andrus was determined that no one else would commit suicide while under his supervision.

The problems did not go away. "Although they were watched by guards sixty seconds every minute, sixty minutes every hour, twenty-four hours a day, seven days a week," Sgt. Peter Misko said, "they did manage to acquire items for self-destruction." Misko once found "a four-foot piece of binding tape in a roll of toilet paper." Colonel Andrus himself admitted to even more finds: "We raided the cells of Hess, Goering, Jodl, von Ribbentrop, and Keitel the day the trial started. The searchers found: Ribbentrop had two tablets (one large, one small), three half-tablets, and four larger tablets wrapped in tissue paper concealed in one of his garters, and one sharp piece of metal measuring one and a half by two inches. Jodl's cell had one nail, one piece of wire six inches long and one-sixteenth of an inch in diameter, tooth powder, nine assorted tablets, and some stringy rags. Keitel had hidden away one small piece of sheet-metal, one tube of aspirin tablets, one tube of belladonna tablets, one half-inch screw, and two nails. Goering and Hess were 'clean.' "

Goering remained "clean" throughout the trial. Despite the constant observation and thorough searches, no item of contraband was ever found on his person or in his cell. This remained true until the evening of October 15, 1946.

4
Death in Cell #5

When Lt. Jean Paul Willis reported for duty as officer of the day in the prison on the morning of October 15, 1946, he immediately sensed that something unusual was about to happen. There was greater activity and more of a sense of urgency than he had noticed during the preceding two weeks, the period of time that followed the sentencing of the convicted war criminals. Though all knew that the day of the executions could not be far off, no one in the prison, aside from a selected few, was sure when the day would actually arrive. But Willis soon had reason to believe that October 15 would be the last day of life for Hermann Goering and the other condemned men. As Willis relieved the previous officer of the day, he was told, "You have got lucky. They brought in the coffins last night." Checking, Willis found the eleven coffins neatly stacked and ready to be carried into the gymnasium, the site of the hangings. To allay any suspicions on the part of the condemned that the hangings were imminent, U.S. Army personnel had carried on a spirited and noisy basketball game in the gymnasium during the night. The clamor covered the thudding sounds of the hammers used to construct the three gallows

Willis, now believing that the Nazis would be hanged during his period of duty, set about the task of inspecting the men under his command, telling them when and where they were to be posted and explaining their duties once again. For most of the men, it was old

43

hat; they had already performed the duties dozens of times. They were unaware, if they had not heard the prison rumors, that today would be the last time they would stand duty outside the cells of Goering and the others.

Though there is no direct evidence, it may be assumed that the morning of October 15, 1946, began for Goering as had all previous mornings in the prison. According to the "Prison Routine Schedule," the prisoners were awakened shortly before breakfast. Once up, Goering was given an opportunity to wash himself in a basin of water brought to his cell and later taken away by one of the trusted German employees of the prison. There was no sink or running water in the cell.

Having washed himself, Goering dressed in the gray jacket, pants, and high riding boots that comprised the Reichsmarschall uniform he had worn during the halcyon days of Nazism. But the effect was no longer the same. The ornate shoulder boards, the collar tabs, and medals had long been stripped from the jacket by Sergeant Raabe, and the collar and cuffs were stained with grease and dirt. Only the high riding boots, coveted as a souvenir by every GI in the prison and prized by Goering, looked as good as new. They had been a subject of much discussion when Goering was brought to the prison a year before. It was obvious that the obese Goering could not remove the boots without assistance, and Colonel Andrus did not wish to allow him to keep them. "No way," Andrus told Sergeant Raabe, "are we to be a servant to that man!" The impasse was finally resolved by detailing German workers to help Goering with his boots, thus allowing him to wear his uniform to the courtroom. After he lost weight, he no longer needed assistance with his boots.

Goering's breakfast was brought to his cell by a German prison employee at 7:00 A.M. The American guard on duty thoroughly inspected the U.S. Army mess kit before it was given to the prisoner. After Goering finished eating, the employee returned to the cell to fetch the empty mess kit, making sure that the spoon—the only eating utensil allowed the prisoners—was accounted for. After eating, Goering usually put his personal items in order.

Only in Goering's case was one of the German employees used for the more strenuous tasks of cell cleaning, such as sweeping and mopping. This was a concession allowed Goering all the while he was in the Nuremberg prison. He had long suffered from attacks of tachycardia and a high pulse rate, and Ludwig Pfluecker, the German POW doctor, observed that these attacks were particularly severe on Fridays, the day set aside for cell cleaning. Eventually the prison administration, acting on a suggestion by Dr. Pfluecker, assigned a German worker to clean Goering's cell, a minor victory of which the former Reichsmarschall was very proud.

Prior to October 1, 1946, the date of sentencing, it had been customary for the prisoners to be allowed to walk in the prison courtyard. But this was no longer permitted. Instead, the condemned men were allowed to exercise only in the hallway outside their cells, and then only if handcuffed to a guard. Since October 7, the date of his last visit with his wife, Goering had refused to leave his cell, neither for exercise nor the weekly shower.

Consequently, Goering spent most of the morning of October 15 lounging on his cot reading a German novel. He also received and wrote several letters. The table on which he wrote was bare of all but the most necessary of his belongings. After he had said farewell to his wife on October 7, Goering removed his family pictures from the table, placed them in an envelope, and sent them to his lawyer. Then he broke down and cried. Despite this momentary lapse of self-control, a prison official told newsmen that of all the prisoners, Goering generally "retained the most dignity."

The first testimony on the events of October 15 is that of Pfc. M. C. Parton, the American guard who escorted Dr. Pfluecker to Goering's cell at approximately 8:30 A.M. Parton said that after they entered the cell, the doctor took Goering's pulse. The two Germans talked for ten minutes or so, after which Goering read some papers to the doctor. After several more minutes of conversation and laughter, Pfluecker and Parton left the cell. Parton, who spoke no German, said that he had no idea what the two had discussed and that he did not remember Pfluecker's giving Goering any medicine, nor did he see the doctor hand anything to Goering or leave anything in the cell. "I saw nothing strange happen while we were in there," Parton concluded.

At approximately 9:50 A.M. Pfc. M. C. Odum and the prison barber, another German POW employee, entered Goering's cell. "I kept a close watch on them," Odum said, "and there was nothing suspicious while we were in the cell."

Little else is known of Goering's morning activities. If one again assumes that normal routine was observed on that last day, Goering was served lunch in his cell at noon. The method of delivery and pickup would have been the same as at breakfast, with the cell guard again examining the mess kit.

At approximately 3:15 in the afternoon, Otto, the German librarian, brought Goering a book, which was inspected by the cell guard and then given to Goering. Some tea or coffee was brought to Goering by one of the white-uniformed German kitchen workers at 3:30. Prior to the arrival of the kitchen worker, Otto had returned to the cell with some writing paper that Goering had requested. Goering sat at his table and began to write a letter. According to the cell guard on duty at the time, "He kept on writing with the tea alongside him on the table. As he was writing the doctor came in accompanied by a guard. They sat and talked about 10 minutes during which time he handed him a white envelope which he placed on the table. Then the doctor and the guard left. Goering took the coffee or tea and placed it on the chair in which the doctor had sat. He took the envelope and put his right hand in it opening it, then poured what looked like a white powder into his tea or coffee."

Sgt. Denzil R. Edie, the guard who had escorted Pfluecker to the cell, remembered only that the doctor had again taken Goering's pulse and had given him one small white pill. He made no mention of an envelope. When Edie went off duty at 4:30 P.M., he noticed Goering stretched out on his cot "sleeping with his arms across his chest."

Between 7:30 and 7:45 P.M. Chaplain Henry Gerecke, a Lutheran minister from St. Louis whom Goering had gotten to know well during the many months at Nuremberg, paid his last visit. To all outward appearances, Goering had been one of the chaplain's most faithful supporters in attending services and sitting in the first row, booming out hymns in his rich voice. However, inwardly Goering remained what he always was: a believer in God but not a member of any organized church nor an adherent to orthodox theology. "Pastor, I believe in God," Goering had told Gerecke. "I believe He watches over the affairs of men. But only the big ones. He is too great to bother about little matters like what becomes of Hermann Goering." Because of this attitude, the chaplain had, a few days earlier, refused to allow Goering to take part in the Sacrament. "Some people will think me narrow," Gerecke explained, "but on that point I have fundamental scruples. I could not grant the Lord's Supper to a man denying the divinity of the Savior who initiated this rite."

Still, Gerecke attempted to minister to Goering's religious needs. The chaplain brought with him to Goering's cell a devotional that he had written in German, and he offered it to him. Goering accepted the devotional with a promise to read it later but refused to kneel beside Gerecke while the chaplain prayed. He listened respectfully but remained seated on his cot.

The chaplain said Goering "seemed lower than other days, which to me was not surprising in view of things to come." Goering asked about Fritz Sauckel, another of the condemned men, and complained because he was not allowed to see "poor Sauckel" in order to help him through the day. Gerecke turned the topic of conversation to religion again, asking Goering for "complete surrender of heart and soul to his Savior." Goering evasively replied that he considered himself to be a Christian but that he could not accept all the teachings of Christ. He became more depressed after Gerecke insisted that he could not meet his daughter in heaven if he refused "the Lord's way of salvation." Despite his low spirits, Goering told the chaplain that he felt at ease and hoped he could rest that evening. Convinced that he had done his best to save the condemned man's soul, Gerecke left the cell. It was the last time he would see Goering alive.

The London *Times* revealed a significant detail of Gerecke's last visit with Goering, one that the chaplain did not mention to the board.

The *Times* reported that Goering anxiously quizzed the chaplain about the exact time the executions were scheduled to begin. Gerecke confirmed this in an interview he later gave to the correspondent of a St. Louis paper. According to this correspondent, "all of the condemned men except Goering had the fixed idea in their minds that they would be put to death" on the morning of October 16 at the traditional hour of dawn. "Whether as a result of secret information or just a hunch, Goering apparently suspected the hour would be earlier." Throughout the day of October 15, Goering "plied Gerecke with questions on this point, questions so sharp and clever that the chaplain was forced by military duty to reply with a falsehood. He told Goering he knew nothing about it."

After Gerecke left Goering's cell, Lt. James H. Dowd accompanied Dr. Pfluecker on his evening rounds. At about 9:20 they passed by Goering's cell, and when Lieutenant Dowd asked the doctor if he was not going to see Goering, Pfluecker replied, "I will see him later." The lieutenant looked into Goering's cell and was amazed at the composure of the condemned man. He remembered that "Goering was flat on his back, and the feature which struck me was that his hands were absolutely flat on the top of the covers, and he seemed perfectly asleep. This naturally struck me funny as conduct for a man who must know that his time had nearly arrived. I was struck with the calmness that could allow him to be asleep at such a time. I passed by again twice more that I remember, and both times looked in. He was exactly the same position both times."

Joseph Kingsbury-Smith, one of eight reporters admitted to the prison that night, was also struck by Goering's outward composure. He wrote:

> His body was covered by an ordinary khaki United States Army blanket. One bluish-clad arm was outstretched. The other was folded over his chest with the fist closed. He was lying absolutely motionless with his head resting on one side and his eyes closed, as if in sleep. Goering was the only one of the condemned men in bed at this hour. I turned to the duty officer of the guard, a young lieutenant standing by, and said, "Is he asleep?" The lieutenant shrugged his shoulders and said he did not

know. A few minutes later, Colonel Selby Little, the deputy security commandant, said to me, "Isn't that just like Goering, going to sleep on his last night?" I still thought it strange and so remarked to one of my colleagues.

But Goering was not asleep. He was waiting for Dr. Pfluecker. Lt. Arthur McLinden and the doctor entered Goering's cell at 9:30. McLinden said that Pfluecker gave Goering a pill, which he swallowed as they looked on. The doctor then took Goering's pulse and spoke with him in German. When they left the cell, Goering shook hands with Pfluecker. "I noticed nothing unusual," McLinden said.

Of special interest is the testimony of Pfc. Gordon Bingham and Pfc. Harold Johnson, the two guards who were on duty outside Goering's cell during the last hours of his life. Bingham, who held the watch prior to Johnson's, recalled:

> I went on post as a member of the 1st Relief at 2030 [8:30 P.M.] as a cell guard on Goering's cell. When I arrived at the cell I looked in and Goering was in bed on his back wearing his boots, pants and coat, holding a book in his two hands. He laid there for about 20 minutes, then sat up and laid the book at the head of his bed. He then got up and urinated, then sat on the bed and took off his boots, put on his slippers; picked up the book laying on the left side of the pillow; got up off the bed and went to the table, picked up his glass case and looked in it, then laid it back down on the table. He then picked up his writing materials, which were on the table, putting them on the chair. He then picked up his glass case and looked in it as he laid it on the chair, then handed it to me through the open cell door.

After Goering put his cell in order, he undressed and got into bed, "putting a blanket over his legs and then laid on his back, putting the blanket under his arms, then laid his arms to his side on top of the covers." He remained motionless in that position for approximately fifteen minutes, then he began restlessly moving his hands. "His left hand he kept continually moving between his body and the wall above the covers. He also kept moving his right hand to his forehead and massaging his forehead."

Bingham recounted what he remembered of the 9:30 visit to Goering's cell by Dr. Pfluecker:

> The doctor talked with Goering in German for about 3 minutes and then handed him a pill or capsule which Goering swallowed; then they talked some more. Then the doctor took Goering's pulse with his right hand of Goering's left, then said a few more words in German and got up and shook hands with Goering and left the cell followed by Lt. McLinden. Then I locked the cell and looked in and Goering was looking at me with his body close to the port and lifted off the bed a little and then laid on his back on the bed with his arms at his side above the covers.

Bingham found one aspect of the doctor's visit significant. "From the time Goering sat up in bed when the doctor came in his cell to the time he laid his hand to his side, I could not see his left hand."

After the doctor and Lieutenant McLinden left the cell, Goering lay flat on his back with his hands to his sides. After fifteen minutes or so, he folded his hands on his chest and turned his head toward the wall. Bingham then accidentally knocked the light aside and had to readjust it to shine into the cell. "When I looked in he was looking at me and pointing his fingers at me with his right hand." Goering returned his hand to his side and remained in that position for another few minutes. He then laced his hands over his chest. With his hands still laced, he put them over his eyes, finally returning them to his chest. Goering then unlaced his hands and returned them to his sides. He then put his right hand "under his armpit close to his eyes; then brought his arms to his sides; then lay there for about 10 minutes; then looked at me and then turned away." At this point, Bingham's relief arrived, causing enough commotion to make Goering once again look toward the door. The guard was changed, and Bingham walked away from the cell.

Concluding his statement, Bingham said:

> The only other thing I care to mention is the fact that he looked in his glasses case twice during the late evening tour. The glasses were in the case and he picked them up and looked, carried them away from the table, then turned around and put them back. He then picked up his

suspenders and pencils, put them on the table and then picked up the case and looked in again. I have nothing else to say or anything that would seem of any import in the happenings of that evening and the morning of the next day.

Bingham's period of duty was followed by Pfc. Harold Johnson's, the cell guard who actually saw Goering kill himself. Johnson testified:

I came on duty as a member of the 2nd Relief on Goering's cell at 2230. At that time he was lying flat on his back with his hands stretched out along his sides above the blanket. He stayed in that position for about five minutes without so much as moving. Then he lifted his left hand clenched, as if to shield his eyes from the light, then he let it fall back down to his side above the covers. He lay perfectly motionless till about 2240 when he brought his hands across his chest with fingers laced and turned his head to the wall. He lay that way for about 2 or 3 minutes and then placed his hands back along his sides. That was at 2244 exactly, as I looked at my watch then to check the time. About two to three minutes later he seemed to stiffen and made a blowing, choking sound through his lips. I called the sergeant who was Corporal of the Relief immediately. He was on the second tier and came down as quickly as he could. I told him there was something wrong with Goering, so he took off to the Prison Office on the double.

Johnson then related the frantic coming and going into Goering's cell by the various prison officials. The corporal of the guard returned swiftly to the cell with Lt. Norwood G. Croner and Chaplain Gerecke. Johnson unlocked the door. Croner and Gerecke went in. Goering's right hand hung down off the bed. The chaplain took hold of it as soon as he entered the cell, Johnson remembered. Checking Goering's pulse, the chaplain exclaimed, "Good Lord, this man is dead!" Hearing this, Croner ran out of the cell to fetch Dr. Pfluecker.

Pfluecker remembered that he had, after his farewell visit with Goering, returned to his own room around 10:50. Croner found him there and immediately told him to return to Goering's cell. When he arrived, Pfluecker found Gerecke already in the cell. Contradicting Gerecke's statement that Goering was dead before the doctor arrived, Pfluecker said that "Goering lay back and made one short expiration." Pfluecker took Goering's wrist and found that the pulse was fading away. Goering's face was already turning blue green. It appeared to the doctor as though it were bathed in artificial light.

> I told the officer that Goering was dying and that nothing could be done. I didn't have any experience in dying from poison. I told the officer who was standing in the doorway to call for the American doctor. Then I removed the blanket because I had to examine his heart and then I saw the envelope in one hand. I told the Chaplain to look at the envelope that I found. He took the envelope and felt it and saw that there was a cartridge case in it and 2 or 3 pieces of paper. I did not take the paper out. I tried to open the cartridge shell. There was nothing in it. I put it back in the envelope and gave it to the Chaplain and asked him to please remember that I had found it in Goering's hand. It must have contained the poison. I asked the American doctor to please look at his mouth because if the powder has been in the phial, maybe some of the pieces of glass would still be there.

Pfluecker later wrote that he had been reminded of the suicide of Heinrich Himmler and that a "good spirit" had given him the idea "that Goering probably had taken cyanide and that one might be able to find the glass splinters of the vial between his teeth." Pfluecker was glad that he had had this thought, because finding glass splinters would prove that Goering had actually used cyanide and not the sleeping pills that the doctor had been giving him on a regular basis.

The American doctor to whom Pfluecker addressed his request to look for the glass splinters was Lt. Charles J. Roska. Roska was not sure of the time that he had been summoned by telephone to come to the prison, "about 1030 or 1100 hours," but he rushed to Goering's cell. As soon as he entered, Roska recognized the distinctive odor of cyanide. He examined Goering's body, carefully noting his findings for the report he was later to submit to the board. Roska observed that Goering was lying on the cot, his hands folded over his upper abdomen. Though his body was still warm and showed no signs of rigor mortis, his skin appeared to have a "grayish cyanosis." Goering's eyes were open, but the pupils did not react to light. An examination of the nose and ears showed them to be free of foreign bodies or inflammation. The mouth was partly open and Roska found numerous pieces of glass on the tongue. "They ranged from 0.1 mm in length to 3 mm and were about 0.1 mm in thickness. The larger pieces were shaped as if they had been part of a tube." Goering's umbilicus was of particular interest to Roska. "It was coated with a brownish-black, friable material which extended beyond the periphery about 3 mm. It was easily peeled off with forceps."

Based on the result of his examination of Goering's body and what he had been told by the cell guard, it was Roska's opinion "that death was due to cyanide poisoning."

Arriving at Goering's cell even later than Roska was Capt. Robert Starnes, chief prison officer. Starnes recalled that he had entered the west end of the prison block at approximately 10:50, where he was met by Sgt. Daniel Hauberger, who excitedly told him that Goering was dead. Starnes hurried to the cell, where he found Gerecke and Pfluecker bending over Goering. As Starnes entered the cell, Gerecke told him, "He's dead." Pfluecker repeated this information, assuring the captain, "He was really dead." At the same time, Pfluecker handed him "two white envelopes, letter size." Starnes reached into one of them and withdrew a brass cartridge with a cap. According to Starnes, "Pfluecker explained that he had been summoned to the cell by the Prison Officer and arrived and found Goering dying or dead. He stated that in his examination of the body he heard a rustling noise under the blankets and removing the blankets found two envelopes underneath his hand against his stomach or the middle part of his body."

After briefly examining what Pfluecker had given him, Starnes sent someone to fetch Colonel Andrus "and when he arrived explained to him what I knew of the occurrence and gave him the two envelopes, including the brass cartridge case with cap."

Colonel Andrus recalled the night of October 15, 1946, very well. It would haunt him for the rest of his life. He was, he later wrote, in the guardroom with the Quadripartite Commission "going over the last details of the execution." There had been a demand on the part of the Soviet member of the commission that the condemned men be handcuffed when they were led from their cells to the execution site, but Andrus refused to consider the idea. As they were discussing the matter, a guard rushed in shouting, "Come on, Chaplain! Goering's having a fit!" Andrus raced down the corridor, arriving in the cell just after Gerecke. Someone, Colonel Andrus could not remember who, handed him "a single folded sheet of paper, with the comment that it had been found in Goering's hand. I took the paper, unread, along to the Commission office, where the suicide investigation would almost immediately begin. I did not even try to read the note because if I had, it could have led to 'prejudice.' As Goering was in my charge when he died, I would be the man immediately held responsible for the happening."

The members of the Quadripartite Commission were incredulous when Andrus informed them that Goering had killed himself. They went to the cell to see for themselves. Lieutenant Willis was present when they entered. "And I will never forget," he said, "the Russian general hauling off and slapping Goering across the face. The British general asked him why he had done that, and the Russian answered: 'You can't fake death. The eyes will always move.' " The Russian was satisfied; Goering was indeed dead.

Goering's death panicked the prison officials, and there was, for a few minutes, some discussion among the officers about hanging the corpse. It was proposed that the body be strapped to a stretcher, carried into the execution chamber with the explanation that Goering had fainted, and then be hanged. But cooler heads prevailed, and the plan was quickly dropped when it was pointed out that too many people already knew of Goering's suicide to keep the matter secret. For the time being, the body remained in the cell.

Still shaken by the suicide, the officers in charge of the executions appeared more nervous than those who were to be executed. Whatever dignity and solemnity the occasion called for was all but lost as the remaining ten men were hurried to their deaths. When Hans Frank entered the execution chamber and attempted to speak to Colonel Andrus, he "was not allowed to finish what he was starting out to say. The major, standing at the door, grabbed him and shoved him toward the gallows." Andrus observed that "ruthlessness was not confined to the Germans. A man was experiencing his last seconds on earth and yet he had to be treated so brutally."

The brief agony suffered by Goering was merciful compared to what his condemned comrades had to endure. According to eyewitness reports, the hangings were terribly bungled. Jodl took eighteen minutes to die. Keitel struggled in the air for twenty-four minutes before he died. None of those hanged was blessed with the almost instantaneous state of unconsciousness that precedes death when the neck is broken. The condemned of Nuremberg slowly and painfully strangled to death.

Cut down from the gallows, the bodies of the hanged men were stretched out on top of their coffins behind a partition at one end of the gymnasium. Early in the morning hours of October 16, Lieutenant Willis was ordered to bring Goering's body to the gymnasium. "Four of the escort guards and I loaded Goering onto a stretcher, carried him into the gym, and laid him out next to the others. When Goering's body was brought in, Colonel Andrus, who had been recording the time each man was hanged, contemptuously scribbled beside Goering's name '2:54—carcass delivered.' He then ordered that the blanket covering Goering's body be removed in order for the witnesses to see that he was truly dead. Photographs were taken of all the bodies, both clothed and nude, and they were then placed in the coffins. The ropes used during the hangings were placed with the bodies.

Arrangements were already made for the disposal of the bodies. Lieutenant Willis remembered what happened: "Nick Carter, who had graduated from the West Point Academy, was commanding Service Company of the 26th Infantry. Nick sent two trucks that day for a prison detail. They had arrived and were told to wait. The caskets were loaded into these trucks. The two truck drivers took off with an armed escort in unmarked cars. Wanting to know where the bodies were taken, I called Nick, and Nick said: 'I don't know what happened to those drivers. They never returned, and have been taken off the rolls for the convenience of the Army.' "

What Willis never found out—until I told him—was that the bodies had been taken from Nuremberg to a crematorium in the Ostfriedhof, a cemetery in Munich. A U.S. Army officer had arrived there at 5:00 A.M. on October 16, telling the German attendants that trucks would arrive at 7:00 A.M. with "the bodies of 11 American soldiers, killed and buried during the war, whose ashes had been requested by their families." The bodies did not arrive until 9:00 A.M., at which time the crematorium was surrounded by U.S. Army guards. The eleven caskets were carried into the basement of the crematorium, where the fires were already blazing. The caskets were not opened, and army officers stood watch over the proceedings. The cremations lasted all day, ending at 11:00 P.M. The German attendants "had not exactly been fooled. As soon as they heard the news, they speculated that the need for investigating Goering's suicide had probably delayed the arrival two hours."

The next day, at U.S. Army Mortuary No. 1, at Heilmannstrasse 25, formerly the villa of a wealthy Munich merchant, a small group of army officers walked down a stairway leading from the garden of the villa to the Contwentzbach, a small stream that enters the Isar. Somewhere along this stream, "11 bright aluminum cylinders, some 16 inches high and six in diameter, were lined up in the mixed sand and high grass along the water. One by one, the cylinders were chopped with axes, smashed open with boot-heels, and their contents sifted into the water."

It was hoped that the secret disposition of the eleven bodies would be the last chapter of the Nuremberg Trials. But such was not to be the case. Back at the prison, a furor had been growing ever since Goering's suicide.

After the bodies had been carried away from the prison, Colonel Andrus made his way to the area in which the world's press corps had anxiously been waiting. None knew at this time that Goering had committed suicide. Painfully, Andrus read an announcement to the correspondents:

> Goering was not hanged. He committed suicide at 10:45 last night by taking cyanide of potassium. He was discovered at once by the sentinel who watched and heard him make an odd noise and twitch. The sentinel called the doctor and chaplain who were in the corridor and who found him dying. There were pieces of glass in his mouth and an odor of cyanide of potassium on his breath.

Andrus said that Goering's hands had not gone beneath the covers, nor were they observed to go near his mouth. He told correspondents that "an investigation is now going on to learn how he could have concealed the poison when he was subject to daily and rigorous searches, both of his clothes and his person."

Colonel Andrus's announcement created pandemonium in the press room. The news that Goering had committed suicide was as disastrous and embarrassing to some of the correspondents as it had been to Andrus. Some correspondents, unable to curb their impatience and acting on false tips, had already cabled their newspapers that Goering was the first of the Nazis to hang. It was too late for many to correct their earlier reports, and they seethed with frustration and anger.

The night of the executions would be forever etched into the memories of those reporters who were at Nuremberg. Several later recounted their recollections. "I waited in the press room most of the night," Dana Adams Schmidt recalled. "Some of the correspondents grew impatient. They felt sure that all of the condemned would be executed, and in the early hours of the morning some of them gave way to impatience and filed stories saying that all had been executed. I was one of the last hold-outs. How could I inform the [New York] *Times* unless I was sure? But, at last, finding myself almost alone, I gave in. I typed a cable that read something like: 'All war criminals executed.' As I walked toward the cable office, one of the members of the press pool burst in, yelling, 'Goering committed suicide, cyanide!' I grabbed my cable and quickly added the words, 'except for Goering, who suicided cyanidewise.' "

And G. K. Hodenfield, an AP correspondent who did not give in to impatience, said, "All of the reporters were at the Palace of Justice by 6:00 on the night of the executions, masses of reporters stumbling over each other. Press wireless was set up near the press room to handle the copy. But no official came around to tell anyone what was going on. As far as was immediately obvious, there were not going to be any executions or anything else that night. But they did leave the lights on in the press room and in the hallways."

Working in the dark, figuratively if not literally, Hodenfield and Thomas Reedy, another AP correspondent, "were working our sources for all we were worth, but we weren't learning a thing. Nor was anyone else." Hodenfield recalled that DANA, the American-controlled German news agency, first broke the story that all of the war criminals had been executed. Then most of the reporters caved in and sent similar stories. "Reedy and I were catching hell from New York and from the German bureau in Frankfurt. How come we didn't know what everyone else seemed to know? We could have followed the herd. Our sources indicated that it was all over." But Reedy was adamant that no story could be filed until they *knew* that all of the war criminals had been executed. Hodenfield was torn between desiring to file his report along with the other correspondents and heeding the advice of Reedy. "I thought that my short and happy career with AP was over, and that I'd probably be fired for not having the story that everyone else had." But the counsel of Reedy prevailed, and Hodenfield continued to wait.

The news conference took place at 6:00 A.M. After Andrus told the correspondents that Goering had committed suicide, there was a moment of complete silence as many of the reporters realized that their impatience had caused them to make a terrific blunder. The silence was broken by Reedy, who stood up and shouted, "Yeahh, you smart-ass sons of bitches!" The correspondents then made a mad dash to the cable room in an attempt to correct their earlier reports.

Standing almost alone and forgotten in the emptying press room, Colonel Andrus slumped dejectedly, his customary panache completely gone. Goering's death was a personal disaster for him, as the commandant had set great stock in the "smooth running" of the trial and the executions. Andrus had tried hard to do what was expected of him. According to Hans Fritzsche, one of the defendants, Andrus had "asked us to help and work together with him" in order that the trial might give "the best possible picture" to the outside world. Once, after Goering had loudly cursed a hostile witness, Colonel Andrus again spoke to the defendants, emphasizing "the importance he placed upon a peaceful, undisturbed, and worthy manner of the proceedings." With one act, Goering had rendered null and void all of Colonel Andrus's work.

What Andrus might not have realized at the time was that much more than just his personal career was to be called into question by Goering's final act of contempt for his captors and the trial to which they submitted him. The first reaction of a member of the United States prosecution team when he heard the news of Goering's suicide was that "Goering has wiped out all the work of the Tribunal!" Goering's suicide was beginning to show international ramifications.

5

Why Suicide?

It has never been a mystery why Goering, with certain death facing him, elected to kill himself. The reason was not, as suggested by Dr. Gustave Gilbert, the prison psychologist, that Goering's nerves "would probably not stand up under an approach to the gallows." Gilbert should have known better. The two had often discussed death, and once when they were considering the inevitability of Goering himself being sentenced to death, Goering told the psychologist, "Hell, I haven't been afraid of death since I was twelve or fourteen years old!" During a later conversation with Gilbert, Goering philosophized, "Ah, but you musn't value life too highly, my dear professor. Everyone has to die sooner or later. And if I can have the chance to die as a martyr, why so much the better. Do you think everybody has that chance? If I can have my bones put in a marble casket, that is, after all, a lot more than most people achieve."

Goering did not like Gilbert, and he resented the doctor's repeated insinuations that he would not have the courage to face his court-imposed fate. Tired of arguing with Gilbert, he challenged him to come to the hangings "and see how I handle myself."

Before Goering's suicide, Gilbert told reporters that the Nazi leader had said that he "would take some secrets to the grave." Gilbert also said that Goering believed his secrets would enable Nazism to revive within ten to twenty years, and he was spending his final days in contemplation of a "secret revenge" on the Allies. However, Gilbert had no idea of the nature of the "secret revenge" planned by Goering, and he dismissed this threat and Goering's insistence that death held no terror for him as sheer bravado.

Two psychiatrists who examined Goering at Nuremberg disagreed with Gilbert's opinion of him. Dr. Douglas M. Kelley said of Goering: "He faces his fate in a philosophical fashion. He expects to hang and there is no psychiatric problem. There is little expectancy that he will break at any point. . . ." Lt. Col. William H. Dunn said that Goering "will face his sentence bolstered by his egocentricity, bravado and showmanship" and perceptively predicted that Goering "would seize any opportunity to go out fighting."

Goering knew all along that he would be sentenced to death by the tribunal, and he often discussed the matter with Dr. Kelley. He told him, "What is there to be afraid of? After I have given orders to hundreds of thousands of men to go into battle, frequently knowing full well that many would not come back, plain soldiers who had no choice in the matter, should I, their leader, cringe when called on to face the enemy?"

Kelley never believed Goering's words were empty ones but considered them to be an accurate gauge of his true feelings. A few years after Goering's death, Kelley wrote: "At Nuremberg, Goering assumed that he would be found guilty and condemned to death. He accepted this fate—maintaining constantly that he was being punished as a German patriot rather than a war criminal—and throughout the trial concerned himself with keeping his name as free as possible from the taint of atrocities and war crimes."

While Goering had accepted as a foregone conclusion that he would be sentenced to death, he could not reconcile himself to the manner in which the sentence was to be carried out. In his mind, hanging was fit only for criminals, and he never considered himself to be a criminal but a defeated soldier. He had long before told Dr. Richard Worthington, another of the Nuremberg psychiatrists, that he and the other Nazi leaders would be executed, not because they were guilty of any crimes but because they had lost the war. He told

Dr. Gilbert shortly after sentence was pronounced, "At least I should be spared the ignominy of the noose. I am a soldier. I have been a soldier all my life, always ready to die by another soldier's bullet. Why shouldn't a firing squad of my enemies dispatch me now?"

Goering's attitude was no different from those of Field Marshal Wilhelm Keitel and Col. Gen. Alfred Jodl, who had also been sentenced to hang. Dr. Gilbert graphically described their utter horror and dismay upon hearing that they were to die on the gallows:

> Keitel was already in his cell, his back to the door, when I entered. He wheeled around and snapped to attention at the far end of the cell, his fists clenched and arms rigid, horror in his eyes. "Death—by *hanging*!" he announced, his voice hoarse with intense shame. "That, at least, I thought would be spared. I don't blame you for standing at a distance from a man sentenced to death by hanging. I understand that perfectly. But I am still the same man as before. If you will please only visit me sometimes in these last days."

Jodl's reaction was much the same. Dr. Gilbert wrote of a visit to his cell:

> Jodl marched to his cell, rigid and upright, avoiding my glance. After he had been unhandcuffed and faced me in his cell, he hesitated a few seconds, as if he could not get the words out. His face was spotted red with vascular tension. "Death—by *hanging*! *That*, at least, I did not deserve. The death part—all right, somebody has to stand for the responsibility. But that!" His mouth quivered and his voice choked for the first time. "That I did not deserve."

For the military men, hanging was an affront to their honor, the only thing left to them. Goering also acutely felt the shame shared by Keitel and Jodl. Gilbert recorded that he returned to his cell in a state of extreme agitation after sentence was pronounced. "His eyes were moist and he was panting, fighting back an emotional breakdown." Goering did not want to talk, and he asked Gilbert to leave him alone for a while. Only later did he give in to his anger.

Goering did not appeal, but his lawyer petitioned that the death sentence be commuted to life imprisonment. Goering himself wished no commutation but asked only that the mode of execution be altered from hanging to shooting. He knew full well that no lessening of the penalty would be granted, but he did hope that he could, at least, be spared the shame of the gallows.

What Goering did not know was that the method of execution was unalterably fixed. The members of the tribunal had already quarreled among themselves on this very matter. The French member, Donnedieu de Vabres, had suggested that shooting be used as "a more honorable" form of execution, and Francis Biddle, his American counterpart, agreed that shooting be employed as a form of "mitigation." General Nikitchenko, the Soviet member of the tribunal, violently disagreed with his colleagues. "Even the thought of using a form of capital punishment as a kind of mitigation did not catch Nikitchenko's fancy, and he decried the waste of time taken up by a discussion of what he termed 'ridiculous trifles.' " The Russian insisted that hanging was the only method of execution that could be considered, and the other members of the tribunal, in an effort to maintain solidarity acceded to Nikitchenko's demands. Thus Goering's manner of execution had been long decided, and his request to be shot was never considered.

This information was conveyed to him by Dr. Gilbert and came as no real surprise. Resigned to the fact that he would not face a military firing squad, Goering jokingly commented, "Well, if they won't alter the sentence, perhaps it is just as well, as I have heard that the Americans can't shoot straight." Colonel Andrus, for one, was not fooled by Goering's studied nonchalance. Many years later Andrus wrote, "It was probably at that moment that the defeated and deflated Reichsmarschall made his last terrible decision. *He would kill himself.*"

Dr. Gilbert, who saw him for the last time only three days before his death, testified that Goering was even more bitter than usual. Gilbert told the board Goering had complained "that the Control Council might at least have given them another method of execution." Even Gilbert was forced to admit to the board that Goering's suicide was motivated "by a desire to escape the ignominious picture he felt he would make in history as one who was hanged for his crimes." Chaplain Gerecke said that on the very day of the executions, Goering

"was again critical of the method of execution. Called most dishon-
orable for him because of his former position with the German people."

The same theme was present in Goering's letter to Colonel Andrus,
in which he alluded to the reason for his suicide: "Dr. Gilbert has just
informed me that the Control Board has refused the petition to change
the method of execution to shooting." In his last letter to his wife,
Goering was even more explicit: "After careful consideration and heart-
felt prayers to God, I have decided, rather than to allow my enemies
to hang me, to kill myself. I would at any time accept death by shooting.
But the hanging of Germany's *Reichsmarschall* cannot be allowed."

Some tried to brand the suicide as an act of cowardice. Justice
Robert H. Jackson, who prosecuted him, said that by his suicide Goering lost any chance to become a German martyr: "If Goering had
been made of the same stuff that could walk to the gallows voicing
some patriotic sentiment such as Nathan Hale's regret that he had but
one life to give to his country, he might well have become a German
martyr. When he took his own life he killed the myth of Nazi bravery
and stoicism and deep conviction."

Colonel Andrus told reporters that Goering had disgraced himself
by his suicide: "If he had the courage of a mouse, he would have tried
to hang on to his life as long as possible."

Others disagreed with Jackson and Andrus, both of whom Goering
had embarrassed during and after the trial. Gen. Henry H. Arnold,
former chief of the U.S. Army Air Force, told reporters that he was
not at all surprised by the manner of Goering's death. The former air
commander said that the way Goering died "was typical of the German
mind. Knowing the temperament of Goering, I expected something
like this to happen. He was very dramatic and always tried to do the
unexpected." In a classic understatement, Arnold added: "The average
German does not want to hang."

Surviving members of the German officer corps were also impressed
by the manner of Goering's death. His decision to kill himself had all
the positive psychological effect that Goering could have hoped for,
restoring somewhat his tarnished reputation even among those German
generals who had previously despised him. Typical was the reaction

of Col. Gen. Heinz Guderian: "Only in prison and by the manner of his death did Goering do something to atone for his past negligence. By taking his own life he escaped from his terrestrial judges, after having openly defended his own past actions."

Even Dr. Jacob Leistner—the German public prosecutor, an avowed anti-Nazi, and a witness to the executions—was forced to admit that "a number of Germans will regard Goering's action as a last vestige of courage and will rejoice that the man who was second in command to Hitler did not have to die a different death."

None of Goering's subsequent biographers have suggested that the manner of his death was cowardly. On the contrary, his suicide only added to the "Goering legend." Typical, if more fulsome, is the comment of Charles Bewley:

> Suffice it to say that Hermann Göring did not hold, and could not be expected to hold, the Catholic view of the sacredness of that human life which has been conferred on the individual by his Creator. He had been brought up in the pagan military tradition that under certain circumstances suicide is not only a legitimate, but the only honorable way out of the difficulties of existence. Moreover, it may be reasonably contended that the preference of death by poison to death by the hangman's noose was no suicide, but a mere choice between methods of meeting the inevitable end. Nor, regarding it from another point of view, can it be suggested that Göring, like Hitler, Goebbels and Himmler, was by taking his life evading the responsibility for his acts before and during the War and leaving it to others to suffer the penalties which should have been his. His duty had been done according to his lights and in leaving the world he left no task unfulfilled.

Some might not accept all the sentiments expressed by Bewley, but the Board of Officers was not in total disagreement. The board never considered cowardice to be the reason for Goering's suicide but concluded that he had killed himself to "avoid a means of execution he bitterly opposed."

With the reason for Goering's suicide already known, the board had yet to determine *how* he had managed to kill himself.

6

The Investigation

Goering's suicide eclipsed even the hanging of the other ten condemned men, and almost immediately an investigation was begun by army authorities. A three-man Board of Officers was appointed to investigate Goering's suicide less than an hour after he swallowed the poison. The board was ordered into existence by verbal command of Brig. Gen. Roy V. Rickard, the American member of the Quadripartite Commission. The purpose of the board was "to investigate and report on the suicide of Hermann Goering, convicted war criminal." General Rickard's verbal order was later confirmed in writing by Gen. Joseph T. McNarney, commander in chief of all United States armed forces in Europe. Thus the investigation carried the highest possible military sanction.

General McNarney approved Rickard's appointment to the board of Col. B. F. Hurless, Lt. Col. William H. Tweedy, and Maj. Stanley T. Rosenthal, all of whom were to work in complete anonymity. Colonel Hurless, as ranking officer, headed the board—an appointment that probably came as a surprise to him, because he had been sent by Third Army Headquarters to act only as an official witness to the executions. The other two officers were members of the 6850th Internal Security Detachment, the unit that had been responsible for prison security at the time of Goering's death.

The board was charged with two specific tasks:

1. The board will investigate all matters connected with the safe-guarding of the major war criminals confined in the Nuremberg Jail, establish the manner by which Prisoner Goering obtained the poison with which he took his own life and fix any responsibility in connection therewith.
2. The board will submit its report to the Allied Commission for the Control of Major War Criminals.

Work began almost immediately after the suicide. At 11:45 on the night of Goering's death, the officers of the board went to Cell #5, "which still contained the remains of Hermann Goering, the former occupant, for the purpose of making an examination of the contents thereof." A special guard was placed at the door of Goering's cell to prevent entrance by unauthorized persons. An itemized and detailed list was made of everything found in the cell. "Except for the remains of Goering, the bunk, and bedding, the cell and its contents were thoroughly examined and searched for clues which might shed light on the suicide." Few clues were found, but the board was suspicious of a "cellophane envelope containing a white powder" and took it for examination. The search was concluded at 1:50 A.M. on October 16.

At 2:45 A.M. the remains of Goering, still clad in silk pajamas, were removed from the cell and taken to the gymnasium for further inspection and preparation for disposal. Accompanied by the board, Lieutenant Roska and Lieutenant Martin, both medical officers, closely inspected Goering's corpse. The pajamas were removed and searched. Nothing of significance was discovered, other than what Roska had already noted when he viewed Goering's body in the cell earlier that night. "The body," the board found, "was clean and absolutely free of eruptions, abrasions, wounds and bruises." It was also noted that the navel "was abnormally large but too small to conceal a tube the size of Exhibit 'A,' " the poison container.

Goering's body was placed on top of his temporary coffin and pictures were taken. His right eye remained open and his left one closed, as if he were winking at the officers on whom he had played his final, macabre joke.

The board returned to Goering's cell, where it then conducted a "thorough search of the bedding and bunk." Nothing significant was found "except several rents, including one conspicuous rip at the foot" of the mattress. According to the statement of Lt. John West, "When this mattress was inspected at approximately 1945, 14 October 1946, this mattress was not torn on either side." Nevertheless, the board decided that the filling of the mattress "had not been disturbed to the extent to indicate the mattress had been used for a protracted place of concealment."

After its inspection of Goering's cell, the board decided to take to the Criminal Investigation Department (CID) laboratory at Frankfurt the following items:

1. A small brass container made from a cartridge case
2. Particles removed from Goering's navel
3. A cellophane envelope containing a white powder
4. A sample of putty from the window of Goering's cell
5. Goering's Bavarian-style pipe

The board worked throughout the night and adjourned at 6:00 A.M. on October 16.

The members assembled again at 11:00 A.M. on October 19 and conducted an examination of Goering's personal effects that were still in the prison baggage room. There, hidden in a jar of skin cream in Goering's elaborate vanity case, the board found yet another brass cartridge. This one still held its vial of clear liquid. The cartridge was sent to the 385th Station Hospital in Nuremberg where the vial was broken open and the contents analyzed. The board closed its meeting at 6:00 P.M.

The next meeting of the board was on October 23, during which time it heard the personal testimony of those close to Goering who had not prepared written statements during the night of October 15. Heard by the board were Colonel Andrus, Lieutenant Roska, Dr. Pfluecker, Captain Starnes, and Maj. Frederic C. Teich, Jr.

Those in charge of security in the prison were placed in a very difficult position after Goering's suicide. They could protest that they had done everything reasonably possible to ensure that their charges had no means to kill themselves, but the unalterable fact remained that Hermann Goering was able to commit suicide with relative ease and at a moment of his own choosing. It could be presumed that the security system in the prison had been less than effective if Goering was able to smuggle the poison into the prison and then hide it in various places throughout the trial. Worse yet would be the discovery that someone within the prison had given Goering the poison. If either negligence or conspiracy were found, Colonel Andrus knew he would be held responsible. Consequently, he made a spirited defense of the security measures he had initiated and of the loyalty and dependability of the men he had picked to staff the prison.

After he had taken the oath administered by Colonel Hurless, the prison commandant detailed for the board the stringent security regulations and searches he had initiated. "I have always thought the searches were thorough and that no one could keep anything concealed with which he could take his life," Andrus assured the board.

Undeniably, Goering had kept something hidden with which he was able to take his own life, and the board required from Andrus additional information on prison security regulations. He said that the baggage room where the personal and valuable property of the prisoners was kept was always locked and under the supervision of an officer. If it was necessary for a prisoner to get something from the baggage room, he was "accompanied by an escort guard and permitted to get whatever he wanted with the officer watching him." Colonel Andrus insisted that there was one piece of luggage to which Goering had never been given access—"a vanity case containing bottles, jars, nail file, scissors, etc." It also contained, the board knew, the second container of poison.

When asked about restrictions on visitors to the prisoners, Andrus said that they were "never permitted any visitors within the jail and were visited only by members of my staff in their cells. They were brought to interrogations conducted by Allied interrogators in the interrogation rooms. They were accompanied by escort guards whose duty it was to see that they were not subjected to insults or indignities. Nothing was given them to take out of the interrogation room."

Meetings between the prisoners and defense counsel, Andrus explained, were even more stringently supervised: "To meet with their defense counsel they were taken to a room where they consulted with the defense counsel across a barred partition made of windshield glass. If they had to pass documents back and forth they had to get permission from the sentinel, who had to open the slide. But the lawyer could not give anything to the prisoner unless it was first searched. Anything given back had to be searched."

Andrus admitted that security in the court was more lax. He said that documents were passed back and forth with much more freedom and that the sentinel "could only make a cursory search of anything passed. The prisoners and defense counsel passed notes back and forth constantly."

Despite the greater amount of freedom permitted by conditions in the courtroom, Andrus paid tribute to the guards posted there. He recounted the example of a lawyer who passed a document to one of the prisoners at the end of the dock only to have the guard immediately snatch it and reprove the lawyer. He also recalled one instance when Adm. Karl Doenitz attempted to shake hands with his lawyer, "and the guard reached up with his stick and shook his hand away." Still, Andrus conceded that the vial of poison could have been passed to Goering in the dock, "possibly by one of the lawyers, if the lawyer were a sleight of hand artist."

The possibility that one of the German employees in the prison might have given the poison to Goering was rejected by Andrus. He told the board, "I believe the German employees of the jail are absolutely loyal and wholly unsympathetic toward the condemned men. They were prisoners themselves and had no opportunity to get any poison. When I was at Mondorf I was given 250 Wehrmacht PW's. When I came to Nuremberg, I selected for my staff only the best 26 out of that 250. 2 new employees came to me since then to relieve losses I sustained."

Andrus explained that these Germans were never allowed to leave the prison during the course of the trial. After he discovered the trial would be lengthy, he "made arrangements with the Military Government to have them put on an employee status. They signed contracts to remain with me on a full prison status and getting a wage scale for their particular qualification." Only after the trial was concluded, Andrus said, were the German employees allowed to leave the prison at will.

In support of his trust in the German employees, Andrus related the story of the German kitchen worker who, after Goering had complained of the poor quality of the food, severely rebuked the former Reichsmarschall. "I believe," Andrus stated, "the tone of that reply was characteristic of the attitude of our help toward the defendants." When Andrus was asked if he believed that this remark reflected the attitude "of all your German help," he replied, "I believe that. I believe that everyone of them blamed the defendants for the plight that they themselves were in and that the working class in general are resentful and that all of them were pleased when they heard the sentences of these prisoners."

Andrus was asked where the vial of poison could have come from, and although he was unable to answer the question, he elaborated on where it could *not* have come from: "The phial of poison could not have been smuggled to Goering by messenger. No messenger brought anything to these prisoners. The only way he ever received anything in his hand was from my staff. He received his food from the kitchen under a guard. They received books from the prison library. These books were cleared and inspected by the Military Government before they were ever placed in the library. They received documents from their lawyers, and after they had been in session and documents were passed to them, they were examined. Paper was examined for color and odor before it was passed to them, because paper saturated with poison would cause death. Food was served under supervision and the cooks could not have had any poison."

Colonel Andrus admitted, however, that had any of the prisoners the means with which to take his own life, it would not have been difficult for him to determine the most opportune day to do so. The prisoners were sentenced on October 1, and on the same day, they were informed that they had the right to petition for clemency. "On the 13th of October the decisions . . . were received back here." All of the petitions, including those of the military men asking to die before a firing squad, were rejected. This information was relayed to the condemned men, all of whom knew that the charter governing the trial procedure provided for the executions to commence within fifteen days after sentence was pronounced. "The condemned men," Andrus told the board, "had every reason to believe that the executions would occur on the date that they did." It was *not* through negligence or any breach of security, Andrus insisted, that the prisoners had this information, but through official channels and deductive reasoning.

Andrus was asked if any poison had been found on Goering or in his luggage "at any time after Goering was turned over to you." The commandant answered, "Yes, there was. A brass tube containing a phial assumed to by cyanide, which all the top Nazis were reported to have had, was found in Goering's baggage when he was first imprisoned. This tube was found in a can of coffee."

One of Andrus's replies might be misleading to someone who had no information other than what is contained in the report. After he was asked how long Goering had been in Cell #5, Andrus replied: "All of the prisoners were changed from the cells into which they were first placed. I don't remember just when this was done, but the records will show." Andrus was telling the truth; *all* of the prisoners had been switched from the cells that they originally occupied after entering the prison. But this was done in October 1945, a full year before Goering's death. After sentence was pronounced in October 1946, only those who were given prison terms were again moved—this time to cells on the second tier. The condemned remained in the same cells that they had occupied for the past year.

Colonel Andrus was followed on the witness stand by Lieutenant Roska, one of the two American doctors who had attended Goering at Nuremberg. Roska said that he visited Goering only periodically, but when Pfluecker discovered illness in any of the prisoners, "I would check what they had and what kind of medicine he gave. And periodically, Lt. Martin and I would check on them ourselves." Roska told the board that every time Pfluecker went into one of the cells, a security guard accompanied him, "but when I went in alone, only a door guard."

Roska said that he had last seen Goering "about three days before he was to be executed." He said of their last meeting: "That evening I went into his cell, sat down and talked to him. He talked about literature, the Russians, and told me about some of the secret army work in the Russian army by former Germans. I asked him how he felt. He seemed in good spirits. He was not depressed. During the two weeks he was waiting for execution, he knew he had to die and told me that his father had told him to do anything he ever wanted to do and do it with a smile. That was the way he conducted his life."

The board expressed an interest in Roska's personal knowledge of cyanide. "Isn't it true," they asked, "that you worked in a laboratory where cyanide was used?" "Yes," he answered, "I have smelled cyanide many times before." Roska was then asked several technical questions about the effect of cyanide, most of which he was unable to answer with any degree of certainty.

The board was also interested in the dark brown substance that had been found around Goering's umbilicus. When he was asked if this matter had ever been noticed on any physical examination given Goering prior to his suicide, Roska answered that it had not.

Strangely, Roska was the only witness questioned who professed not to know when the executions were scheduled to take place. He was asked, "Do you have any reason to believe that anyone outside of the certain designated authorities knew of the execution date?" Roska answered, "No, sir. I didn't know it myself until that afternoon when a conducted tour of the prison was made."

After several questions about Goering's general health, his loss of weight, and medication prescribed him, the board concluded its examination of Lieutenant Roska.

Roska was followed on the stand by Dr. Pfluecker, who more closely attended the prisoners and who had been with them throughout their incarceration. Of all the German employees, Pfluecker had the most free and frequent access to Goering. He saw him twice a day during the trial and more frequently after sentence was pronounced.

Pfluecker, a former major in the German army, told the board why he had been picked for the position of prison doctor: "I was a prisoner of war for 14 weeks in France. About the 10th of July [1945] an American medical officer came to the camp where I was a prisoner of war, looking for a German doctor. As I speak a little English, he took me, although I was old. As we got to Mondorf, he told me that I would have a job which a young doctor had until now, but this doctor was too young and could not handle the men. I saw a whole lot of high ranking German officers and the prison officer, Capt. Biddle, told me, 'You will handle the top Germans. What do you think about this work?' "

If Pfluecker had any distaste for this work, he did not express it to Captain Biddle. Instead, he set about winning the trust and confidence of his new patients. Pfluecker told the board that "my top patient was Goering." The former Reichsmarschall was in a very bad state of health. He suffered from heart problems and bronchitis. In addition, he was undergoing treatment for addiction to paracodeine. "The cure was difficult," Pfluecker said, "and it was not so easy to handle him at first, but because Goering was a very clever man and saw he had no power with his doctor, he gave in."

"Goering often had heart attacks," Pfluecker said. To alleviate the stress that promoted these attacks, the prison authorities gave Pfluecker permission to administer sedatives to Goering, who was also given phenobarbital every day and two sleeping pills every night.

The board wanted to know how these pills were doled out to Goering and whether he might have had an opportunity to accumulate enough of them to kill himself. "I always gave it personally and saw him swallow it," Pfluecker said of the medication. Still, the doctor was distrustful of his "top patient." Pfluecker told the board that he had often talked with Goering, imploring him never to attempt to conceal any of the tablets. "It would be great trouble for me," Pfluecker told him. Goering replied, "Doctor, I will never bring you any trouble." But Pfluecker was not totally convinced, telling the board, "I wouldn't trust him very much."

Questioning by the board revealed that Pfluecker had reason to be wary of Goering because the two had on several occasions discussed suicide and sleeping pills: "I talked with him sometime and he asked me how many sleeping pills would be dangerous and I told him 20 or 30 would bring a deep sleep. It is not so easy to die from sleeping pills. Another thing, he was very oriented about poison. He told me he knew he would never die from taking sleeping pills. They are not sure." The board then asked how often Goering had discussed suicide and poisons with the doctor. Pfluecker replied, "One or two times. I had the impression that he knew enough about sleeping pills and how difficult it was to die. He could take 40 pills of paracodeine, so he couldn't think of committing suicide with sleeping pills." When asked if there had been any talk about suicide after October 1, Pfluecker answered, "Surely not. It was long before."

Despite the fact that they had discussed suicide on several occasions, the doctor insisted that Goering had given no indication that he was seriously thinking of taking his own life. "I was very surprised," Pfluecker told the board. Asked if he thought that Goering "may have received the poison in the last month," Pfluecker said, "That is too much speculation." However, when he was then asked if he thought that Goering had always had the poison while in the prison, Pfluecker readily agreed that this was his opinion. "He never said anything that would indicate that he might have poison in his cell or on his person?" queried the board. Pfluecker did not answer the question directly but stated, "He was always a man to try to show sincerity, but it was not easy to trust him." The board had a final question on poison: "To your knowledge, had Goering approached anyone else on the subject of poison?" Pfluecker replied that he did not know.

Pfluecker told the board that on the night of October 15, he had given Goering only one actual sleeping pill. The second was filled with sodium bicarbonate. His reason for doing so, Pfluecker told the board, was that he did not wish to give Goering two strong sleeping pills "and have him be asleep and then be awakened for the execution. And therefore, I did not give the strong sleeping pills because he would be awakened ½ hour afterwards and maybe get excited."

Pfluecker was asked if Goering knew that it was the night of the executions. "He told me, 'I know it.' He was a clever man. He saw the lights burning and I am sure he knew it was the night." The doctor added that it was "common knowledge" among all the condemned. "Somebody asked me if he could take off his clothes and I told him 'I don't know.' "

The board sharply questioned Pfluecker about his shaking hands with Goering during their last visit, asking if it was a common practice. He said he knew that shaking hands was a violation of the rules, "but the last time it was difficult for a doctor not to shake hands." However, Pfluecker admitted that he had shaken hands with Goering "since the sentences were delivered." "Each night?" asked the board. Growing uneasy, the doctor tried to hedge his answer, "I don't remember. I felt every evening and every morning, his pulse." The board was not satisfied with this reply and again asked the doctor how many times he had given Goering his hand. Pressed, Pfluecker admitted that he had done so "about 5 or 6 times," after the two had "deep talks." Pfluecker recalled one "deep talk" followed by a handshake took place after Goering saw his wife for the last time. Appealing to the board, Pfluecker explained, "If you had been with this man for 15 months you would understand." The board dropped the matter, and Pfluecker was excused.

The board then summoned Captain Starnes, chief prison officer, whom they closely questioned about prison security. Starnes, who reported directly to Colonel Andrus, was also in a difficult position. He told the board: "Goering had an American sentinel on duty at his cell 24 hours a day, to my personal knowledge, since the 26th of November last year. [This was after Dr. Ley's suicide.] During the time court was in session, Goering was moved from his cell to the court room and back again daily except on those days when there was no court. He was also moved from his cell to other places, such as, rooms 54 and 56 for meetings with his lawyers and later with his family. At any time he was away from his cell there was an American sentinel with him. Only when he was in the exercise yard in or near the prison did the guard get more than two or three paces away from him. While court was in session and Goering was away from his cell, it was searched regularly by a member of the prison staff, one of the wardens under the supervision of an officer."

Starnes told the board that Goering was taken to the interview rooms on only seven occasions from October 1 to October 15. "On each trip to an interview he was under guard of two United States Army soldiers, handcuffed to his cell guard and accompanied by a member of the Prison Escort Guard."

Goering's clothes were sent to the laundry each week, Starnes told the board. The clothing passed through the hands of the German civilian workers in the jail, who carried it to the laundry and brought it back to the prison for distribution. The clothing was carefully inspected by the cell guard when it left the cell and when it was returned. When Starnes was asked if Goering was ever stripped and a simultaneous search of his clothes and person made, he replied, "Yes, he was. On some occasions, when we were suspicious of him, we made a search of all his clothes. He was held when he returned from court. He was caught at the time of his return and searched immediately before he could get rid of anything. His clothes were taken off."

Starnes, too, discounted the possibility that the German kitchen workers could have passed the poison to Goering. "All this food passed in front of the American sentinel who had orders to examine any food and other articles passed into the cell."

If Goering ever wanted anything from the luggage room, Starnes said, "he was required to furnish a written report or to make a verbal request to the German civilian, Streng, who would transmit that request to me." There were very few times that Goering requested anything, and Starnes could not remember "any instance currently." He did know that Goering received an exchange of uniforms from the luggage room so that he could appear "neat and clean" for court.

The board turned its attention to the German workers with whom Starnes worked very closely. "During the period 15 October," the board asked, "did you notice any suspicious actions or activities by any of the German help in that part of the prison?" Starnes replied that he had not. He was then asked, "Do you feel confident that none of them would participate in a plot to give one of the condemned a vial of poison?" Starnes answered, "That is rather a difficult question as far as my personal judgement goes. I trust those men. If I had distrusted them before that time I would have restricted their actions or had them watched more closely, but I did not and I trust them. Right now I trust them as much as anyone else, as well as Americans. They gave me no reason, at any time, to distrust them."

After Starnes was asked if searches were made of the living quarters of the German workers, he answered, "Yes, several." However, he had to admit that none was made "within six weeks to two months" preceding Goering's suicide.

Starnes also told the board that, in his opinion, there were enough unusual happenings on the night of October 15 that Goering could probably deduce the executions were about to take place. "The fact that eight reporters visited the jail at a late hour was very unusual. I would say a man could construe the activities to mean that."

The baggage room remained a source of interest to the board, and Starnes was followed by Major Teich, the officer whose responsibility it had been to enforce security regulations pertaining to the prisoners' personal belongings stored there. Teich told the board, "When a prisoner comes to the prison he is divested of all his baggage except those items which are absolutely necessary. Goering had 4 pieces of baggage which contained every imaginable type of item. He had 2 large suitcases, one hat box, and one small fitted bag. Subsequent to the time when they are processed and placed in cells, many of the prisoners make requests for certain items from among the pieces of their baggage, which have been placed in the baggage room. These requests, if they are reasonable and necessary, are granted."

Teich said that he always checked the items removed from the baggage room, but he could recall "no instance in which Goering requested any items from his luggage and there is no record in his file of such a request." When he was asked if anyone could have given Goering anything without first getting approval, Teich replied that the prison officer would have a key to the baggage room. However, he added, "I feel certain that nothing has passed through the grating of room 57 that was not inspected by an officer." With this comment, Teich completed his testimony.

Teich was the last to be questioned by the board. Following the parade of witnesses, there was the board's consideration of the reports from the 385th Station Hospital and the 27th CID laboratory. The former was the more succinct.

Capt. Milton Silverman, who was given the suicide device found in Goering's vanity case, reported: "Ampoule contents submitted for analysis, 23 Oct 46, qualitatively shown to contain cyanide or a cyanide derivative by Prussian Blue Test."

The CID report was much more lengthy and complex. Various techniques were employed in examining the brass cartridge found in Goering's hand. Material was removed from the top, bottom, and rim of the cartridge. Examined microscopically, these specimens showed remarkable similarity of color, texture, and organic structure. As the CID lab was not equipped for bacteriological work, the specimens were taken to the 4th Medical Laboratory at Darmstadt. There they were examined by Capt. Milton Silverstein, the European theater chief serologist.

Various media for culturing bacteria were prepared by Silverstein, and they were inoculated with material from the shell case. When the cultures were examined, they were found to be mostly negative for any type of bacteria. Silverstein suspected a preservative had been added to these specimens that, although preserving the bacteria, did so in an inactive or dead state, which prevented them from multiplying in culture media. Nevertheless, Silverstein came to the conclusion that "all of the characteristics of these specimens under the microscope indicated that they were faeces."

The matter from Goering's umbilicus was also submitted to intense scrutiny. It consisted, according to the CID report, of a "piece of dark brown material about 1 cm x 1 1/2 cm, with hairs attached." It was described as gray on the inside and dry, hard, and brown on the outside. In order to reconstitute it, the specimen was placed in normal physiological saline solution for a period of six hours. The result was then examined.

Both animal and vegetable fibers were found to be present in the solution. Two hairs were also found. "Both of these hairs present typical characteristics of human body hair. They are too fine to be pubic hairs and could have come only from the back or abdomen of a light skinned human being." (Dr. John K. Lattimer, a personal friend to whom I showed the CID report, stripped it of all jargon. He told me, "The material they analyzed sounds like the dirt that accumulates in the umbilicus of unwashed fat people.")

The remaining items of evidence were also examined by the agents. The mysterious white powder in the cellophane envelope proved to be dental cleanser, and there was no evidence that the brass cartridge had ever been in contact with it. Comparison of the putty from the cell window with material found on the brass cartridge was not considered necessary because the material found on the case was of human origin. Goering's pipe "was very closely examined but nothing of interest was noted."

The last item of evidence considered by the board was supplied by Goering himself. It was the letter found in his hand after his death. Addressed to "The Commandant," and dated October 11, 1946, Goering's letter read:

> I have always had the capsule of poison with me from the time I became a prisoner. When taken to Mondorf I had *three* capsules. The *first* I left in my clothes so that it would be found when a search was made. The *second* I placed under the clothesrack on undressing and took it to me again on dressing. I hid this in Mondorf and here in the cell so well that despite the *frequent* and *thorough searches* it could not be found. During the court sessions I had it on my person in my high riding boots. The *third* capsule is *still* in my small suitcase in the round box of skin cream, hidden in the cream. I could have taken this to me twice in Mondorf if I had needed it. None of those charged with searching is to be blamed for it was practically *impossible* to find the capsule. It would have been *pure accident*.

After he signed the letter, Goering added a postscript: "Dr. Gilbert informed me that the Control Board has refused the petition to change the method of execution to shooting."

Having questioned the various witnesses and having read the lab reports and Goering's letter, the board adjourned for the day.

On October 24 Colonel Hurless and Colonel Tweedy went to

Goering's cell, where they closely examined the toilet. Their observations were included in a report they prepared:

> Entering the cell the toilet is located in an alcove in the right corner adjacent to the door. The bowl of this toilet is porcelain and typical of the standard quality sanitary toilets manufactured in Germany between the years 1920 and 1925. The seat which is integral of this type bowl has two concealed recesses at the rear, near the orifice through which the water is introduced for flushing. Examination and experimentation proved conclusively that the metal case found in Goering's hand at death could be concealed in the recesses mentioned above, and could have remained there indefinitely undiscovered. Also the metal case could be placed in and recovered from these recesses by a person while ostensibly making use of the toilet without attracting undue attention even of a guard watching through the door.

The inspection of the toilet in Goering's cell brought the investigation to an end. All that now remained was to fit together the pieces of the puzzle.

7

The Board's Findings

The board had an undigested mass of information that now had to be considered and evaluated before they could determine how Goering managed to obtain the poison, hide it, and then kill himself. The report (prepared by the board) contains a detailed summary of the development of the thought processes that ultimately led the board to conclude that Goering had always had the poison while in American captivity and that no one assisted him in his escape from the gallows.

The officers' discussions began with the well-known fact that all of the leading Nazi officials were supplied with poison during the last days of the war and that most were able to retain the poison even after capture. It was recalled that a small vial of poison had been found in a can of coffee in Goering's luggage shortly after he was brought to Mondorf. It was also noted that another such device was found in Goering's luggage in the prison baggage room four days after his suicide. Therefore the board concluded: "Inasmuch as two such devices were actually found in Goering's baggage, it is logical to conclude that he was in possession of a third." The board cited Goering's letter to Colonel Andrus as corroboration for this conclusion.

This evidence, the board stated, "is believed sufficiently strong to eliminate the possibilities of procurement by other means." Rejecting the possibility that one of the German prisoner workers or an American guard could have given Goering the poison, the board stated:

The attitude of the civilian prison workers toward Goering, their unquestioned loyalty to American authority and the fact that Goering was
not in a position to offer remuneration for any services performed, removes any shadow of suspicion from this category. Insofar as American
or Allied personnel are concerned, it can be said without fear of contradiction that this category would have left no stone unturned to insure
that Goering met his fate on the gallows.

In support of the conclusion that Goering had no means of re-
munerating a confederate by a bribe from his valuables stored in the
prison baggage room, the board stated that "the evidence shows that
articles of personal property not required by the prisoner or classified
as valuable were kept in the prison store room which was kept locked
at all times and were at no time accessible to the 21 accused except
on approval of the Operations Officer."

The most difficult questions the board had to answer were how
Goering managed to smuggle the poison into the two prisons (first
Mondorf, then Nuremberg) and how he kept it hidden throughout his
lengthy incarceration. The board frankly admitted that "the method
by which he was able to originally conceal the container is not known."
However, it advanced two theories in answer to this all-important
question: "It could possibly have been concealed by swallowing or by
insertion in his rectum." It was pointed out by the board that the
laboratory tests revealed that excretal matter was found on the cartridge
case and that this was persuasive evidence that the cartridge had indeed
been in Goering's rectum. Thus the board concluded that Goering
had brought the capsule into the prison either by swallowing the capsule or by inserting it into his rectum, the emphasis being placed on
the latter possibility.

Concluding that he was in possession of the poison from the time
of his surrender to American forces, the board was forced to make the
reluctant admission that Goering, "subtle individual that he was, outwitted his guards by clever maneuvering of the suicide device, despite
constant observation." It was postulated by the board that Goering
could, "without serious injury to his health," continue to swallow and
subsequently retrieve the brass cartridge, hide it for periods of time in

his rectum, or carry it in his pocket, tobacco pouch, or elsewhere on his person. Admitting that it would be difficult to do so, the board theorized that he could have "concealed the small brass container in his navel."

However, the poison's longtime place of concealment, the board decided, could have been "under the rim of the toilet" in Goering's cell. The board said that it had tested this theory and established that "the container was difficult to locate when inserted in the recess of the toilet, even though they knew where it had been placed."

Having concluded to their satisfaction the questions of how Goering managed to bring the poison into the prison and hide it, the officers of the board went on to other considerations. It would not have been difficult, they decided, for Goering to have known exactly when to use the suicide device, because

> the Charter which was furnished the accused prisoners provided that should execution be the sentence of the Court, it would be carried into effect after the elapse of 15 days after the sentence was announced, excluding Sundays, and that all of the condemned prisoners knew with almost certainty that the executions would be performed on the 16th day after pronouncement of sentence.

With this advance knowledge, the board theorized that "Goering extracted the poison vial from its case and introduced it into his mouth without attracting the attention or rousing the suspicion of his guard." He had probably obtained the poison earlier, the board maintained, while using the toilet and not in full view of the cell guard. "Moreover, the vial could have been introduced into his mouth at any time between the evening meal and his demise." The board speculated that Goering's "large jowels and sagging flesh from the loss of weight" prevented the guard from noticing that he had the poison in his mouth.

"It can be assumed," said the board, "that Goering, being the clever man that he was, was reasonably sure that the execution would be performed on the night of his suicide and decided that he had waited as long as he safely could before committing suicide."

The board determined that Goering committed suicide because

"he was sentenced to death by hanging—a means of execution he bitterly opposed."

The most important conclusion reached by the board was that Goering's success in committing suicide was due to his own cunning and "not to dereliction on the part of any individual or group of individuals connected with the administration of the prisons in which he has been confined." The board emphasized that "reasonable safeguards had been planned and executed for the prevention of suicide by any one of the condemned."

Completing their review of all the evidence, the officers of the board found:

1. That the small brass container, containing the suicide poison was in possession of Goering at the time he was taken into custody by the American Army.
2. That all reasonable safeguards were taken in the guarding of Goering, and that he was able to retain the poison in his possession through his own cleverness and thoughtful planning and that no individual or individuals connected with the prison be held responsible for the death by suicide of Hermann Goering.

Colonel Hurless, Colonel Tweedy, and Major Rosenthal affixed their signatures to the completed report and forwarded it to the Quadripartite Commission for approval. The endorsement was not long in coming. The commission issued a report of its own, stating:

The Quadripartite Commission for the detention of Major War Criminals, having reviewed the report of the Board of Officers . . . and having conducted their own further inquiries, find:
1. That Göring had the poison in his possession when apprehended and retained it until he employed it on the night of 15th October, 1946.
2. That there is reason to support the view that at one time Göring could have carried the poison secreted in the cavity of his umbilical.
3. That there is evidence to prove conclusively that it was not there throughout his imprisonment and that at some stage it was in his alimentary tract.

4. That an obscure recess in the inside of the toilet under the overhanging rim could have concealed the container for a time without detection except by an extraordinary search.
5. That the security measures taken were proper in the peculiar conditions of the Trial and were satisfactorily carried out.
6. In particular
   (i) That no blame for dereliction of duty is ascribed to the sentry on duty at the time of Göring's death.
   (ii) That no blameworthy action or negligence is ascribed to the other prison guards of the U.S. Army.
   (iii) That there is no evidence tending to involve the German workers in the special prison.
7. That this case shows that in order to have complete security in cases of this kind it is necessary to have medical personnel thoroughly experienced in prison work, and to conduct a thorough examination of all internal cavities of the body and to employ x-ray.

The Quadripartite Commission then released its report to the members of the press, who had been impatiently and angrily demanding an answer to the question of how Goering managed to escape the court-imposed sentence of hanging.

8

The Press versus the Army

Those who are old enough to remember Goering's suicide may also recall the very real sense of disappointment and outrage which followed the news that he had escaped retribution. Today it is difficult for postwar generations to imagine the furor and controversy that his death triggered. Of all the Nazis, Goering was the most prominent to have been put on trial; Hitler, Himmler, and Goebbels had killed themselves to escape capture and punishment at the hands of the Allies. Goering, then, more than anyone else in the dock, personified the Nazi system and was, in a sense, a substitute for Hitler and the others who escaped trial. Many Americans can still remember the famous picture of Sergeant Woods, the Nuremberg executioner, displaying the heavy rope with which he planned to hang Goering. A Gallup survey taken at the time of the trial revealed that two out of three Americans wanted Goering to receive the death sentence, and when he did not hang, there quickly developed the feeling that he had "cheated" the American public as well as the hangman.

The bitterness felt by the American public was quickly articulated and magnified by the nation's press, which had long been at odds with the army over what it considered to be the scornful and demeaning treatment of those who were trying to secure information for their readers. In pouring out abuse and derision after the suicide, it seemed as if the press was demanding that a scapegoat be found to hang in

Goering's stead. And the army, which had supposedly allowed Goering to slip between its fingers, appeared to be the chosen victim. The fury of the press, except in degree, should not have been unexpected by army authorities as they had long been subjected to harsh criticism for their handling of Goering and the other defendants.

Even before the trial, the press had taken a special interest in Goering. Shortly after he surrendered to the American army, the press took to task various high-ranking officers for their friendly treatment of the Nazi leader. Brig. Gen. Robert J. Stack, to whom Goering was sent, observed hitherto accepted customs of military courtesy, saluting Germany's Reichsmarschall, and treating him with respect. Later, Goering was taken to Seventh Army Headquarters at Kitzbühel, where he was feted with cocktails and a dinner party. Pictures were taken of the beaming Reichsmarschall in full uniform and resplendent with medals, standing with champagne glass in hand and surrounded by high-ranking officers of the United States armed forces. The press, not in sympathy with this exaggerated concept of military chivalry toward a defeated enemy, took a very dim view of the whole affair, and extremely hostile reports on the dinner party were to be found the next day in all major newspapers. For maximum psychological effect, pictures taken in the newly liberated concentration camps were often juxtaposed with those of army officials enjoying a warm camaraderie with the smiling Goering.

Stung to the quick by the hostile reports, the army high command was not long in responding. General Eisenhower, acknowledging the fact that "the Press of the United States has reacted bitterly and justifiably against what is alleged to be the friendly and hospitable treatment that certain high Nazis . . . have received upon their capture," reprimanded the officers involved and ordered that henceforth Goering should be treated as an ordinary prisoner of war. For the first time, but not for the last, the press caused the army to have its fingers slapped for its treatment of Goering.

Goering was taken to the Palace Hotel at Mondorf, where he was turned over to Colonel Andrus. It was then that Andrus's running battle with the press began. Though the name "Palace Hotel" belied the fact that after the drastic modification of his room, Goering's accommodations were extremely primitive and lacking any type of convenience, much less luxury, a reporter soon filed a story entitled "It Pays to Be a Nazi!" Another reporter, taking a different but equally biased position, called Andrus "The Mondorf Monster." Alternatively, the army was accused of either pampering or mistreating its prisoners.

Once Goering and the others were taken to Nuremberg, the press followed in droves. It was necessary to build in the courtroom a press box large enough to hold over 250 reporters who had come from all over the world. From the start of the trial, they focused much of their attention on Goering. "Every day," Colonel Andrus wrote, "reporters were tapping out their hundreds of thousands of words about the trial. If Goering swore under his breath at a witness (and he often did), the oath would be ringing around the world within minutes." When the trial was over, it was estimated that over fourteen million words had been sent from the Palace of Justice. Much was critical of the army and Colonel Andrus.

Andrus believed that the press had never been fair with him: "I always had the problem of satisfying the Press. If no information was given out, I had something to 'hide'; if one news agency was given a titbit, then the other had to be treated the same way. Either way I couldn't win!"

The press was particularly critical of Andrus after the suicide of Dr. Ley. AP reporter Hodenfield recounted a story about another correspondent, "name long forgotten," who supposedly marched into Andrus's office after Ley's suicide, placed a pistol on the colonel's desk and told him, "I trust you will do the only honorable thing." While the story is probably apocryphal, it does illustrate the intensity of the dislike for Andrus held by many members of the press. Hodenfield himself remembered Andrus as "a pompous ass" and said that no one tried to cultivate him for stories.

From the time of Ley's suicide, Andrus and his superiors began to regard the press as a potentially dangerous foe, and an attempt was made by the army to control what the correspondents wrote. According to Werner Maser, "Reports on the IMT [International Military Tribunal] were allowed to contain only what the Allies wanted. Anyone who was not prepared to comply with their instructions did not get a seat either in the Palace of Justice or in the old Nuremberg school," the meeting place for correspondents, reporters, and all those not officially connected with the trial. "Here, if they had special passes, they could have meals (not without their attraction in 1946), exchange information, and discuss Nuremberg 'news' on the spot. Many knew each other so well that they seemed like a large family—and felt themselves to be so."

If army officials felt any kinship with this "family," it must have been tinged with the smug and condescending attitude that the well-to-do reserve for poor relations. Tania Long, a correspondent for the *New York Times*, filed a story bitterly complaining about the conditions under which the members of the press were forced to work and live and of the treatment meted out to them by army authorities. Though the correspondents were housed in a castle near Nuremberg, living conditions were less than primitive. Correspondents packed ten to a room found the plumbing so inadequate that they often left for the courtroom without first brushing their teeth or shaving. In what was known as "the villa," an annex to the castle, one bathroom served forty-two people. Kitchen facilities were worse; there was an epidemic of intestinal disorders that forced many correspondents to miss important sessions of the trial. Worst of all, they felt, was the attitude of the military: "Underlying all this is the Army's very noticeable hostility against correspondents and foreigners. Some Army officers complain that the correspondents 'had Patton fired' although they obviously did not." Long charged that the army's attitude toward foreigners, "explainable only as chauvinism of the worst sort," was bitterly resented by the non-American members of the press. "This attitude," she wrote, "is reflected right down to the behavior of the enlisted men who have been heard making outrageous remarks . . . in front of the visiting correspondents."

From the beginning of the trial there was a deep gulf between the press and the army, and correspondents were kept far away from prison officials. Only shortly before the executions did prison officials, on orders from the Allied Control Commission in Berlin, lift a corner of the curtain of secrecy that had been drawn over the prison. Prison officials began a series of two daily press conferences. The first was presided over by Major Teich, who refused to answer most questions, saying that no details of the executions were available. The unfortunate Teich did answer one question, however; he said that precautions against suicide were "so good that they could not be improved upon."

The army's defensive posture against the press continued to the time of the executions. An attempt was made by the Allied Control Commission to bar the press from the executions. However, Hugh Baillie protested to General McNarney, the American member of the commission, saying that "secret executions are liable to give rise to rumors of all sorts; such as some of the guilty were not killed at all, but were secretly reprieved for various reasons." Although the Allied Control Commission reversed its decision, the press continued to have difficulty with the army in getting information. *PM*'s Victor Bernstein reported, "Despite the prodding of an angry press corps at Nuremberg, officials gave a stock 'I don't know' answer to all questions about time, place, method and personnel" pertaining to the executions. Even on the very night of the hangings, "no one *ever* told us where and when the executions were to take place," Hodenfield recalled bitterly.

While Bernstein and Hodenfield and other reporters were restricted on the night of the executions to the Palace of Justice, eight representatives of the world's press were selected for a tour of the prison and to later witness the executions. Even this compromise was allowed only grudgingly. Kingsbury-Smith, one of the eight taken on the prison tour, said, "I do not believe that Andrus was keen about the visit of the correspondents to the condemned block, but they had made a formal request some days ago and he had been authorized . . . to take them through that last night."

As a witness to the executions, Kingsbury-Smith did not send an erroneous report of Goering's death. "But I regret to say that one of our international news service reporters did. He contacted a French officer who had witnessed the executions, and asked him if they were all dead. The French officer replied affirmatively but did not add that Goering's death was due to suicide."

The correspondent Kingsbury-Smith referred to was Lowell Bennett, who was remembered by his colleague Hodenfield as "the most unfortunate reporter at Nuremberg." Hodenfield said of Bennett, "By chance he ran into a French general, a friend of his, who had been an official witness. Lowell asked him if it was all over and the general said, *"Oui, tout c'est fini."* Lowell broke for his typewriter. He had no reason to suspect anything out of the way, and the French general just assumed that Goering's suicide had been announced. Incidentally, the pool reporters who had witnessed the executions were held incommunicado until after the Andrus announcement. There was no way to check with them what happened."

Equally unfortunate as Bennett was UP correspondent Clinton B. Conger, who erroneously cabled that Hermann Goering "has already walked to the gallows and is swinging limply at the end of a hempen noose." Relying on these advance stories, the London *Times* told its readers that Goering "was hanged this morning in Nuremberg prison."

Brig. Edmund Paton-Walsh, the British member of the Quadripartite Commission, told newsmen that he "regretted that false information" had appeared in various newspapers and said that this mistake "was largely to be ascribed to the efforts of the American news agencies" trying to compete with the correspondents within the prison. The resulting embarrassment did nothing to improve the already poor relationship between the army and the American press.

The criticism that Andrus and the army endured after the suicide of Dr. Ley was nothing compared to the storm that broke after it was announced that Goering had killed himself. Andrus knew that he and his men would draw most of the lightning from the storm. "A suicide in his prison is a serious matter for any commandant," he said, "but, with the eyes of the world on the confined leaders of Nazi Germany . . . the matter was doubly serious." Andrus said this of Ley's suicide, but it was all the more true in the case of Goering, as Andrus was soon to learn.

The *Washington Post* pointedly observed that the brunt of Goering's suicide fell squarely upon Colonel Andrus because he had maintained ever since the suicide of Ley "that self-destruction would be 'impossible' in the Nuremberg jail." Remembering Teich's assurance that suicide precaution in the prison "was so good that it could not be improved upon," reporters snorted in derision when Teich offered the lame excuse, "When an individual has twenty-four hours a day for a year to think up ways of concealment, he can think up some pretty clever things."

Press criticism of Andrus and his officers was so strong that a military spokesman had to deny rumors that the army was considering immediate proceedings against them. The *St. Louis Post-Dispatch* maintained that "rumor had it that high official heads would roll and that eagles would take wings and flit away from certain shoulders." As a colonel, Andrus wore on his shoulders the eagle insignia of his rank.

Hounded by the press for immediate answers, Andrus could only reply that an investigation was ongoing and that he had nothing more to tell them. Teich told the anxious press that the board hoped to come to some conclusions within two days and all one could do was wait.

The press waited and waited and waited. On October 18 the London *Times* told its readers:

> The four-power delegation representing the Allied Control Council, on whose authority this statement is issued, has nothing to say about investigations now proceeding into circumstances of Goering's suicide. Complete silence is maintained about the activities of the board of inquiry set up to investigate the affair and the contents of three pencilled notes found in Goering's cell which are said to have been turned over to the control council.

Already angered by the army's high-handed treatment, the press became openly and unreservedly hostile toward Colonel Andrus in particular and the army in general. Now the shoe was on the other foot; the press had the army on the defensive, and the correspondents pressed the attack. "Vanished were the arrogant briefing officers," reported the *Post-Dispatch*, "who were accustomed to grin scornfully when correspondents begged to be told at least how many paces the doomed prisoners were able to take at their exercise." The newspaper said that these officers shrank from the task of explaining Goering's suicide and the long delay that preceded its announcement.

Outrage over the army's handling of the Goering affair was world-wide. The deceived British newspapers were particularly vocal in their criticism of the United States Army's mismanagement of information; the London *Daily Mail* blamed army "bureaucratic bungling" for the delay in announcing Goering's suicide. The Russians, while nurturing deep suspicions and waiting for party-line instructions on how to handle the affair, registered their displeasure over the way the army had handled the news. Capt. Boris Vladirovic, correspondent of Tass, the Soviet news agency, said, "It was after eight o'clock in Moscow when we were released from security and that is too late for any paper." *PM*'s Victor Bernstein said it looked to him "as if the arrangements were hit or miss and as though trained correspondents in Nuremberg were suffering under severest handicaps in attempting to fulfill their duty in getting information out to the waiting world with speed and accuracy."

Editors, as well as correspondents, began to blast the army and prison officials. Printed under the title "The Army Bungles Again," the following editorial is typical of those that could be found in almost every newspaper in the United States:

> The United States Army has proved itself the most efficient in the world at fighting and has succeeded in claiming for itself the title of the stupidest in the handling of news. Now, our military handlers of news have bungled again. It is high time the War Department saw fit to place some responsibility on its men connected with news handling to see that the Americans are kept informed speedily. It is time for sense and brains to replace stupidity.

While this editorial did not call for Colonel Andrus's replacement, *Time* magazine singled out the unfortunate colonel to blame for the whole fiasco:

> It happened because the Army had placed in charge of the prison a pompous, unimaginative, and thoroughly likeable officer who wasn't up to his job. Colonel Burton C. Andrus loved that job. Every morning his plump little figure, looking like an inflated pouter pigeon, moved majestically into the court, impeccably garbed in his uniform and a highly shellacked helmet. His bow to the judges as they entered was one of the sights of Nuremberg. He loved to pen little notes: "The American

Colonel invites the distinguished French prosecutor and his staff to accompany him to a baseball game."

Time further charged that there was no real security in the Nuremberg prison and offered highly exaggerated, if not untrue, examples of laxity. One individual, *Time* claimed, "pasted a dog's picture over his own [identity card] and went in and out of the courthouse for days." Another example was that of a woman reporter who, with a forgotten pistol in her purse, passed by all the guards. "She could have leaned over and shot Goering—or the Chief Justice." *Time* also said that any one of the German lawyers could have given Goering the poison. "During the recesses, throngs of people milled about the dock and papers were passed back and forth," making it very difficult for the guards to observe the lawyers.

What was Colonel Andrus doing all the time these breaches of security were taking place? He was, according to *Time*, puttering around, "occasionally stealing a dentist's tool from the prison dentist's office just to see if it would be missed." It always was, *Time* was forced to admit.

Aside from the petty carping about supposed negligence on the part of the prison staff, the reports on Goering's suicide took on another and more devastating aspect. The army, the press charged, had allowed Goering to make a mockery of the whole trial, robbing it of all meaning. *Time* said that Goering, in the midst of humiliation and defeat, had managed to become a "hero" in the eyes of the German people, thus "virtually destroying the positive psychological effect of the trial."

> On the day after the executions, bowed Nürnberg suddenly straightened up. Men with glistening eyes stopped for excited talks with one another. Little knots gathered before the *Hauptbahnhof*. Germans who had avoided the eyes of Americans the night before now looked at them frankly with derisive smiles. You heard over and over again from passersby on the streets: "*Unser Hermann.*" Goering's one sharp breath-taking act wiped away ten months of painstaking work.

Newsweek said that the defiant Goering "had succeeded in wrecking" the planned psychological effect of the trial and that attempts by the Americans to brand Goering's suicide as an act of cowardice were not working. "Few Germans saw it in that light. They took grim satisfaction in the knowledge that the Allies couldn't hang 'Unser Hermann' after all."

The *New York Times* observed that all other aspects of the trial were "completely overshadowed" as thousands of Germans chuckled over the trick that Goering had played on the occupying powers. "Goering's dramatic gesture in death appeared to have helped these Germans forget his crimes, the millions of deaths in the concentration camps. . . and the lessons of the ten-month trial." The article concluded that "the event that was to have been a weapon in the hands of democracy suddenly became one in the hands of unrepentant German nationalists." The London *Times* echoed these sentiments:

> In German eyes the manner of Goering's death is bound to take something away from the Nuremberg judgement in making a legend of a man whose end was in keeping with his arrogant but by no means uncourageous deportment throughout the trial. There are many Germans. . . who will think of Goering with pride. Worse, perhaps, a good deal of mocking laughter was to be discerned today among the population of Nuremberg. Nuremberg, with its united appeal from the scaffold to purely nationalist sentiment, could yet be a rallying point.

While the western press insinuated only that the United States Army was guilty of negligence in allowing Goering to kill himself, the Russians took another tack. Only four hours after Goering committed suicide, the Soviets were openly accusing the Americans of giving him the poison. It was an accusation they never officially retracted.

There is no doubt that Goering's suicide while under American supervision was a potentially valuable propaganda tool for the Communists. Adept and unscrupulous in their use of propaganda, the Russians had long been working to tar the United States and its allies with the charge of being in secret sympathy with the Nazis. In 1945 they accused the West of hiding Hitler and Eva Braun in the British zone of occupation, though the corpses of the two had already been discovered and identified by Russian military personnel. At the conclusion of the Nuremberg Trials, the Russians expressed their vehement dissatisfaction with the court's decision not to hang all the defendants and particularly with the decision to free von Papen, Schacht, and Fritzsche. The Russians claimed that the Western powers wished to save the Nazis as future allies against Communism. When Goering killed himself, the Communist press of the world went into a paroxysm of hysterical denunciation and accusation.

Illustrative of the tack taken by the Communists is the October 17, 1946, issue of the *Daily Worker*. This American Communist newspaper, undoubtedly reflecting the official Moscow line, made a cause célèbre of Goering's suicide. In huge black letters, the *Daily Worker* demanded an answer to "WHO HELPED GOERING CHEAT NOOSE?" Commenting on the release of the three defendants and Goering's suicide, the newspaper claimed there existed the most sinister and far-reaching of conspiracies:

> The acquittal of the financier, the diplomat, and the propagandist of Naziism robbed the American people of the fruits of victory. Those Nazis, as well as Hess and others sentenced to jail, belonged on the gallows. A still more insistent question which cries for an answer—is how Goering was able to cheat the gallows. What officers or officials were implicated in the conspiracy which smuggled the poison vial into the hands of Hitler's crown prince?

Answering its own questions, the *Daily Worker* claimed that "a chain of events points an accusing finger against those powerful men in government and the army who have been appeasing the fascists." These "powerful men," accused the *Daily Worker*, allowed Goering to escape hanging in order to "assume a mock pose of martyrdom among the German people."

Thus the United States Army, depending upon which accusation one accepted, found itself charged with allowing Goering to escape the gallows either through negligence or complicity, and in either case, of permitting Goering to make a farce of the whole trial, robbing it of all meaning and preparing the way for a rebirth of the German ultranationalism that had so recently been defeated at the cost of so many lives. Goering's suicide was no longer simply a case of one of the prisoners escaping punishment, it was an incident threatening not only the prestige of the United States Army but the interests of the nation itself.

The report by the Board of Officers, which was endorsed by the Quadripartite Commission, killed the furor. Some correspondents grumbled that details of Goering's suicide were still "hazy," but they accepted the army's explanation. Typical of the stories that followed the release of the board's findings was *Newsweek's* "P.S. to Nuremberg":

> A four-power board of officers last week wrote the official postscript to Hermann Göring's suicide. After studying reports from prison officials and doctors, the board concluded: (1) Göring had the 2½-inch vial of cyanide at the time of his arrest seventeen months ago; (2) he hid it at various times in his navel, his alimentary tract, and possibly in "an obscure recess" of his cell toilet, and (3) nobody was to blame.

Until this very day, this has remained the "official" explanation of Goering's suicide.

9

The Donovan Connection

It was no surprise that the board did not investigate the possibility that the United States government or one of its agencies might have been involved in the Goering suicide. Apart from the Russians and their political allies, no one in 1946 seriously suggested that Goering's death could have been the result of a "high-level plot" on the part of the United States government. However, by the 1980s the willingness of the American people to believe in governmental conspiracies was much greater than at the end of World War II, and the mystery of Goering's suicide was not exempt from this suspicion.

Personally, I could not accept the idea that Goering's suicide was in any way connected with a governmental conspiracy. True, there were some to whom I spoke and wrote who suggested this possibility, but the suggestion was always made quite casually, and no evidence of governmental involvement was ever offered me. Consequently, I did not plan to go into this area of research. Later, I was forced to change my mind.

I had completed a first draft of my manuscript, and I was sitting in my living room visiting with a former Nuremberg prison official. This gentleman, who had read my manuscript, had been very helpful to me in my research. I found his memory to be sharp, his knowledge of personalities and events of the trial firsthand, and I had come to respect his opinions. Nevertheless, I was totally surprised and unprepared for the questions he raised during our visit.

For quite some time as we talked, this gentleman wore a perplexed look on his face, much as if he felt that I had made a fundamental error in my conclusions or had omitted a crucial part in my research. After discussing the board's findings and the secrecy surrounding them, he said to me, "It's like they were saying it never happened, isn't it?" He thought that the report answered very little, and I told him that I thoroughly agreed with his assessment of the investigation.

My visitor sat silent for a moment. Then he broached the subject that had been troubling him: "I don't know whether I am shooting you a curve or not, but I think that you had better give some consideration to the possibility that the United States was involved in this. I mean, was the United States government involved?"

I was astounded by the thought; but the man sitting in my living room was quite serious, and it appeared to me that his suspicion was founded on more than idle speculation. "Do you really think the government might have been involved?" I asked incredulously.

"I think it's possible," he replied. "After all, our government has done some strange things."

"But what motive would the government have for allowing Goering to escape the gallows?" I asked.

Pausing for a moment, my guest answered, "Well, we need a 'star,' don't we? Take away that 'star' and those trials are meaningless. Goering was the 'star.' "

I had to admit that what my guest said made sense. The trial would have lacked much of its effect if Goering, rather than having played a key role, had actually done what he told Dr. Gilbert, the prison psychologist, he wished he could do. Once, when he was enraged by the testimony of a German witness, he told Gilbert, "Dammit, I just wish we could all have the courage to confine our defense to three simple words: *Lick my arse!*" If expressed in cruder terms, this sentiment did not radically differ from the comment Goering cynically wrote on Gilbert's souvenir copy of the indictment before the trial opened: "The victor will always be the judge, and the vanquished the accused!"

Throughout the trial Goering never wavered from his stance that the tribunal lacked authority to try him. Even when he took the witness stand in his own defense, he protested to Gilbert, "I still don't recognize the authority of the court—I can say, like Maria Stuart, that I can be tried only by a court of peers."

Yet Goering actively participated in the trial process, giving it the "star" quality that it needed. He did not lack the courage needed to tell the court, "Lick my arse!" nor did he have any hope of saving himself. In November 1945 he told Gilbert, "As far as the trial is concerned, it's just a cut-and-dried political affair, and I'm prepared for the consequences. I know what is in store for me. I'm even writing my farewell letter to my wife today." If this was Goering's attitude toward the trial, why did he eventually agree to play the winners' game?

"Goering made a deal with Wild Bill Donovan," said the former Nuremberg prison official, referring to Col. (later Maj. Gen.) William J. Donovan, wartime director of the Office of Strategic Services (OSS), the forerunner of the CIA.

"Where did Donovan fit into all this?" I asked. "Why was the head of the OSS involved with Goering and the trials?"

"Donovan was given the assignment of getting everything ready for the process," came the answer. "He had the responsibility for its smooth-running. When it was all over, he got his promotion and Andrus didn't. Why?"

Startled by the implications, I could only ask, "Do you mean that Donovan made a deal with Goering, a deal in which he would not hang if he cooperated during the trial?"

"Yes, he might have," came the answer. "Perhaps I am being absurd about this, but I know that Donovan talked to Goering, and after that Goering's whole attitude changed. I think you need to look into this."

I did not believe that my guest was being "absurd," but I was still skeptical of any "high-level plot," as suggested by the Russians. However, this former U.S. Army soldier in no way shared the Soviet mentality, and he seemed to have some basis for his suspicions. Consequently, I decided that I would have to consider the possibility of government involvement, via the Donovan connection, in Goering's suicide.

There was little mention of Donovan in the literature on the Nuremberg Trials. Even in the two biographies of the OSS chief, which were published right at the time my interest in the man commenced, there was scarce reference to his role in Nuremberg. However, I learned that Donovan had been appointed special assistant to Justice Robert H. Jackson, United States chief prosecutor, and in this position had wielded considerable influence and power before the trials, though he was in continual conflict with Jackson.

Donovan and Jackson did not see eye-to-eye from the start. There was a serious and fundamental difference of opinion between the two on how the trials should be conducted. Jackson wanted to base the prosecution's case on captured German documents; Donovan, on the other hand, advocated the use of witnesses. Donovan believed documents would be dry and uninteresting and would not in themselves be sufficient to prove that there had been a criminal conspiracy among the leaders of the Third Reich, Fascist Italy, and Imperial Japan to rule the world. Donovan, therefore, was very strong in his belief that the use of witnesses in lieu of documents would be more effective. Despite the fact that Jackson was in total disagreement, Donovan proceeded to lay the groundwork for conducting the trial along the line of his own thinking. He recruited the "star"—Hermann Goering.

It was no easy task. Goering's hostile attitude toward the proposed trial was well known to Donovan. The OSS chief, hoping to impress Goering and meet with him on a soldier-to-soldier basis, donned his dress uniform with all medals and went to Goering's cell. Goering knew of Donovan, and he was grateful, in those lonely days, to be treated again with the respect he felt he deserved.

Consciously attempting to win Goering over, Donovan began by saying that he did not personally believe the Reichsmarschall had ever wanted war, nor did he believe that Goering had ever played a part in the extermination of the Jews. Goering vigorously nodded in assent. "Still," Donovan continued, "you were the second man in the state;

and the crimes of the Hitler regime were so monstrous!" Goering said
nothing and waited for Donovan to get to the point. Appealing to
Goering's injured vanity, Donovan then said, "You are the one of all
the accused who most stood in the middle of things and I want you
to have the opportunity to draw a faithful picture of the history of the
last ten years."

Goering was intrigued by the idea but asked why he should do
this. Donovan answered, "If this trial is to have any meaning, it can
only be to bridge the abyss that Hitler has placed between peoples."
This could be accomplished, Donovan explained, only through the
German people's condemnation of the crimes for which the Nazis
were responsible. It was his opinion that if the German people were
told by the Allies of the Nazi crimes, they would not believe them.
But if the most popular man of the Third Reich admitted that the
charges were true, he would not only convince the German people
but would also allow the world to understand the fantasy in which the
Germans had been living under Hitler and the pressure to which they
had been subjected all those years.

Goering was in full accord with these goals, but he immediately
spotted the hook in the bait. "So I am to be your chief witness against
Hitler?" he asked.

"Yes," Donovan admitted, "but you need not say one word more
than what you have already said a thousand times against Hitler and
the regime. Only in this way will the trial have any meaning and only
in this way can Germany find its way back to the democratic peoples
with whom it belongs." Left unsaid, but certainly in the minds of both
men, was the understanding that these "democratic peoples" would
form the new bulwark against the Communists in Europe and the rest
of the world. It was an argument that could not help but appeal to
Goering.

Goering thoughtfully considered Donovan's proposal. Finally, he
said, "You are entirely right. What happens to me personally is not
of the slightest importance. It is only important that Germany be
understood and that the German people receive justice."

Then began a rambling discussion during which Goering was delighted to hear Donovan say that he personally rejected the idea of "collective guilt" of the German people and that he thought a dangerous precedent was being set in branding as war criminals military officers who had obeyed the orders of their superiors. Goering had been saying the same thing for months, and he believed that in Donovan he had met a man in whom he could trust. When Donovan left the cell, Goering began to prepare his defense. A "deal" had been struck.

However, Donovan was not fated to remain for the trials. His oft and finally publicly stated reservations about trying the German General Staff widened the breach between him and Jackson. When President Truman agreed that the General Staff should be regarded as war criminals, "Donovan objected, first gently, then forcefully." After Jackson refused to advise Truman to reject the Russian demand for the indictment of the corps of officers, Donovan decided to leave Nuremberg to return to full-time directorship of the OSS.

Donovan's departure from the Nuremberg scene was a heavy blow to Goering. Dr. Gilbert recorded in his diary that Goering felt he had lost a "good bet." Nevertheless, the disappointed Reichsmarschall went through with his part of the bargain, giving the trial the "star" it needed.

So my guest had up to a point been correct. There had been a meeting between Goering and Donovan; and there had been a "deal" struck between the two, after which Goering agreed to take part in the trial proceedings. But the "deal" did *not* include any type of consideration of Goering's personal fate. In fact, after the two had reached agreement on Donovan's proposal, the OSS chief said quietly but firmly to the man of whom he was asking so much, "But, Herr Goering, I cannot save your head!"

The board, I therefore concluded, was correct in its decision to ignore the Russian charge that the United States government was in some way involved in Goering's suicide. It was one of the few correct decisions the board made.

10

The Hiding Spot

Taken at face value, the report written by the Board of Officers is persuasive evidence that Goering had the poison from the time of his surrender, was clever enough to hide it throughout his incarceration, and had no assistance in escaping the gallows. The absolute loyalty of both the American and German prison personnel ruled out the possibility that he could have gained possession of the poison any time subsequent to his surrender. Leonard Mosley, the author of a biography of Goering, had access to the board's report and was thoroughly convinced by it. Mosley wrote, "Ever since Hermann Goering killed himself on the night of his execution, people have speculated about the way in which he did it. Who passed him the poison? In fact, the answer was really quite simple. He brought it into Nuremberg Jail himself."

But was the answer really as "simple" as Mosley supposed? Do the facts actually support the conclusions reached by the Board of Officers and endorsed by the Quadripartite Commission? In order to answer these questions, we must critically examine the actual testimony contained in the report and consider many sources and much evidence not available in 1946. Such an effort will show that the riddle of Goering's suicide was far from solved by the board. Indeed, it will reveal that the board was wrong in almost every one of its conclusions. The officers of the board were so often wrong that one must wonder

105

if they simply accepted whatever conveniently fit into a preconceived and accepted theory, even if it defied logic. In all too many instances this seems to be the case.

The most important question the board had to answer was how Goering managed to smuggle the poison into the Nuremberg prison. The board admitted this could not be determined with certainty but theorized that Goering either swallowed the poison container, inserted it into his rectum, or concealed it in the cavity of his umbilicus. The first theory is highly unlikely, the second is unsupported by the facts, and the third is patently ridiculous.

If one actually held the brass cartridge in one's hand, it would immediately become apparent that the theory that Goering could have swallowed it is, to say the least, farfetched. To say that he could have swallowed it, "continuing to pass it through his alimentary tract" and "without serious injury to his health," is to ignore the probability that he would have choked to death in the process! Swallowing the cartridge would be the equivalent of swallowing a small tube of lipstick. And had he managed to swallow it, Goering had no guarantee whatsoever that the twist-off cap would not become separated from the case, releasing the fragile glass vial of hydrocyanic acid into his stomach. Goering was no fool, and it is difficult to believe that he would have taken such a chance.

Even if one grants, for the sake of argument, that Goering did swallow the capsule, its recovery would have been no easy matter. It would have taken quite a while to pass through his alimentary tract, and if it were not lost, Goering would have had to examine carefully each of his stools. That he could have done so undetected in a small cell lacking all but the most primitive of washing facilities (he had a pan of water) and under constant observation by a guard just outside the door defies logic.

The presence of excretal matter on the cartridge is evidence that Goering had the poison in his rectum at one time or another, but it is *not* proof that he smuggled it into the prison in this manner. There is considerable evidence that he did not.

Colonel Andrus wrote that when the prisoners arrived at the prison, "they were immediately stripped naked for a complete physical examination by the prison doctor." The doctor knew exactly what he was looking for as the recent suicide of Heinrich Himmler by cyanide had made the Americans wary of their captives' capacity for self-destruction. Even a routine physical examination, to say nothing of one specifically conducted to look for a poison cartridge, includes a rectal examination. Lieutenant Roska told the board that "a simultaneous examination" of all of Goering's orifices was made when he (Goering) first came to Nuremberg, "but not since I have been here." Dr. Pfluecker also told the board that Goering's rectum had been examined by "Major Kelley and two others."

For confirmation that high-ranking Nazi officers upon capture were routinely and thoroughly inspected for poison capsules, I wrote to Dr. Donald G. Brownlow, a historian of the Third Reich and a former U.S. Army intelligence officer. He replied, "I do know that all of the prisoners were searched—even into scars and very personal areas. We were fully aware that all of the 'brass' had the poison capsules and that suicide was a strong possibility. When we learned that the top Nazis had the vials for such a purpose, they were all given very thorough examinations upon capture or very soon thereafter. We were extremely upset to learn of Himmler's death in the hands of the British, and this made everyone more apprehensive of the other top brass. Such medical exams were always given by the army medical teams, and I must assume that this was done in Goering's case as well."

K. Robert Wilheim, an interrogator at Mondorf, told me that he was positive that the internees were given a thorough physical examination while there. "There was a young American M.D. captain for such examinations," he explained, "and I do recall that he once remarked to me, 'Never during my medical studies did I expect that I would have to examine Goering's rectum!' "

Positive proof of a similar physical examination of Goering's rectum upon his entry into the Nuremberg prison came to me from another source. Sgt. Richard Raabe, the supply warden at the prison, told me that when Goering entered the prison, he was immediately taken to a cell and thoroughly searched. Raabe supplied me with a written affidavit stating:

> I was present in the cell of Hermann Goering during his physical examination on entrance to Nuremberg. The procedure was that all twenty-two of the first war trial prisoners were given a complete examination; i.e., besides checking teeth for a hollow tooth or two to hide cyanide, *all* areas of the body were examined, including navel and rectum. Present at the examinations were an army officer, army dentist, army doctor, plus yours truly. No poison was found on Hermann Goering or any of the other twenty-one.

During a subsequent telephone conversation, I asked Raabe how thorough this physical examination was. "Complete!" he answered. "I was very surprised when they later claimed that Goering had the poison in his rectum." According to Raabe, there was "no way" that the doctor could have missed the poison had it been there.

Nevertheless, though it was far from proven and despite considerable evidence to the contrary, the board concluded that Goering had originally smuggled the poison into the prison either by swallowing the cartridge or inserting it into his rectum.

Perhaps influenced by the unknown dark substance found in Goering's navel after death and the fact that the usually meticulously clean Goering had refused to bathe since early October, the board may have at first believed he had concealed the cartridge in the cavity of his umbilicus. The board decided that while this would have been "difficult," it could have been possible.

Could the poison ever have been concealed in Goering's navel as the board suggested? Aside from the fact that Raabe said that Goering's navel had been inspected, this theory lacks all credibility. The brass cartridge is too large to have been concealed in Goering's navel. The board itself, during the October 15 visit to Goering's cell, came to that conclusion. "The navel was abnormally large," the officers noted, "but too small to conceal a tube the size of Exhibit 'A.' " Lieutenant Roska, too, examined Goering's navel and told the board that it measured "about 1 cm deep and 0.6 cm in diameter." The cartridge measures almost four and one-half centimeters (nearly two inches), which is *far* too large to have been inserted into Goering's navel. After the board reversed its decision of October 15 and decided the cartridge could have been in Goering's navel, it tried to get Roska to admit that it was possible. But he refused to do so, saying that it was impossible for him to believe this. Pressing, the board asked Roska if "from the standpoint of anatomy" it was possible for the cartridge to have been in Goering's navel even for a short time. Again, Roska said that he did not believe this was feasible and pointed out that when he examined him after death, there was not the slightest sign of irritation or inflammation around Goering's navel.

From the testimony of Lieutenant Roska and consideration of the physical evidence, it would seem there were no grounds at all to conclude that the poison was ever in Goering's navel.

If the board was far wrong in concluding that Goering smuggled the poison into the prison by either swallowing the cartridge or inserting it into his rectum and later hiding it in his navel, was it any closer to the truth in finding that Goering had hidden the poison in his cell toilet? Again, there is no proof for this conclusion, and there is actually evidence against it.

Captain Starnes told the board that "the toilet was searched on routine searches." Asked if the entire circumference of the toilet bowl was ever examined, Starnes admitted that he did not know. He was forced to agree, at the board's suggestion, that the examination probably "consisted mainly of looking into the toilet bowl."

The answers given by Starnes, though honest, are totally misleading. It was the first time that the board had asked anyone about the toilet in Goering's cell, and Starnes, off guard and unprepared, undoubtedly answered without thinking. He did not point out to the board that "looking into the toilet bowl" alone was not as negligent as it was made to sound. The toilet in Goering's cell was extremely simple in design; it consisted solely of a porcelain bowl on a supporting neck. There was no water compartment. The water was introduced into the bowl through a thin metal pipe that ran from the top of the recessed alcove into the bowl. As a matter of fact, there was nothing to examine *except* the bowl of the toilet. It is ludicrous to imagine that guards did not search the overhanging rim of the bowl and all orifices but merely looked into the bowl, as if they might find some instrument of suicide floating on the water. More likely, Starnes did not have the information necessary to answer the board's questions and compliantly went along with whatever was suggested to him by his superiors. In any case, the board made no effort to further resolve the matter; not a single guard actually responsible for searching Goering's cell was asked about the toilet.

My own research on this matter was more thorough than the board's; I asked former prison guards about the cell toilet. They all insisted that the toilets were searched regularly and thoroughly. One of these guards, James LeMay, told me that the toilet in Goering's cell was inspected "very often." When I asked him if he thought it possible that the poison could have remained hidden in the toilet throughout Goering's incarceration, he immediately replied, "Impossible!" Peter Misko, another of the guards, told me, "Yes, [the toilets] were inspected thoroughly by qualified persons each and every time a prisoner left the cell, i.e., when they went to the exercise yards, interrogation, trials, etc." There seems, then, to be little question that Goering's cell toilet was a very unlikely hiding spot for the poison.

The most disturbing aspect of the "toilet bowl theory" is from whom it came and in what manner. It was Dr. Pfluecker who first suggested that Goering had hidden the poison in the toilet. After the board, in a rather abrupt change of subjects, asked Pfluecker if he had any idea where Goering might have hidden the cartridge, the doctor replied, "If I could see the cell maybe I could find the spot." Considering the fact that the board and the guards who had searched Goering's cell for over a year had looked in vain for "the spot," this was a rather surprising comment. However, it was not even necessary to show the cell to the doctor, who, during and after the trial, had seen it hundreds of times before, because he then said without hesitation, "You can hide poison in the toilet." Displaying an amazing amount of information about the inner recesses of Goering's toilet and the opportunities for concealment which they offered, he volunteered, "The toilet has a border and this is hollow and if you take a newspaper you could hide anything in it."

Dr. Pfluecker, with no apparent strain and off the top of his head, gave the members of the board the answer that had long eluded them. If they felt anything other than gratitude for the amazing intuition of the doctor, they did not express it. Nor did they ask for any explanation of such an incredible piece of detective work. They just accepted it. Once the theory was suggested by Dr. Pfluecker and the cell toilet was examined by Colonel Hurless and Colonel Tweedy on October 24, the theory became "fact" and was incorporated into the final report as an official finding of the board. From there, it passed into history as "the answer" to one of the most puzzling questions raised by Goering's suicide.

Then what can one say of the board's assertion that Goering, "subtle individual that he was, outwitted his guards by cleverly maneuvering the suicide device" from his rectum and the cell toilet to "his pocket or tobacco pouch"? This, too, is sheer nonsense. It is almost as if the board had not read its own report. It would have been the height of stupidity for Goering to have ever carried the poison on his person. He was subject to too many routine and unexpected searches, both in and out of his cell. The report states, "The evidence indicates that frequently when an accused was returned to his cell he was searched by a member of the security guard, daily when the accused persons were absent from their cells, and, on certain occasions when in their cells."

Colonel Andrus told the board that the prisoners' clothes were brought to them only after they had "passed inspection." Captain Starnes was even more specific when asked if Goering was ever stripped for a simultaneous search of his person and clothes: "Yes, he was. On some occasions, when we were suspicious of him, we made a search of all his clothes. He was held when he returned from court. He was caught at the time of his return and searched immediately before he could get rid of anything. His clothes were taken off."

Despite the testimony of Andrus and Starnes and the inherent improbability that Goering would be foolish enough to remove the poison from its hitherto undiscovered location in the cell and then "hide" it in his pocket, the board decided that this probably had been the case.

Goering's tobacco pouch, too, seems an unlikely hiding place for the poison. Speaking with correspondents shortly after Goering's death, Colonel Andrus said, "We searched the prisoners' cells completely. We even found bits of glass hidden in a tobacco pouch. You can see how thorough we were." Andrus was emphatic in his insistence that Goering could not have had the poison in his possession throughout the trial. "I took a similar vial from him when he was captured. It is impossible that he could have concealed another."

But Goering must have—even if only for a short period of time. It has been suggested by some that he came into possession of the poison when he later regained some of his personal belongings. Even if the board was unable to determine the hiding place for the poison, others believe that they have come up with the answer.

The suggestion that Goering hid the capsule in the bowl or stem of his favorite pipe, from which he was rarely separated, has often been put forth. This theory first surfaced in the newspapers only two days after the suicide. It has, since then, been widely repeated and believed. Albert Speer told me in a letter: "The theory that Goering's capsule was concealed in his long pipe, which he broke at the last moment, is . . . quite plausible." And Edward A. Schaefer, a longtime friend of mine, said that Baldur von Schirach, the former Hitler Youth leader, told him the same thing. However, despite the presumed authority of Speer and von Schirach, the theory of the poison being hidden in Goering's pipe is baseless.

This theory evidently originated in a story related by Hermann Willkamp, the prison barber. Willkamp said that Goering told him at the time of their farewell, "I would like to give you . . . my pipe, but I can't. When I leave this cell for the last time, I will break it to bits and throw it out of the window." Willkamp told eager reporters that he did not at the time understand Goering's "strange smile," but later "everything became quite clear: he could have hidden his ampule of cyanide of potassium only in that pipe."

The conversation reported by Willkamp and evidently read and believed by Speer and von Schirach is a complete fabrication. Pvt. M. C. Odum, the American guard who accompanied Willkamp during the barber's last meeting with Goering, told the board that "the only conversation between the barber and Goering was greetings when entering the cell and thanks by Goering when the barber finished." The report makes it quite clear that Goering's pipe was found in his cell on the night of October 15 and that it was part of the evidence turned over to the CID agents for examination. A picture of the pipe (Exhibit 'E') is included in the report, and it is clearly intact. The lab report stated that the pipe was closely examined, "but nothing of interest was noted."

It is nonsense to assume that the brass cartridge could have been hidden for any length of time in the large bowl of the pipe, much less in the narrow stem. If it were hidden in the bowl of the pipe, it would have to have been removed and rehidden every time that Goering smoked, which was every day, or the heat generated by the burning tobacco would have shattered the glass vial. Major Teich correctly told correspondents that it would have been "impossible" for Goering to have smoked the pipe had the poison been in it.

Equally unsubstantiated is the persistent rumor that Goering hid the capsule in an incision which was cut into his abdomen for that purpose and then allowed to heal. According to the *Washington Post*, prison doctors found a "1-inch wound on the abdomen . . . of Hermann Goering after his death and he may have kept there, just under the skin, the poison container." A usually reliable informant said that doctors had pried up Goering's layers of fat and "found blood around the navel." This theory particularly fascinated correspondent Clinton B. Conger. His dispatch to the *New York Daily News* appeared under the headline "Hint Fatso Hid Vial in Abdominal Wound." Unfortunately for Conger, this erroneous report was quickly denied by both Colonel Andrus and Lieutenant Roska, and the newspaper printed the denial the next day.

If the theories put forth by the board and others are in error, then how did Goering smuggle the poison into the prison and manage to hide it for the year prior to his suicide? Perhaps the most obvious answer is the best one, though it will immediately raise a new set of questions. The board itself came very close to this answer when it concluded: "Inasmuch as two such devices were actually found in Goering's baggage, it is logical to assume that he was in possession of another." Though the board did not follow through with this line of thought, it is equally logical to conclude that the *third* vial of poison remained in Goering's luggage, securely hidden away in his myriad personal possessions until he needed it. If this is true, it would answer the question of how Goering brought the poison into the prison and make totally superfluous all the ridiculous and farfetched theories of how he subsequently hid it during the year that preceded his suicide. There is much evidence to suggest that the poison did remain in the baggage room.

It is obvious that the contents of Goering's numerous pieces of luggage, despite what the board was told, were never properly searched. How else would the poison hidden in the jar of skin cream have escaped detection until October 19, four days *after* the suicide? Walther Funk, who was imprisoned with Goering, remembered that Goering "always appeared fearful over the prospect of being removed from the prison and compelled to leave all his belongings behind." Adm. Karl Doenitz, another of the defendants, recalled that Goering had "pestered" him about this possibility. With his fate sealed, it is clear that Goering's preoccupation with the thought of being separated from his luggage was motivated by something other than fear of material loss. Dr. Pfluecker, when writing his memoirs, belatedly became "convinced that the very clever Goering had the opportunity to withdraw the poison while taking clothes out of his luggage, and bring it back to his cell."

Is it possible that Goering had access to his personal belongings in the baggage room and, despite testimony to the contrary, could reach them without going through official channels? How secure was the baggage room?

Teich's statement that Goering's four pieces of luggage contained "every imaginable type of item" is something of an understatement. Dr. Kelley wrote that Goering brought with him to Mondorf "three large rings, truly massive baubels, each set in heavy platinum mount." Another item that Goering had with him was "a monstrous unset emerald, a truly tremendous stone measuring one inch by one-half inch." According to Kelley, Goering also had in his luggage gold cigar and cigarette cases, gold pens and pencils, and four jeweled wristwatches and traveling clocks. Colonel Andrus, too, was impressed with the vast amount of miscellaneous and valuable items that Goering brought with him into captivity. His inventory of Goering's personal possessions almost filled an entire page of his book. Though the gems seen by Kelley are missing from Andrus's inventory, the other items and many more are faithfully reported.

Both Andrus and Teich insisted that the prisoners were allowed access to their luggage only under the strictest of security measures, and Starnes said he could not remember a single instance in which Goering requested anything from the baggage room. The report itself, however, proves that security was not always observed as closely as it should have been.

There was the example of the blue briefcase that Goering unaccountably had in his possession at one point during the trial. When Starnes was asked if he had given the briefcase to Goering, he denied he had done so. Further, he could not name the individual who had given it to Goering. He admitted that the briefcase came from the baggage room, "as it matched with another piece of luggage" still there. Though neither Starnes nor Teich knew who was responsible for procuring the briefcase for Goering, they said it could have been given to him by any one of the officers who had a key to the baggage room. Teich explained, "There was a constant flow of prison officers and some changes in our own staff. The brief case could have been taken from the baggage room properly and legally." However, the prison records revealed nothing pertaining to the briefcase.

The board required from each of the officers who had a key to the baggage room a sworn and signed deposition that he had not given anything to Goering and that Goering had no access to his personal and valuable belongings. However, due to the limited time scope of the investigation, the depositions covered only the period from October 1 to October 15, 1946. Nothing was said of the many months that preceded this period, and it was never ascertained who gave Goering the blue briefcase.

Nevertheless, the fact remains that Goering did have in his personal possession a briefcase that was very elaborate and contained several compartments, and it had come from the baggage room. When no one accepted responsibility for having given it to Goering, there was no way to verify that the blue briefcase had been inspected and found to be "clean" before it came into his possession. The poison capsule *could* have been in the briefcase. There is, however, no proof of this, and the incident is mentioned here only to illustrate that Goering, one way or another, did have access to his luggage.

If this were the only instance in which the security of the baggage room failed, it would have little significance. However, there was at least one other instance that did not come to the attention of the board.

In April 1976 I visited a small town in Texas not far from where I live. There I talked with a woman whose first husband had been an officer assigned to the Nuremberg prison. Her husband, Lt. Jack G. ("Tex") Wheelis, then deceased for some years, had left her some souvenirs that Goering had given him. At the time of my visit, she showed me a solid gold Mont Blanc fountain pen with Goering's name inscribed on the cap, a large and elaborate Swiss wristwatch bearing his name in facsimile signature, a solid gold cigarette case, and a handsome pair of suede gloves. All of these gifts, she told me, were given to her husband "for favors done on behalf of Frau Goering and her little daughter." I purchased all of these items from her, and after a few minutes of friendly conversation, I departed.

When I reached home, I immediately checked Colonel Andrus's book, looking for the inventory of Goering's personal items that had been stored in the prison baggage room. I found that at least two of the souvenirs I had purchased—the fountain pen and the Swiss wrist-watch—were clearly identifiable as having been there. Colonel Andrus specifically mentioned them in his book.

I wrote to Andrus, with whom I had been corresponding about the continued incarceration of Rudolf Hess, and naively asked him to further verify the authenticity of the items I had bought from the former Mrs. Wheelis. Andrus immediately terminated our correspondence, and despite several follow-up letters, I never heard from him again.

Only years later, after reading the board's report on the investigation into Goering's death, did I realize what a raw nerve my request—with its evidence of a serious breach of security on the part of one of Andrus's own officers—must have struck in the colonel.

The Wheelis incident, combined with the delivery of the briefcase to Goering, contradicts one more conclusion reached by the board. The two incidents suggest that the prison baggage room was not as secure as the board maintained.

If the poison had been cleverly concealed in one piece of Goering's luggage, it is possible that someone could have removed that piece from the baggage room without authorization or proper search, given it to Goering, and so inadvertently supplied him with the poison. It is also possible that someone, in collaboration with Goering, might have deliberately removed the poison from the baggage room and given it to him.

But the latter alternative would require that someone within the prison be in *sympathy* with Goering. Despite his apparent willingness to allow Wheelis to obtain souvenirs from his personal belongings, Goering was in no position to bribe him or anyone else. Wheelis, for example, could have taken the souvenirs with or without Goering's permission, even without his knowledge. Therefore, bribery could *not* be the motive for anyone aiding Goering.

The board maintained that no one in the prison, either German or American, had any sympathy for Goering and the other prisoners. But were the officers of the board any more correct in this conclusion than they had been about the hiding place of Goering's poison?

11

Sympathies: German and American

The board concluded that "the attitude of the civilian prison workers toward Goering, their unquestioned loyalty to American authority and the fact that Goering was not in a position to offer remuneration for any services performed, removes any shadow of suspicion from this category." Only in its assertion that Goering was in no position to offer remuneration was the board correct in its conclusion regarding the German workers.

Judging from the questions asked by the board and the reports in the press after Goering's death, suspicion at first rested heavily on the German workers assigned to the prison. But after Colonel Andrus and Captain Starnes defended the German employees, the board decided that all were loyal to their American employers.

However, one cannot help but wonder if the board was in any position to accurately gauge the true attitudes and loyalties of the German workers. Its opinion that these Germans, who had until very recently sworn unquestioning allegiance and obedience to Adolf Hitler and those very men then locked in the cells, were now loyal and devoted to the Americans seems a bit naive. One should never forget the massive destruction and economic chaos that Germany faced after the war. Desperate Germans would have paid lip service to the devil himself if such hypocrisy would have brought them position, food, money, and a place to live. German workers at the Nuremberg prison

118

may well have served the Americans, not because of any sympathy for the victor's cause nor any antipathy toward their former leaders but because Colonel Andrus offered them "full prison status" and "a wage scale for their particular qualification," conditions that they scarcely could hope to find anywhere else in postwar Germany.

It might have been surprising to the board to learn that Albert Speer remembered these German workers with gratitude. "They behaved helpfully toward us whenever there was no supervisory personnel around. They managed to whisper to us a good many bits of news from the papers as well as good wishes and encouragements." Sergeant Raabe, who closely worked with the German employees of the prison, said that the ones who made the rounds with him were so openly friendly with the prisoners and so often spoke to them without permission that he was forced to watch them constantly. His suspicion of the German workers was so great that when he first heard of Goering's suicide, he immediately thought that one of them had given him the poison. "I always had the feeling that, some way or another, the poison came in through the Germans."

Other than Dr. Pfluecker, no German was questioned by the board— a prime example of the board's failure to critically examine and evaluate the Germans' true attitudes and sympathies. Indeed Goering's having "contrived to commit suicide after Pfluecker's visit at first placed the doctor in a highly precarious position." Pfluecker himself realized that he must be suspect and so told the board, "I entered the prison office to see if I would be arrested. I was afraid that I would be blamed." *Time* reported that one of the theories advanced in answer to the puzzle of the suicide was that Goering had faked the gurgling sounds that had attracted the guard; "thereupon the guard summoned the doctor, who then administered the poison." However, Pfluecker had little to fear from the investigation; the board showed scant interest in him.

Colonel Andrus later wrote that Dr. Pfluecker "had a deep pride in his profession and was absolutely trustworthy," adding that the doctor had "a thorough distaste for the Nazis." During his testimony to the board, Andrus discounted any possibility that the poison could have been in Pfluecker's possession as "he had absolutely nothing when he reported to me at Mondorf except the class X clothing he was wearing." Lieutenant Roska told the board that Pfluecker was, in his opinion, fully reliable and that the authorities were justified in putting their trust in him. But as a doctor, Roska's professional opinion of his colleague was a bit more critical. He told the board, "He is an old man, primarily a urologist. He knows what his limitations are. He has always consulted one of us."

Captain Starnes, too, was asked about Pfluecker. The officers of the board wanted to know if anyone, "aside from the humane aspect," had ever expressed sympathy for Goering. Starnes answered, "No, except for the doctor." Not satisfied with this answer, the board suggested that any expression of sympathy for Goering on the part of the doctor could be attributed to "humanitarian" reasons. Starnes, oblivious to the contradiction of his first reply, answered, "Yes, I construed it as such." The board, having the question answered in two diametrically opposed ways, could place whatever interpretation it wished upon Pfluecker's expression of sympathy. No other questions about the doctor's sympathies were asked of anyone.

Other evidence, however, reveals that Pfluecker had a great deal of sympathy for Goering and probably was not as hostile to the Nazi regime as Andrus maintained. The doctor was an older man and had lived through the defeat in the First World War, the humiliation of Versailles, the Red Menace that swept Germany, the rise and triumph of Hitler, and the ultimate collapse of the Third Reich. Like many Germans of his generation, the accomplishments of the Hitler regime were not totally forgotten by him. Even with those Germans who did not share the Nazi ideology, Goering enjoyed popularity. Dr. Pfluecker was no exception to this.

Despite the fact that Colonel Andrus told the board that Pfluecker had been selected for his position on the basis of his hostility to the Nazis, Pfluecker himself said that he was chosen because he could speak English. His memoirs reveal that his being "already washed and shaved" also played a part in Biddle's decision to select him rather than another doctor. Once at Mondorf, and later at Nuremberg, Pfluecker walked a thin line trying to please his American employers and at the same time enjoy the trust and the confidence of his German patients. "It was natural," he wrote, "that we Germans stuck together in the bad times." Pfluecker said that it was not easy in the early days when conversation between him and the prisoners was forbidden to express this feeling of solidarity. "Only by a look could we let the prisoners know that we had sympathy for the alteration of their status."

After Pfluecker told Andrus that the health of all the prisoners was declining because they had no opportunity for normal conversation among themselves or with others, the doctor was given permission to speak with his patients on matters totally unrelated to health. Over the many months, Pfluecker became a frequent and welcome visitor to Goering's cell. As a fellow German and an educated man, he was the one man in whom Goering could confide and find commiseration. They discussed everything from suicide to Goering's growing concern for the welfare of his wife and daughter. It was Pfluecker whom Goering turned to after seeing his wife for the last time. Totally crushed, he told the doctor, "I saw my wife for the last time, my dear doctor. It was a very bad moment, but my wife wanted it. She was wonderful. She is really a great woman. She was about to give way only towards the end, but then she took hold of herself and was quite composed when we said goodbye."

Goering was devastated by the farewell to his family and told Pfluecker that the Americans could do anything they wanted to him; in his own mind he was already dead. It was shortly after this visit that Goering removed the pictures of his wife and child from his cell. His anguish was so great that the doctor himself was greatly moved. The scene stayed with him all his life, and he recounted it in his memoirs with obvious sympathy.

Goering's gratitude to Pfluecker evidenced itself in a signed portrait he gave him shortly before he committed suicide. It was a family picture depicting Goering and his wife adoringly looking at little Edda. It was not the type of official portrait Goering used to present to underlings but the type he reserved for close friends and family. It was a remembrance that Pfluecker treasured and allowed to be printed in his memoirs.

Those who still remember Dr. Pfluecker recall a different man from the one represented to the board. Col. Richard Nalle, who was present during the trials and the executions, told me he "would not trust Pfluecker an inch." After Colonel Nalle heard that Goering had committed suicide by poison, the thought that he had received the poison from the German doctor was the first that came to his mind. Many years after his testimony to the board, Dr. Roska said to me that Pfluecker was extremely respectful toward the prisoners and considered them still to be his superiors, clicking his heels and standing at attention when speaking with them. Sergeant Raabe, too, saw this exaggerated mark of respect "many times." Speaking of the personal relationship between Goering and the doctor, Raabe said, "There was still this aura about Goering in Pfluecker's eyes, that he was his superior." Reflecting upon the doctor for a moment, Raabe added, "I don't think that he was ever completely loyal to us. If he had a choice, German or American, I am sure he would have followed his German instincts immediately."

There is evidence that Pfluecker did follow his "German instincts" on at least one occasion when he had to choose between loyalty to the Americans and siding with his fellow Germans, and the matter proved to be not a trivial one.

One of the most puzzling questions about the suicide was how Goering knew that the executions were to begin at midnight October 15 and not at the traditional hour of dawn. *PM* posed the questions, "Did Goering know when he took his own life that he was but two hours away from the hangman's noose? If he did know, how?" The answer probably is that Pfluecker told him.

All of the condemned, Chaplain Gerecke said, had the "Wednesday bug," but only Goering correctly believed that the executions would begin shortly after midnight. Pfluecker denied to the board that he had this information. The board asked him, "Did anybody tell you that [October 15] was the night for the executions?" Pfluecker answered, "We knew it from the newspapers." But the newspapers had never said beforehand just when the executions would begin, because they did not know; one would have to assume, then, that Pfluecker did not know either—or at least he did not know "from the newspapers." He further denied to the board that he had even told the condemned that the night of October 15 was selected for the executions, much less the exact time they were scheduled to begin. When he was asked by "somebody" (apparently Pfluecker could not remember who it was when questioned by the board) if there was any sense in getting undressed that night, Pfluecker, according to his testimony in 1946, answered only, "I don't know."

Some years later, when he wrote his memoirs, Pfluecker's memory improved greatly. He then remembered it was Goering who had asked the question and that he had rather cryptically replied "that a night was very short sometimes, but that I could not tell him anything definite." Pfluecker's memory also improved on another point. He suddenly remembered he had known the exact time the executions were scheduled to begin. "On October 15, at 3:30 P.M., the foreman, Herr Streng, and I were ordered to the office. There, we were . . . told to be ready at 11:00 P.M. Those who had been condemned to death would be awakened at 11:45 and told that their executions were imminent."

The timing of the imparting of this information is highly significant. Within minutes of receiving it, according to what Private Bingham told the board, Pfluecker had gone to Goering's cell with the ostensible purpose of taking him an envelope containing the white powder that Goering poured into his coffee. It is almost impossible to believe that in the ten minutes of conversation that ensued, Pfluecker did not tell Goering of the time set for the beginning of the executions. If he did, this would answer the question of how Goering had such precise information.

But the officers of the board never asked Pfluecker what he and Goering had discussed. Nor did they ask him any probing questions. Perhaps they were afraid that the answers to these unasked questions might contradict their assertion that all of the German workers were loyal to their American employers and had no sympathy for the condemned. In the case of Dr. Pfluecker, at least, their fear was well founded.

What, then, of the U.S. Army personnel assigned to the prison? Were they as capable and loyal as the board maintained? Would all of them "leave no stone unturned" to deliver Goering up to the gallows? It is impossible to determine from the report in what manner the board came to this conclusion. Not a *single* question was asked of any of the witnesses about the attitudes and sympathies of the American guards and officers assigned to the prison! It is as if the officers of the board deliberately wished to avoid this subject. Perhaps they did not wish to have placed in the report what they knew some might say.

It was a well-known fact at the time that Goering's skillful defense and courageous demeanor during the trial had won him much respect and admiration, even from those who prosecuted him. Sir Norman Birkett, who was present throughout the trial as an alternate judge, wrote:

> Goering is the man who has really dominated the proceedings, and that, remarkable enough, without ever uttering a word in public up to the moment he went into the witness box. He has followed the evidence with great intentness when the evidence required attention, and has slept like a child when it did not; and it has been obvious that a personality of outstanding, though possibly evil qualities, was seated there in the dock. Nobody seems to have been quite prepared for his immense ability and knowledge and his thorough mastery and understanding of the detail of the captured documents. Suave, shrewd, adroit, capable, resourceful, he quickly saw the elements of the situation, and as his self confidence grew, his mastery became more apparent. His self control, too, was remarkable and to all the other qualities manifested in his evidence he added the resonant tones of his speaking voice, and the eloquent but restrained use of gesture.

Leo Kahn, of London's Imperial War Museum, wrote:

> Not only did Göring manage to become the focal point of public attention, but in the process he also created for himself a surprisingly large measure of more or less grudging respect and sympathy. Journalists, visitors, tribunal personnel, even some of the judges and prosecuting attorneys were impressed; the more so as the general public, misled by the popular press, had badly underrated him, picturing him as a brainless

thug, who would cut a miserable figure when deprived of his splendid uniforms and countless glittering medals.

Some at Nuremberg even developed a grudging personal liking for Goering. Typical was Airey Neave, a British officer and former prisoner of war of the Germans, who was selected to serve the indictments on the accused. "Murderer he might have been," Neave wrote of Goering, "but he was a brave bastard too." Neave said that when he heard of Goering's suicide, he "could scarcely repress a laugh. The old rascal had got away with it." As Kahn remarked, "Many people were not sorry when he managed to commit suicide before he could be delivered to the hangman."

Dr. Kelley's admiration for Goering showed plainly in a book the prison psychiatrist later wrote:

> He had faced the International Tribunal with courage but denied its rights to judge or sentence him. He stoically endured his long imprisonment that he might force down the Allied Tribunal and browbeat the prosecuting lawyers on their own terms. By these methods he established himself with the German people. In his last moments of life, he took matters into his own hands, and once again the dominant figure, cheated the hangman of the Allied nations. His suicide, shrouded in mystery and emphasizing the impotency of the American guards, was a skillful, even brilliant, finishing touch, completing the edifice for Germans to admire in time to come.

Kelley ended his paean to Goering by suggesting that history "may well show that Goering won out in the end, even though condemned by the high court of the Allied powers."

There is no question that Goering was an extremely engaging and personable individual when he chose to be. Dr. Gilbert wrote that he "presented a front of utter amiability and good-humored bravado to the American officers, whom he was obviously trying to win over." Whether obvious or not, Goering was often successful. If he was able to win the respect, admiration, and even sympathy of those of greater maturity and judgment, there can be no doubt that his efforts succeeded with others younger and more impressionable. Albert Speer told me that "many of the American GIs and officers of lower ranks were very friendly with us during the trial, and Goering was very popular with them."

His popularity with the American guards was deliberately cultivated by Goering, who was a master of psychology. John Pearsall, a former guard at Nuremberg, related a typical occurrence: "A common custom, especially when a new GI came on duty for the first time, was to have all the prisoners autograph dollar bills. This seemed to please Goering. In fact, he would kid the guard by asking him if he intended to sell the autograph in the United States for a lot of money."

Pearsall remembered that Goering, unlike some of the prisoners, never refused to give an autograph, "and was always willing to talk with the Americans." He rarely entered the courtroom without a wink and a joke directed toward the Army personnel assigned to guard him and the other prisoners. The result was, as an early biographer of Goering wrote, that the American guards were "wax" in his hands.

Sergeant Raabe, who was in close contact with Goering for many months, remembered Goering as friendly and amiable. "I never had any problem with him," he said. Raabe explained that once the trial started, the reserve that formerly characterized the relationship between the prisoners and the guards began to dissolve. "The guards were walking and talking with them." If Goering had "half an ounce of psychology," Raabe commented, "he is going to be nice to these guards." Goering had the prerequisite knowledge of psychology, and the result was, Raabe said, that there gradually developed among the guards the feeling that Goering "really was not such a bad guy," and even "hey, he's a nice person."

Goering's knowledge of psychology was so great that his verbal duels with Dr. Gilbert were often a source of great amusement to the American guards. Col. Bud Jones told me of the time he was present at a meeting between Goering and Gilbert. "Goering seemed to be in complete control. It was so obvious that both guards had smiles on their faces and it was all they could do to keep from bursting out in laughter" at Goering's facetious answers to Gilbert's Freudian questions. "It was obvious," Jones said, "that Goering was so much smarter than the doctor. He was a man of great wit and intelligence. It was difficult not to admire him."

Even those who were farther removed from Goering than the guards with whom he came into day-to-day contact were impressed by the former Reichsmarschall. Chaplain Carl Eggers said Goering "had the highest IQ of any of the prisoners, which isn't widely known. And he had a great personal charm; perfect manners, a good sense of humor. He knew the Bible, too, which surprised me. I looked forward to seeing him. He was always interesting." Eggers summed Goering up as a "good-natured charmer."

Even the Catholic chaplain, Father O'Connor, who did not minister to the spiritual needs of the Protestant Goering, seemingly admired the former Reichsmarschall. "Of all the doomed men, he impressed us the most. You felt that, with his brain, he could have accomplished a lot. He was no fool, even though great stress has been laid on his weight and his many medals and uniforms." Strangely, the two had often discussed baseball. "Who are these Dodgers? What is this baseball business? Is there money in it?" Goering had asked. After Father O'Connor replied that Branch Rickey, the general manager of the Dodgers, was paid ninety thousand dollars a year, Goering said, "Maybe I should have gone into that business." The two must have laughed at the thought of the obese Goering running the bases.

Emma Haynes, who was in charge of the rooms in which the defendants met with their lawyers, had many opportunities to observe Goering, both in and out of the courtroom. She said, "Many Americans in Nuremberg, including myself, developed a feeling of grudging admiration for Goering. He never tried to weasel out of anything that he had done as Ribbentrop and the others tried to do. He seemed to accept the fact that he would be found guilty and would receive the death penalty. But he never allowed the thought of his approaching death to interfere with his interest in life. He was an exceedingly intelligent man in contrast to the many American cartoons of the time that depicted him as a fat clown."

Ray D'Addario, the official army photographer during the trials, recalled that "Goering would always pose for me when I would ask him to. He was really a personable fellow." D'Addario was relieved that it was not his task to take the final photographs of Goering stretched out on his coffin. "They brought in some other officer who took the pictures. I'm glad that I didn't have to. We had been with those men for nine months." Reflecting on Goering's escape from the gallows, D'Addario commented, "A lot of people were happy when Goering didn't hang."

It is certain that many Americans both respected and sympathized with Goering and that others, like Kelley and Neave, did not seem overly saddened by his suicide. Yet this is not proof that anyone was so sympathetic to Goering that he would assist him in committing suicide. However, if one can believe Franz von Papen, he was twice approached by American guards who offered him means of doing away with himself. "The second one," von Papen wrote, "was so insistent that in the end I had to call the officer in charge to get rid of him."

Even if one mistrusts von Papen, there was at least one guard at Nuremberg who might have helped Goering commit suicide, if he had had the means and the opportunity. I sent a first-draft copy of my manuscript to this former guard (who shall remain nameless). He telephoned me several days later and he told me that "cold chills" ran through his body when he read my description of Goering's relationship with his American guards. "I know *exactly* what you are talking about," he said, "because I felt the same way." When he learned that he was to be posted to the Nuremberg prison, he had at first volunteered for any firing squad appointed to shoot Goering. However, after getting to know Goering and often conversing with him, he changed his attitude. His admiration for him grew so strong, he told me, "I would have helped him commit suicide if I could have." But he did not, he quickly added. I believed his denial then and I still do.

However, if the willingness, if not the opportunity, to help Goering kill himself was present in one guard, is it not possible that someone else had both?

Goering's letter to Colonel Andrus seemingly argues against this possibility. But does it really?

12

The Letter to Colonel Andrus

Nuremberg, 11 October 1946
To the Commandant:

I have always had the capsule of poison with me from the time I became a prisoner. When taken to Mondorf I had *three* capsules. The *first* I left in my clothes so that it would be found when a search was made. The *second* I placed under the clothesrack on undressing and took it to me again on dressing. I hid this in Mondorf and here in the cell so well that despite the *frequent* and *thorough* *searches* it could not be found. During the court sessions I had it on my person in my high riding boots. The *third* capsule is *still* in my small suitcase in the round box of skin cream, hidden in the cream. I could have taken this to me twice in Mondorf if I had needed it. None of those charged with searching is to be blamed for it was practically *impossible* to find the capsule. It would have been *pure accident*.

/s/ Hermann Goering

Dr. Gilbert informed me that the Control Board has refused the petition to change the method of execution to shooting.

Goering's letter to Colonel Andrus exists; of that much, at least, I am sure. The Berlin Document Center sent me a copy of the handwritten note, and I am convinced that it is in Goering's hand. That much is certain, though little else of its history is.

It is impossible to determine who found the letter on the night of October 15, 1946. Dr. Pfluecker claimed that he found a single en-

129

velope containing some papers and a brass cartridge and that the envelope was under the blanket in Goering's hand. He also told the board that he called his discovery to the attention of Chaplain Gerecke and that he made a point of asking the chaplain to remember where it had been found and under what circumstances. Gerecke dutifully told the board that Pfluecker had found the envelope in Goering's hand, but he evidently simply accepted the doctor's word for this. However, in a press interview on October 17, he told a completely different story. In this earlier version, Gerecke said that "an officer" found the envelope. "The officer reached over and picked up the right hand which was laying clutched outside the blanket. There was a rustle and an envelope fell to the floor. The officer stooped and recovered it." Some years later, in an article about his experiences at Nuremberg, Gerecke again recounted the events of that night in Goering's cell. In this account, the brass cartridge was not found in an envelope at all but resting on Goering's chest. "Desperately, not knowing what else to do, I leaned close to the unconscious man and spoke Scripture in his ear." According to Gerecke, it was only then that "the prison doctor, a German," entered the cell. Again, Gerecke made no mention of the doctor finding the envelope.

Lieutenant Roska, the American doctor, confirmed that an envelope containing a brass cartridge and some papers were found on Goering's body, but he told the board that it was *he* who had removed it from Goering's hand and long after the doctor had entered the cell.

When the envelope came into the possession of Captain Starnes, it suddenly became "two white envelopes, letter size." He said that he reached into one of the envelopes and withdrew a brass cartridge with cap. Starnes also told the board that both envelopes had "folded paper inside with the writing on them that I recognized as Goering's own handwriting." He told the board that Pfluecker had found the envelopes underneath Goering's hand after the doctor, while examining the body, "heard a rustling noise" under the blankets. Starnes, of course, was not present when the envelopes were found and merely repeated to the board what someone had told him.

The board seemed genuinely interested in the question of how many envelopes were found and by whom, and the record hints that the officers may have suspected that at least one of the letters or envelopes was introduced into the cell after Goering's suicide. Starnes was asked by the board if there were any instructions issued to the guard on Goering's cell "denying persons entrance into the cell." Starnes recalled that no one was permitted to enter the cell. "I placed Sgt. Hauberger on duty in the cell and instructed the sentinel and Sgt. Hauberger to allow no one entrance and allow nothing in the cell to be disturbed or moved without my instruction or that of Colonel Andrus." The board persisted: "Between the time you issued the order and the time the Board entered the cell had anyone entered that cell?" Starnes replied that no one had done so but added, "Dr. Roska had gone in there after Colonel Andrus and had left prior to the time I placed the Sergeant on duty. To the best of my knowledge he did not return."

The questions asked of Dr. Roska also suggest that the board was suspicious of whatever was found in Goering's hand. The board asked, "Did you see anything else [other than the single envelope] that Goering held in his hand that night when you first went into his cell?" Roska replied, "No, sir." "You saw only the envelope with the cartridge in it?" the board asked. Again, Roska replied that this was all he saw.

The board never asked Colonel Andrus about the number of envelopes found and the letter that Goering had written to him, but Andrus recalled the matter years later. He wrote that someone "handed me a single folded sheet of paper." Andrus also wrote that one of the Allied Control Commissioners later told him that Goering had written three letters on that single sheet of paper: "one to myself, one to his wife, and one to the German people."

However, Colonel Andrus cannot be considered a reliable witness in the matter of the Goering letter. By his own admission, he paid no attention to whatever was handed him. Even when writing his memoirs years later, he was still not in command of the facts. Though Andrus quoted in its entirety Goering's letter to him, he had claimed only pages before that Goering admitted in the letter that "he secreted the brass-and-glass vial in his anus and in his flabby navel." Of course, Goering made no such admission in the letter.

As confused as the record is, it seems safe to assume that Dr.

Pfluecker, at one time or another, had in his possession at least one envelope containing some papers and eventually the brass cartridge. If the envelope had any handwriting on it, he did not say. Nor was he asked by the board. Gerecke and Roska also mentioned only one envelope, though Roska claimed he was the one who took it from Goering's hand. Pfluecker, Gerecke, and Roska all were obviously referring to the same envelope because each mentioned that it contained the brass cartridge. Only Starnes, who was a latecomer to the cell, mentioned two envelopes and supplied details of their appearance and contents. Either Gerecke, Pfluecker, and Roska were mistaken about the number of envelopes, or Starnes was. The weight of numbers is a positive factor for the former case, while the amount of detail supplied by Starnes argues the latter.

Even when questioned closely by the board, Starnes doggedly insisted that there were two envelopes and gave further details about what he had had in his possession: "I know there was handwriting on the outside of one. The one that contained the brass cartridge case was slightly torn at the end of the cartridge case. This was further torn by the further handling by myself and Colonel Andrus before he gave the envelope to Brigadier Patonwalsh [sic]."

"Could one of these have been a folded piece of paper?" the board asked. Starnes admitted that it was possible but again insisted, "It looked like an envelope to me."

Shortly after Goering's suicide, an article in the London *Times* specifically referred to a torn envelope bearing Goering's handwriting and containing three penciled notes. Therefore, the *Times* confirmed Starnes's recollection of details, if not the number of envelopes found.

The puzzle of the number of envelopes found in Goering's cell and by whom they were found was never resolved by the board. They made little effort to do so besides asking a few superficial questions that skirted the issue. If the board suspected that one of the envelopes may have been smuggled into Goering's cell *after* his suicide, which would resolve the conflict in testimony between Starnes and those who were earlier in the cell, it did not follow the line of questioning that it should have.

Pfluecker's claim that he found an envelope in Goering's hand *under* the blanket was in direct conflict with all other testimony about the position of the hands before death. All other witnesses, including Private Johnson, who watched as Goering killed himself, insisted that Goering's hands were always on top of the blankets as prescribed by prison regulations. The *New York Times* reported that Johnson, a few days after the suicide, still insisted that such was the case: Goering's hands had never gone below the covers, and he had nothing whatsoever in them, certainly nothing as large and obvious as a white envelope.

The *Washington Post*, quoting a newsman who had observed Goering in his cell shortly before his suicide, said that all the while he was being observed, Goering's hands were outside the covers and that his right hand appeared to be clenched. Dr. Kelley wrote that it was the jail's "strict rule" that the head and hands of a prisoner be visible at all times. Even prisoners who inadvertently broke this regulation while asleep were brusquely awakened by worried guards and forced to conform with the rule. Von Papen complained that this was often done to him during his "snatches of sleep."

On the very night of the executions, Alfred Rosenberg complained about the regulation requiring him to keep his hands above the covers. The reason for complaint was that his hands became cold in the frigid cell. At least two other prisoners made the same protest on the night of the executions. Lieutenant Jean Paul Willis, officer of the day, later told the board, "During my tour of duty frequent inspections were made of the cell guards, and at no time were any unusual incidents reported to me prior to 2240. To all outward appearances there was no change in Hermann Goering's appearance." Over thirty-five years after the event, Willis still insisted Goering had never thrust his hands beneath the covers. During a lengthy conversation, I questioned Willis closely on this point. He told me he stood by his 1946 statement to the board. "Goering's hands *never* went beneath those covers!" He was at a complete loss to explain how the board could have concluded otherwise.

Considering the testimony of an officer who made regular inspections of the cells along with the testimony of all the other witnesses who reported that Goering's hands never went beneath the covers, there is no reason to believe that the prison's "strict rule" was relaxed on the night of October 15.

The question of the position of Goering's hands is not a trivial one. If Dr. Pfluecker was correct in stating that the letter was found in Goering's hand under the blankets, then the board's conclusion that "no blame for dereliction of duty is assigned to the sentry on duty at the time of Goering's death" is not a proper one. If Pfluecker was correct about the position of Goering's hands, Private Johnson had allowed Goering to break one of the cardinal rules of the prison. However, if Johnson and the other witnesses are correct in their insistence that Goering's hands never went beneath the covers, the matter is even more serious. Pfluecker's story of finding the envelope cannot be true.

Faced by the dilemma of deciding which story was the correct one, the board neatly sidestepped the issue by ignoring the contradiction; Pfluecker had found the envelope in Goering's hand under the blankets, but Johnson had never allowed Goering's hands to go under the blankets, the board concluded. The only way that such a thing could have happened was for Goering, in the throes of death after swallowing the poison, to have spasmodically thrust his hand beneath the blankets and clutched the envelope in a death grip.

The report goes to great lengths to deny that the board, during deliberation, was influenced by Goering's letter to Colonel Andrus. Three times in as many pages the board states that a major conclusion was reached *before* it received the letter on October 23. In all cases, the letter provided corroboration for the board's conclusions but was not, the report insists, the basis for them. Brigadier Paton-Walsh told the press that the letter "had some relation to the event, but the commission drew its own conclusions." If one is to believe the report and the statement of Paton-Walsh, the board concluded independently and without prior knowledge of the letter's contents, that Goering brought the poison with him to Nuremberg, that he managed to hide it throughout his imprisonment, and that no one assisted him in any way with his suicide.

The assertion that the board was unaware of the contents of Goering's letter until October 23 and had conducted most of its investigation in the dark is very difficult to believe. Colonel Andrus said that he had not read the letter but took it to the office of the commission, where it presumably remained until "received" by the board on October 23. It is most probable, if not absolutely certain, that the board knew at an earlier date what Goering had written. If not, it is a strange coincidence that on October 19 they managed to find the second brass cartridge in the prison baggage room exactly where Goering's letter said it was hidden.

Colonel Andrus inadvertently provided evidence of the board's prior knowledge of the letter's contents when he said on October 23, supposedly *before* the board considered the letter, that the vanity case in the baggage room had never been opened until "it was searched for some salve." If the search on October 19 was specifically for "some salve," it is obvious that the board had already read the letter. Otherwise, why would Andrus specifically refer to a search "for some salve" rather than a general search?

If the board truly knew nothing of the letter's content until October 23, it was almost alone in its lack of knowledge. On October 19 the *New York Times* headlined: "Goering Note Said to Explain Suicide." The accompanying story accurately reported that Goering, in one of the three letters he had written, explained how he had retained the poison with which he killed himself. "The letter," the *Times* said, "did not incriminate any individual and even went out of the way to exonerate various persons." The story indicated that "an authoritative source" was the origin of the information. On the same day the *Washington Post* headlined: "Sensation in Goering Death Clears Army, Generals Hint." According to the *Post*, two Allied generals, whose names could not be given, had predicted "a sensational solution" to the mystery of Goering's suicide, "one that will clear the American Army for the blame." The story indicated that Goering's letter would provide the key to the mystery.

Thus, as early as October 18, the date the stories were filed from Nuremberg, "authoritative sources" were predicting the outcome of the board's investigation. If the board members actually knew nothing of what Goering had written, they most certainly were living in a complete vacuum, hermetically sealed off from the rest of the world.

Despite the army's admission that Goering's letter to Andrus played a crucial role in its investigation, the text of the letter was not released to the press. It was only in February 1946 that some details were furnished, seemingly to refute rumors that one of Goering's guards had given him the poison. An anonymous army spokesman in Frankfurt told the press that Hermann Goering's deathbed letter "absolved his GI guards of responsibility for his having his fatal poison capsule." The spokesman admitted that the letter did not reveal where Goering had hidden the poison or how he had managed to smuggle it into the prison, but again emphasized that the "guards were not to blame." In conclusion, the army official faithfully adhered to the board's conclusions that "at one time Goering hid the capsule in his alimentary canal and part of the time he kept it in a hidden recess of the toilet in his cell," but he added that this was concluded on the basis of "surmise and implication." The belated statement to the press sounded more defensive than positive.

Goering's letter to Andrus may have appeared to answer many questions at the time. Upon reflection, however, the letter raises more questions than it answers. First of all, one is forced to consider the purpose of the letter. Ostensibly, Goering wrote it to explain how he procured the poison and managed to hide it while imprisoned. But he never said just where he hid the cartridge. His claim to have hidden it in his high riding boots during the court sessions must be viewed with considerable skepticism as the evidence shows that he was often stopped, stripped, and searched when returning from court. The most inept of guards would not overlook such an obvious hiding place as Goering's boots. Significantly, the board never gave any indication that it believed this story, choosing instead to pass over it in complete silence. To have accepted it would have been for the army tantamount to an admission of gross negligence.

Goering's claim that while at Mondorf he could have twice procured the poison hidden in the vanity case is questionable. While at

Mondorf, he wrote a furious letter to General Eisenhower in which he bitterly complained of the deprivations he was forced to suffer. "Of my toilet articles," he wrote, "I have only a sponge, soap, toothbrush (not even a comb)." Clearly at this time, Goering had no access to his vanity case nor to the second vial of cyanide. The testimony of Colonel Andrus and the often-demonstrated lack of sympathy for the Nazis by Eisenhower make it highly unlikely that Goering was ever given access to his vanity case.

Sergeant Raabe, who placed Goering's luggage and other belongings in the prison baggage room, said that the vanity case remained undisturbed throughout Goering's imprisonment. He remembered it as a large case "like an actor's make-up box, full of all sorts of lotions and creams." It was not the sort of item that would be deemed "essential" for Goering to have.

Goering said in his letter to Colonel Andrus that he had hidden the poison capsule with which he killed himself so well that not even the most thorough of searches could have found it. Dr. Kelley remembered these searches, which sometimes occurred as often as four times a week, as "so thorough that prisoners needed some four hours to restore their cells to order." During these searches, the prisoner was "forced to strip and stand in a corner of the cell while M.P.'s went carefully through bedding, clothing, papers, and other impedimenta." Von Papen later said that he regarded it as extremely unlikely that Goering could have hidden anything in his cell for any length of time; the searches, he said, were much too thorough. Von Schirach, who had experienced these searches with von Papen and Goering, later remarked, "It has always puzzled me how Goering . . . managed to secure and then hide the cyanide with which he took his life."

Goering's letter only added insult to injury as he claimed to have been able, with relative ease and almost immediately, to find a hiding spot in his cell that the combined efforts of many capable officers and guards were unable to match in a year's time. If it was Goering's intention to resolve the mystery of the hiding place for the poison, his letter utterly failed to do so.

It is significant, however, that Goering specifically mentioned the poison capsule hidden in the can of skin cream in the baggage room. He wrote: "The *third* capsule is *still* [Goering's emphasis] in the round box of skin cream." As the search of October 19 was to prove, the capsule was indeed "*still*" there. If Goering had no access to his vanity case in the baggage room, how did he know this? The question does not seem to have occurred to the board.

The letter to Colonel Andrus contained yet another disturbing aspect not considered by the board. It had been written on October 11, four days before the suicide. Lt. John W. West told the board that it was his nightly duty to inspect Goering's cell and that he had last done so on October 14 at 7:45 P.M. "All of his personal effects were searched," West said, "his bedding removed from the bed and shaken, the mattress turned over." Rather than exhibiting any apprehension that the letter might be found, "Goering seemed very happy and talked a great deal." If Goering was acting, it was a superb job.

If the opportunities for hiding the letter in the cell were limited and dangerous, could Goering have employed reverse psychology in keeping it from being discovered? Could he have placed it in one of the envelopes in his stack of personal correspondence, perhaps between the pages of a letter his wife had written, and simply left it on his table? The answer would have to be no in light of the conditions that existed in the prison. All of the prisoners complained throughout their incarceration of the guards' habits of stealing every souvenir, particularly autograph items, they could lay their hands on. Much of Goering's private correspondence, including very personal letters to his wife and daughter, never reached the intended recipient but was stolen by the guards and later sold as choice souvenirs. More than anyone else, Goering was aware of the "collecting" habits of the GIs, and so there is little likelihood that he would have taken a chance with his letter to Colonel Andrus. Therefore, reverse psychology cannot answer the question of why the letter was not found before the night of October 15.

It is difficult to believe that Goering, knowing full well that his cell was subject to both routine and unexpected searches, allowed the dangerous letter to remain in the cell since October 11. "I have always wondered about that," said cell guard William Glenney. "It doesn't make sense that Goering would have left the envelope in his cell 'on trust' that no one would find it and open it."

Glenney's suspicion is well founded. Would not common sense dictate that Goering write a letter holding the key to his planned escape from the gallows as a "last communication," even after a farewell letter to his wife? (Goering's farewell letter to his wife was dated October 15, 1946, the last day of his life.) The answer would have to be yes *if* the true purpose of the letter were simply to confess that he always had the poison. But this was *not* its real purpose.

Perhaps, I thought, Colonel Andrus understood the true purpose of the letter, though he professed that never at Nuremberg jail did he learn what Goering had written. "For twenty years," he wrote in his memoirs, "I wondered about Goering's last thoughts on earth." Yet when Desmond Zwar, Andrus's coauthor, wanted to locate the hitherto undisclosed letter, the colonel was not at all cooperative. "In fact," Zwar told me, "he regarded my persistence in trying to find out the contents of the Goering suicide note as a damned nuisance and told me so several times." Zwar eventually wrote letters to every possible depository where the letter might be found, telling Andrus that if he would sign them, "I'd then leave him alone about the matter." Andrus reluctantly consented, and the letter was found and first published in Andrus's book and newspapers of the time.

Andrus's reluctance to assist Zwar in finding the answer to the question that had been puzzling him "for twenty years" was curious to me. I was tempted to think that the long puzzlement over the letter was Zwar's contribution to Andrus's book and that Andrus himself had long known what was in the letter but did not wish to make its contents known.

Why would Andrus not want Zwar to find and publish the letter? Perhaps Andrus knew that the real and all too obvious purpose of the letter was to protect an accomplice who had procured the poison for Goering only shortly before his suicide. Though the letter was addressed to Colonel Andrus, Goering certainly had no desire to protect the commandant to whom he always contemptuously referred as "the fire brigade colonel," a reference to the shiny helmet that Andrus habitually wore. Andrus admitted that he would be the last to believe "that Goering had any feeling other than resentment for me."

Speaking of the prisoners, Andrus later wrote, "Psychologically, I was a symbol to them of what they were facing. There is always a tendency among people confined in prison to hate their custodians. The custodian is to them the embodiment of the retribution they have to face for the evil they have done."

If someone in the prison had given Goering the poison and had demanded a "confession" for protection before delivery could be made, it was *not* Colonel Andrus.

13

Conspiracy: Yes or No?

The board did not entirely ignore the possibility that someone within the prison gave Goering the poison, but the officers did not pursue the matter in great depth. Though it was accepted for the sake of consideration that Goering could have obtained the poison "from a member of the civilian prison staff, his lawyer, his wife, another prisoner, and, as for that matter, any one of the members of the Armed Forces on duty in the prison," only the German workers aroused even the slightest evidence of suspicion from the board.

Despite the board's lack of interest in Frau Goering, biographer Willi Frischauer said she was "high on the list" of suspects. Even though the phraseology is an exaggeration of Frau Goering's importance to the board, there is little doubt that she would have done anything to help her husband escape hanging. As the wife of a top Nazi official, it was entirely possible that she possessed one or more of the poison capsules.

Frau Goering was allowed to visit her husband for thirty minutes on a daily basis from the middle of September 1946 to the end of that month. She saw her husband again, and for the last time, on October 7, after he had been sentenced to hang. It was during this visit, according to the persistent rumors, that she passed the poison to her husband in a last kiss and embrace.

Capt. Hubert Biddle, the former Nuremberg staff officer who had found the vial of poison in the can of coffee shortly after Goering had been taken into custody, said it was his opinion that the death capsule "could have been passed to Goering in a farewell kiss with his wife." Biddle's theory is open to question because he had long departed the Nuremberg prison and was in the United States at the time of Goering's death. He had no firsthand information.

The chief flaw in Biddle's romantic theory is that Frau Goering had absolutely no opportunity to pass the poison to her husband. All of the visits had been conducted with Frau Goering on one side of a wire-mesh partition and her husband on the other side. In addition, the two were under constant observation by an American guard hand-cuffed to Goering's right arm. Chaplain Gerecke described the con-ditions under which these visits took place: "Each prisoner was heavily guarded when he talked with his kin. They were not allowed to touch each other. In fact, a screen between them ruled out any chance of an object being passed through. Chaplain O'Connor or I, and an officer, were always present on the visitor's side."

Emma Haynes, who was in charge of the rooms in which Goering and the others received visits from their lawyers and relatives, told me that it was "simply ridiculous" for anyone to suggest that Frau Goering could have passed the poison to her husband. "They were always separated by a wire grill and could not even touch each other. Besides, there was an armed guard at Goering's side during every interview."

Other than the meetings behind the mesh partition, there were none between Goering and his wife and even then they were *never* allowed any physical contact. Frau Goering begged Andrus to be per-mitted at least to hold her husband's hand, "but the answer had to be no," he wrote. Pfc. Russel A. Keller, who accompanied Goering to his last visit with his wife, confirmed to the board that "at no time during their visit did Goering and his wife make physical contact in any way, nor was anything in the way of papers, parcels, or anything else passed between them." Keller was so conscientious in performing his duty that when Goering tried to raise his right arm in a final blessing of his wife, he immediately forced it down, tugging on the handcuff linking his arm to Goering's. Evidently Keller was afraid that Goering

TOP: A youthful Hermann Goering in Storm Trooper uniform. At his throat is the Pour le Mérite won as a fighter pilot during World War I. LEFT: The official engagement portrait of Goering and Emmy Sonnemann. Goering wears the uniform of a Luftwaffe general. *Courtesy Lt. Col. Thomas M. Johnson*

TOP LEFT: Goering removes his medals at Seventh Army Interrogation Center, Augsburg, Germany. *Courtesy Lt. Col. Thomas M. Johnson; U.S. Information Agency photo.* TOP RIGHT: Goering after learning at a press conference he is to be tried as a war criminal. Maj. Paul Kubala translates. *U.S. Army.* BOTTOM: Wearing dark glasses to shield his eyes from the camera lights, Goering occupies the first seat in the prisoners' dock. *U.S. Army Signal Corps*

TOP: Goering speaks with Dr. Hans Frank in the courtroom. Free from his immense weight (note baggy uniform) and drug habit, Goering exhibited surprising vitality and keenness of mind. *National Archives.*
RIGHT: Goering in the witness box. His skillful and courageous defense gained him much respect and admiration, even from former foes. *U.S. Army Signal Corps*

TOP: The prison wing occupied by the major war criminals. Goering's cell is in the second row from the bottom, fourth window from the left. *Courtesy Col. Burton C. Andrus, Jr.* BOTTOM: After Dr. Robert Ley killed himself in November 1945, each prisoner was observed around the clock. Goering's cell is on the extreme right. *U.S. Army Signal Corps*

LEFT: Goering eats in his cell from a GI mess kit that had been thoroughly inspected before it was given to him. *U.S. Army Signal Corps.* BELOW: One of the "suicide-proof" cells. It had been stripped of all projections and electrical outlets, and the table was designed to collapse under a man's weight. *Courtesy Col. Burton C. Andrus, Jr.* BOTTOM: A typical cell. In the corner is a toilet like the one in which, it was alleged, Goering hid his poison for over fifteen months. *Courtesy Col. Burton C. Andrus, Jr.*

RIGHT: Shelves in the baggage room where the personal property of the prisoners was stored. Four days after Goering's suicide, another poison vial was found in his luggage. *Courtesy Col. Burton C. Andrus, Jr.* BELOW, LEFT TO RIGHT: Col. Burton C. Andrus, prison commandant, with Col. Robert G. Storey, Justice Robert H. Jackson, and Col. John H. Amen *U.S. Army Signal Corps.* BOTTOM: Dr. Ludwig Pfluecker (*left*), German POW prison doctor, with Dr. Heinz Hoch, POW prison dentist *U.S. Army Signal Corps*

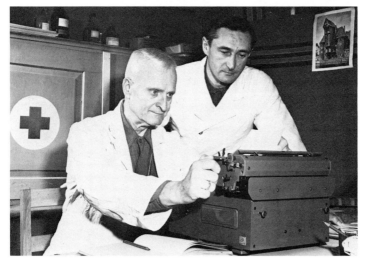

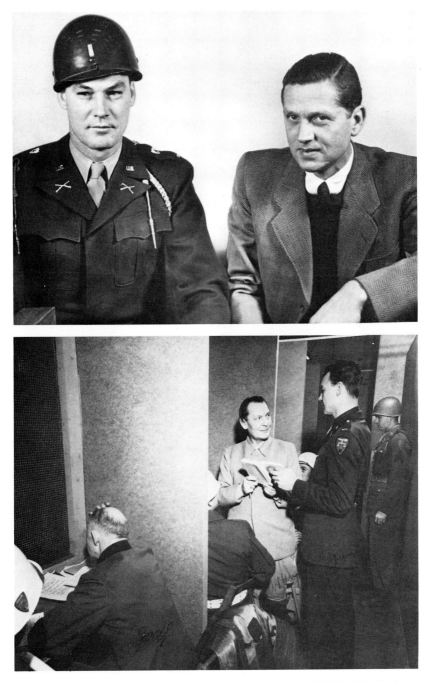

TOP: Lt. Jack G. Wheelis and the former SS and Gestapo general Walter Schellenberg. Wheelis noted in admiration that "Walter" had become a general while still in his thirties. *Jack G. Wheelis Collection, Eugene C. Barker Texas History Center, Austin, Texas.* BOTTOM: Lt. Jack G. Wheelis with Hermann Goering. The reverse side of this picture bears a dedication from Goering to "the great hunter from Texas." *Jack G. Wheelis Collection, Eugene C. Barker Texas History Center, Austin, Texas*

TOP: The corpse of Hermann Goering. Publication of this photo was intended to prevent rumors that the convicted Nazis had not been executed. *U.S. Army Signal Corps.* LEFT: Lt. Jack G. Wheelis wearing Goering's wristwatch, which had been stored for safekeeping in the prison baggage room when Goering first arrived at the prison *Courtesy Mrs. Genelle Salles.* ABOVE: The brass cartridge that contained the vial of poison with which Goering killed himself *National Archives*

was attempting to touch his wife's hand through the screen or about to give the Nazi salute.

Frau von Schirach recalled that when she, with the permission of the guard, attempted to push a cigarette through the fine mesh grill, "it got stuck." If an object as flexible and thin as a cigarette could not pass through the grill, there is no possibility that the brass cartridge containing the poison could have been passed through.

Frau Goering always insisted that she had nothing to do with her husband's suicide. Only hours after it was announced, George Martin, a French journalist, went to the small house in Sackdilling, a small town near Neuhaus where Frau Goering lived in seclusion. The door was opened by a woman who was staying with Frau Goering, and Martin told her that he was a journalist. The woman told him that "housebreakers were more welcome than journalists" and that Frau Goering did not wish to speak to anyone. After Martin requested that Frau Goering be told that it was rumored she had given the poison to her husband, the door immediately swung open, and Emmy Goering confronted the journalist. She told him indignantly, "How can anyone suspect me! You know yourself that not for one second was I with my husband alone and unobserved. Even when Edda was with me, we were so closely watched that the child could not stick even her little finger through the grating. Write in your newspaper that I was never allowed to see my husband alone before his death."

Frau Goering's face stiffened and appeared mask-like. Tears ran down her cheeks. Martin left, convinced she was telling the truth.

Some time later, Frau Goering told Menno Duerkson, a reporter, that it was "utter insanity" to suspect her. It was, Frau Goering maintained, "absolutely impossible considering the conditions under which I was allowed to see him." She told correspondent Marguerite Higgins, "Thank God that I cannot be considered a suspect, since I was separated from my husband during all our talks by a thick wire netting." In discussing the matter some years later with one of her husband's biographers, Frau Goering made a very telling point: "He would not have taken the poison from me; he would not have put me in a position where I might be accused of a crime!"

Major Teich, speaking on behalf of the prison authorities, told the press "it would have been impossible" for Frau Goering to have passed anything to her husband during their visits. The board realized this to be the truth, in light of the prison security regulation with which they were familiar, and Frau Goering was never questioned.

Dr. Otto Stahmer, Goering's lawyer, had far greater opportunity than Frau Goering to give the poison to his client. Colonel Andrus admitted that the lawyer could have done so had he been "a sleight of hand artist." He later wrote that while most of the lawyers were legally and politically respected, "we had to be suspicious of all." Goering, on the other hand, told his wife in a letter that he had the "fullest confidence" in Dr. Stahmer, advising her that she could "discuss anything with him."

Many of those who had attended the trials suspected Dr. Stahmer, or one of the other lawyers, as the most likely channel for the poison to be passed to Goering. Saying that he did not believe Frau Goering guilty, Thomas J. Dodd, United States counsel, suggested that Goering's "lawyer, or someone in that sphere," had given him the poison. Don Spencer, who had observed the court proceedings, told me, "In the courtroom, in front of everyone—he could have received it from any number of people. The defense counsels were accustomed to passing notes back and forth to their clients every day." Rolf Wartenberg, one of the Nuremberg interrogators, wrote me, "There were not so many persons who had access to Goering; naturally, his defense lawyers had access, and I have photos where one of his lawyers is passing Goering a sheaf of documents." Thus, Dr. Stahmer could be considered suspect.

From all descriptions of him, Stahmer seems to have possessed neither the motive nor the "sleight of hand" ability necessary for him to have passed the poison to Goering. Over seventy years old, he was described by Airey Neave as "squeaky and insipid," though possessed of considerable legal skill. Pictures of Stahmer show him to have been, as described by another author, "staid, almost prim." He had had no prior connection with Goering, who, after being shown a list of lawyer's names, including Stahmer's, said, "I do not know anything of the gentlemen on this list. I do not know any lawyers." Obviously, Dr. Stahmer was not tainted by a Nazi background, or his name would not have been on the list. Bradley F. Smith commented, "Generally chosen because they were anti-Nazis or had at least been cool to Hitler's regime, the German defense attorneys in the main considered the defendants to be the source of their own, and their nation's, misfortune."

Like Frau Goering, Dr. Stahmer always vehemently denied that he had anything to do with Goering's suicide. "I would not have helped Goering commit suicide even if I had been given the chance," Dr. Stahmer said. "Neither Goering nor Frau Goering ever even suggested that anything like that was being planned." In support of his denial of complicity, Dr. Stahmer showed the press pictures taken during his conferences with Goering and pointed out to them that "even if Goering had wanted to give me an indication of his intention, that would have been impossible." The pictures showed an American security officer sitting alongside the attorney and between Stahmer and Goering a wire netting with a glass window.

Dr. Walter Siemers, another of the German lawyers, confirmed Stahmer's denials that he had given the poison to Goering. He was indignant at any such suggestion and told reporters, "Dr. Stahmer was the most correct of all the attorneys."

While it was possible for Dr. Stahmer to have done so, it seems unlikely that he had any motivation for taking such a risk. He was never called before the board, but all the guards who had escorted Stahmer to his meetings with Goering stated positively that nothing had passed between them unless it had first been thoroughly inspected by an officer. The board concluded that there was no reason to suspect Stahmer, and he, too, was eliminated from any list.

It has been suspected by many that one of the German prison employees gave Goering the poison, though no individual worker was ever specifically mentioned. AP reporter Reedy wrote that sources inside the Nuremberg jail reported that "12 German employees [were] under constant scrutiny while officials investigate[d] where and how the poison was passed to Goering, and by whom." Suspicions of the German workers linger even to this day. Gen. Samuel T. Williams, former commanding officer of the 26th Infantry Regiment, the unit from which many of the jail guards were drawn, told me that he had "always assumed that Goering got his pill or pills . . . from the German cooks in the prison." Emma Haynes wrote, "During recent years, it has been claimed that he received the poison from a German employee in the prison. This account made much more sense to me." William Stricker, head of the Nuremberg branch of DANA, was equally convinced "that it was one of the Germans used to perform various functions from dentistry to cleaning." He wrote me:

> It is easily possible that during one of their trips outside, one of the Germans could have obtained a cyanide capsule and smuggled it back into the Palace of Justice through a very cursory checkup. As a matter of fact, on the very day of the executions, I asked one of my German staff members to get me one of the capsules which had been distributed by the millions by the German government to citizens to prevent dying a painful death in burning buildings. My reporter returned after less than two hours with a capsule which he had obtained at the Nuremberg railroad station for three packs of cigarettes.

Despite the sympathy shown for the prisoners by some of the German workers and the evident availability of poison in Nuremberg, no evidence has been uncovered to link the two factors. The poison that Goering used to commit suicide certainly could not be purchased on the streets as it was of special manufacture and available only to the most senior Nazi officials. After a brief flurry of accusations had been lodged against them as a group, the German prison employees were dismissed as suspects in the Goering suicide.

Though it appears that no one other than Frau Goering, Dr. Stahmer, and the German workers were ever even briefly considered suspect by the board, one might wonder about some of the others who were in the prison. For example, Dr. Kelley, Dr. Gilbert, and Chaplain Gerecke all had opportunity to give Goering the poison. One might think that any one of these individuals, all of whom had been trained to put personal antipathies aside, might have, out of compassion, allowed Goering to escape at least the final humiliation of hanging.

Dr. Kelley, who displayed an amazing amount of sympathy and admiration for Goering, is often suggested as the one who gave him the poison. Frau von Schirach told me, "I seem to remember that Kelley, who often spoke with Goering, killed himself some years ago with the same type of poison. Perhaps there is a connection here?" Frau von Schirach's memory was correct; Dr. Kelley killed himself on New Year's Day, 1957, with a cyanide capsule that he brought from Nuremberg as a souvenir. However, other than the similar means of self-destruction, there seems to be no connection between the deaths of Kelley and Goering. According to the statement of Kelley's physician, the psychiatrist killed himself for personal reasons totally unrelated to his Nuremberg experiences. Additionally, Kelley left Nuremberg after the first two months of the trial, thereby lessening the chance that he could have aided Goering at all, and certainly not at the time when Goering most urgently required the poison. Despite Dr. Kelley's pronounced sympathy for Goering and the similarity of their deaths, no evidence has been uncovered to suggest that he gave him the poison.

Dr. Gilbert, who remained throughout the trial and after the sentences were pronounced, must also be disqualified as an accomplice. Despite his professional training and the need for objectivity in his work, it is obvious from his statement to the board and even more so from the book which he later wrote that he loathed Goering and had no sympathy whatsoever for him. Gilbert, a Jew who had been forced to flee Austria by the Nazis, would have been the last person to help Goering commit suicide.

Chaplain Gerecke, too, must be excluded from suspicion. According to him, the subject of suicide was alluded to by Goering only once in their many conversations and then only in such a manner that Gerecke concluded suicide was the furthest thing from Goering's mind. After a new security rule had been imposed by Colonel Andrus, Goering exploded to the chaplain, "What kind of foolishness is this? They ought to know that it's impossible here for us to do anything against ourselves." After Goering committed suicide, Gerecke was deeply disappointed that his efforts to bring him to accept the concepts of Christianity had been in vain. Gerecke had thought for a while that

Goering had made a sincere return to his religion as the time for the executions neared. "But it could not have been sincere," Gerecke told reporters, "or I am sure that he would not have ended his life as he did." Gerecke certainly had compassion for Goering, but his own religious convictions were too strong to have permitted him to be an accomplice to suicide. Rightly, the board never considered him suspect.

With most of the obvious suspects eliminated, was there any evidence that a conspiracy even existed? Is there any reason to believe that Goering was not always in possession of the poison? According to the *New York Times* there was.

On October 18, 1946, the *Times* published a story which offered inferential evidence that Goering was not in possession of a means of suicide only months before his death. The *Times* maintained that Goering "apparently made an attempt to obtain a suicide weapon three months ago when he extracted a piece of celluloid from his earphones in the courtroom." The missing piece, the *Times* claimed, was later found in Goering's possession. "If this information is exact," the newspaper observed, "it would explode the theory that Goering had the potassium cyanide phial for a long while, or before he tried to obtain the instrument with which he could have cut his veins."

Was this information "exact"? According to the *Washington Post*, "A prison spokesman revealed that almost two months before the trial ended, a sharp piece of metal, apparently part of the courtroom receiver, was taken from Goering during a routine search of his cell." The prison spokesman was not being entirely candid with the press. Captain Starnes mentioned the incident to the board but admitted to the officers that the missing piece was never found. In either case, despite the difference in terminology between the *Times* and the *Post* and the unclear details of what exactly happened, Goering's intent at that time *is* clear—he wanted something he could use to kill himself.

If Goering already had the poison, why would he go to the trouble and the risk involved in securing this piece from the earphones? (Guards might find his poison while searching for the missing piece of celluloid.) The obvious answer is he did *not* have the poison at the time and must have obtained it later. If this is true, it is almost certain he had aid in procuring it.

Since 1946 various persons have confessed to being the one who gave Goering the poison. Most of these individuals have been dismissed as publicity-seeking cranks; but there was one person whose confession was taken seriously by some segments of the press. Former SS Gen. Erich von dem Bach-Zelewski told American military authorities in 1951 that it was he who gave the poison to Goering. *Time* reported the confession in an article entitled "How Goering Died." According to *Time*, Bach-Zelewski entered the Nuremberg prison at the beginning of the trial with three vials of cyanide. "Because he was a witness, not a prisoner, guards had not searched him." When Goering, who was then in a cell opposite that of the SS general, asked for some poison, Bach-Zelewski obliged. "The transaction, according to Bach-Zelewski, was quite impersonal. 'I had no relations with Goering and did not like him . . . but he was the first to ask me for the poison.' " It had been passed to Goering, *Time* said, in a bar of GI soap.

Heydecker and Leeb revealed in their book how the transaction supposedly took place. Bach-Zelewski told them that for weeks he had been greeting Goering with exaggerated and preposterous marks of respect whenever the two passed on the way to the showers. Much amused, the American guards were lulled into inattention. "By this trickery, claimed Bach-Zelewski, it was eventually possible for him once to shake Goering by the hand, although this was strictly forbidden. On this occasion the poison changed hands."

Bach-Zelewski is now dead, and his story is impossible to prove or disprove. There is, however, a serious flaw in his confession: he totally lacked a motive. When he said he did not like Goering, it was an understatement; the two men loathed each other. After Bach-Zelewski gave unfavorable testimony at Nuremberg, Goering was outraged by what he considered to be "treason." Andrus remembered, "Finally, as Bach-Zelewski stepped down from the witness box and passed Goering, the former Nazi leader snarled: '*Schweinehund und Verraeter!* (Pig-dog and traitor!)' " Dr. Gilbert also remembered Goering's furious reaction to the testimony of Bach-Zelewski: "Why, that dirty, bloody, treacherous swine!! That filthy skunk. Goddam, *Donnerwetter*, the blankety-blank sonofabitch!!! He was the bloodiest murderer in the whole goddam setup!"

Goering later gave his lawyer a series of questions formulated to force Bach-Zelewski, to whom he referred as "that scoundrel," to admit that he was personally responsible for criminal antipartisan activities and that he had sullied German military honor by pressing common criminals into the armed forces to combat the partisans.

Goering's obvious desire was to compromise Bach-Zelewski, thus assuring the SS general, who claimed to have given him the means to commit suicide, of a place of his own on the gallows. It was strange behavior for a man who supposedly had every reason *not* to antagonize his benefactor.

Apart from the fact that Goering and Bach-Zelewski did not like each other, there is additional evidence that the whole story is a piece of fiction. Goering never occupied a cell opposite that of Bach-Zelewski; the two were never even in the same wing of the prison. Further, the analysis of the scrapings from the brass cartridge revealed not the slightest hint that the case had once been embedded in soap. Lastly, Bach-Zelewski's claim is rendered suspect by the fact that the glass vial found in the soap that he later surrendered to American authorities in 1951 differs from the type that Goering used to kill himself. The glass vial used by Goering had a flat bottom and a rounded knob at the other end; the vial given up by Bach-Zelewski was rounded at both ends, much like ammonia vials. Obviously, it was not from the same source as Goering's poison. For all of these reasons, Bach-Zelewski's story must be discounted.

Nevertheless, there are still those who believe that Goering had an accomplice, and their reasons are often persuasive. Goering's biographers Manvell and Fraenkel wrote that Frau Goering, using a code word, twice asked her husband if he had poison; the second time was during their last meeting, only eight days before the suicide. On both occasions, Goering shook his head. Frau Goering told the same story to Dr. Robert Kempner, a German-born member of the United States prosecution team. According to Kempner, Frau Goering asked her husband, "Have you got the comb?" ("Comb" was the agreed-upon word for poison.) Goering answered no, Frau Goering told Kempner.

Henriette von Schirach remembered accompanying Emmy Goering from the prison after they had visited their husbands. Frau Goering was convinced that her husband was going to hang, and she was utterly desolate over the thought. "They can't hang him. Tell me—they can't hang Hermann. Think only—Hermann at the gallows!" Unable to face the prospect of her husband's hanging, Frau Goering deluded herself. "They are obviously deceiving us. . . . They will take him away and intern him on an island like Napoleon." Clearly, Goering had told his wife nothing at this meeting that would lead her to believe that he possessed a means of doing away with himself.

Frau Goering was always consistent in her denial that her husband had told her that he had any poison. As early as October 1946, she told reporters that her husband said he did not have poison on October 7, the date of their last meeting. "I don't know whether he really had not at the time, or whether he did not wish to tell me. He fully trusted in me, but maybe he was afraid that I would blab out in surprise."

It is difficult to believe Goering was afraid his wife "would blab out in surprise," and it is more difficult to believe he would deliberately lie to her, thus robbing her of the one consolation she could expect in the days to come. In all likelihood, he really did not have the poison at the time of their last meeting but was reasonably certain he would come by it. He may have hinted as much to his wife, but she did not understand what he meant.

Frau Goering vividly remembered her last meeting with her husband. It was a trying time for both, but the details of their last conversation remained with her over the years. After asking if Edda knew that he had to die, Goering discussed with his wife what was to come in the next few days. At the end of their conversation, Frau Goering was resigned to the inevitability of her husband's death.

However, the manner prescribed for his death still distressed her terribly. Knowing this, Goering told her in the last few minutes before their final parting: "Another thing. Do not believe that I will hang. I will be given a bullet." Astounded by the conviction reflected in her husband's words, Frau Goering asked incredulously, "Do you really believe you will be shot?" Goering hesitated for a moment as if looking for the right words and then said quite deliberately, "Of one thing you may be sure. They will not hang me!" After a pause, he repeated slowly, word for word, "They will not hang me!"

Goering's confident assurance to his wife that he would not hang seems to contradict his previous statement that he was not in possession of any poison. But one must consider his actual, carefully chosen words: he did not say he would be shot; rather, he would be given a bullet. *"Man wird mir eine Kugel geben."* The phraseology is very strange. A German friend of mine, when asked to consider this sentence, said, "It is not 'German.' It sounds like a foreigner."

Was Goering trying to tell his wife in cryptic fashion that he would not hang not because the Allied Control Commission would grant his petition to die before a firing squad, but because someone was going to give him one of the brass *cartridges*? Technically speaking, these poison containers *were* bullets, and Frau Goering well knew what they looked like. Perhaps Goering was trying to prompt his wife into making the association, and in her agitation, she simply failed to do so.

One thing is clear from Goering's meeting with his wife on October 7: he no longer expected to hang. This was in direct contrast to what he had previously believed. Earlier in the year, he told Dr. Kelley, "Yes, I know I shall hang. You know I shall hang. I am ready." Much later, Goering told Dr. Stahmer that "the practice of hanging will be raised to its highest dignity by the fact that Hermann Goering died that way." Clearly, something had happened between the time of Goering's statements to Kelley and Stahmer and the time of his meeting with his wife. Goering no longer expected to go to his death on the gallows!

Frau Goering later wrote that despite her husband's assurance to her that he would not hang, she was utterly surprised to learn he had managed to kill himself. The way her husband died impressed her more than did the fact of his death. She wrote, "The realization that Hermann was dead did not occur to me in the first moments. I perceived then only the single terrible comfort, like a spiritual release, that he did not have to suffer the dreadful and outrageous death that his enemies had planned for him. I thanked God from an overflowing heart and remembered again Hermann's last words: 'They will not hang me!' "

In this same vein, Frau Goering told Willi Frischauer that she was happy her husband managed to die by his own hand. "If he had been hanged, I could not have believed in God any more!"

Frau Goering's own words graphically illustrate the anguish she suffered over the thought of her husband being hanged; they ring too true to believe other than that Goering had really told her he had no poison. She was *not* expecting him to kill himself.

Together with her daughter, Frau Goering puzzled over the mystery of who could have given the poison to her husband. Finally, little Edda suggested that "an angel" had given him the poison, and Frau Goering tearfully agreed. Only shortly thereafter, she concluded that her husband's "angel" had to be an American. According to Marguerite Higgins, Frau Goering told her housekeeper she was convinced that no German could have slipped the poison to her husband and that it must have been "an American friend of his who did it." She also suggested to NBC's Ed Haaker that an American in the prison was responsible for providing her husband with the poison. Years later, she was still convinced of this, telling Manvell and Fraenkel she believed that an American guard in the prison was the person who slipped the poison to her husband. She also told Dr. Kempner that "a friend" whom she would not name had passed the poison to Goering in his cell. To her close friends, she told the same story. Frau von Schirach, who shared the immediate postwar period in prison with Frau Goering, told me, "Emmy was certain that Hermann got the poison from one of the American soldiers of the guard."

Frau Goering has also been quoted as saying that the letter to Colonel Andrus was "nonsense." Its real purpose, she insisted, was "to protect the man who had given him the capsule at Nuremberg." Dr. Kempner concurred with Frau Goering: "At first, I believed the letter. Today I have my doubts. I am certain that Goering went to Nuremberg without the capsule and that someone gave it to him at

Nuremberg." Dr. Werner Bross, an associate of Dr. Stahmer during the early days of the trial, said that with his letter to Andrus, "Goering wanted only to protect the man who had given the poison to him."

Frau Goering probably knew the identity of the individual who gave her husband the poison, but she never publicly revealed his name. However, she did discuss the matter privately with Charles Bewley, a friend of the Goering family from the days when he was the Irish ambassador to Nazi Germany. In his highly sympathetic biography of Goering, Bewley wrote:

> It is not my intention to discuss here the method by which he came possessed of the phial of cyankali in the night before the execution. Much has been written on the subject; it is one which cannot but appeal to the love of sensation of the international public. In itself it is not of the slightest importance; let it suffice here to say that the correct account of the introduction of the poison into the prison has not yet been published. It is known to the surviving members of Göring's family; if they have not divulged it, their reticence is due in the first place to their aversion to all avoidable sensationalism and in the second place to their desire not to compromise a non-German in the prison who assisted in its procuration.

Frau Goering, if she actually knew who gave the poison to her husband, took the secret with her to the grave. Edda, too, has never publicly broken the silence. However, there is at least one person who has been long convinced that he knows the secret: Dr. Werner Bross, the associate of Dr. Stahmer. According to Bross, a few years after Goering's death, he again met one of the American officers who had been at Nuremberg prison. They discussed Goering's suicide, and Bross asked the officer if he had any idea how Goering got the poison. The officer, with a meaningful gesture, pointed to an expensive wristwatch he was wearing and said, "A present from Goering, understand?" Bross said that he did understand, and from that time on "the puzzle over the capsule was solved for me."

Bross's statement, as quoted in the German newspaper Welt am Sonntag, intrigued me, and I wrote him for verification. He was quick to attest to the accuracy of the report and supplied details of his meeting with the American officer. According to Bross, the two met during the later trials of the lesser war criminals prosecuted by the Americans. The conversation took place in the room where the German lawyers consulted with their clients. The officer, who sat at a desk, seemed to be in charge. It was during this time that he showed Bross the wristwatch. Bross told me that he remembered only that the wristwatch was "very large" and appeared to be quite expensive. However, he clearly remembered what the officer had told him of its source.

Was Dr. Bross telling the truth about the officer and the watch? I think so. Lt. Tex Wheelis's widow still had the wristwatch when we met. I bought it from her.

14

The Lieutenant from Texas

It was Dr. Roska who sent me the articles from *Welt am Sonntag* and only shortly after our initial telephone conversation. I had mixed reactions to the newspaper series in which Jack Wheelis was identified as the man who gave Goering the poison. My first reaction was one of disappointment and exasperation. For thirty years no author had shown any great interest in the mystery of Goering's suicide. Then, after I had become interested enough in the subject to begin my own research, I found that two Germans had already come to the same conclusion as I about the source of the poison, and they had published their findings while I was still working on the preliminary drafts for the first chapters of my own manuscript! I was tempted to abandon the whole project.

However, I soon decided that *Die Kapsel*, the book from which the articles in *Welt am Sonntag* were drawn, actually answered very little and offered no real proof for the accusation against Wheelis. In addition, there was evidence that the German authors had ignored some crucial facts and had manufactured details in order to make their case against Wheelis. There was, for example, the indisputable fact that the poison used by Goering was of German origin and of the same type carried by most of the top-ranking Nazis. Since the German authors had carefully examined the report of the Board of Officers and had quoted parts of it, they had to know this. However, in order to answer the question of where the poison came from, they wrote that Wheelis was in possession of "two cyanide capsules that were given to him during the war" for use in case he was captured by the Japanese. Though Wheelis had served in the marines before joining the army, he never fought against the Japanese, and there was no evidence whatsoever that he was ever given any poison, and certainly not of the type with which Goering killed himself. Therefore, I decided to continue my own research and hoped to find the answers that had obviously eluded the German authors.

I needed much more information, particularly about Jack Wheelis. Who was he? What was his background? Why did some believe that he had given Goering the poison? Did he really do it? If yes, why? Was Wheelis simply a greedy and unscrupulous individual who accepted a bribe in return for the poison, or was he possibly an admirer of the Nazi philosophy that Goering represented? I found the answers to these questions most surprising.

Jack George Wheelis was born in Mart, Texas, a small town near Waco, on April 22, 1913. He was the fourth child of Benjamin and Dorothy Wheelis, preceded by two sisters and a brother. Another brother was born some years later.

Dorothy Wheelis was thought by many to have been an orphan, but this was not quite correct. Shortly before her mother died, and while she was still an infant, her father deserted the family and returned to his native Scotland. Until she married and accepted the quiet security that Benjamin Wheelis offered, Dorothy's life was not an easy one.

Benjamin Wheelis was a farmer, and evidently a good one. Even during the days of the Great Depression, he managed to provide for his family and hold on to his land. Though a good provider, he was a gruff, brusque patriarch who had little time for his children and who was not given to open displays of affection. As soon as his sons were old enough, they were put to work on the farm, "earning their keep" in the family. Despite his natural conservatism in thought and action, Benjamin Wheelis bought his oldest son a car for his sixteenth birthday.

Times had become hard by the time Jack reached his sixteenth birthday, but he was disappointed, nevertheless, when he did not receive a car from his father.

Jack finished high school in Mart. His transcript shows that he was an average student, failing no classes. He was a tall, strong, and good-looking boy who had a strong desire "to be liked" by his classmates and others. That he succeeded in this is evidenced by the memories of him still held by some members of the Class of 1931. One of his classmates remembered him as "an A-No. 1 boy, a perfect gentleman and a great football player." Another recalled that Jack was "honest, conscientious and enjoyed a good laugh." She also recalled that he, true to the storybook romances, eventually married his high-school sweetheart. Both agreed that Jack Wheelis was the type of young man who caught the attention of others.

Most of the attention that Wheelis garnered came because of his good looks and his aptitude for sports, particularly football. After graduating from Mart High School, Wheelis enrolled at Texas Tech, at Lubbock, on a football scholarship. Fresh off the farm and "with a dollar in his pocket," he hitchhiked to college. The year was a disaster for Wheelis. The first semester he made four Ds, a B-, a C; his only A was in military training. The second semester, he did only a little better in some courses but failed mathematics. Again, he made an A in military training. His main interest remained football, and his team was good enough to be invited to a bowl game. However, they made such a poor showing that their coach refused to ride back to Lubbock on the same train with them. Wheelis thought that the coach's pique was extremely funny, and he repeated the story of the fiasco many times during his life.

At the end of his first year at Texas Tech, Wheelis decided—or the college decided for him—that he was wasting his time. With nothing else to do, he joined the marines. He never left the States during his hitch, but military life, with its travel and enforced exposure to persons from all walks of life, caused him to question some of the beliefs he had accepted as a farm boy in Mart. In particular, he learned to question the justness of the racism practiced against blacks, hotly debating the subject with friend and foe. When his tour of duty with the marines came to an end, a more worldly Jack Wheelis reentered Texas Tech in 1937.

Wheelis's grades for the next four years were still not the best, but they showed an improvement. In June 1941 he graduated with a BS degree in agriculture, with a major in agricultural education. Texas Tech was not the type of school that attracted the more affluent and "city-bred" students, nor was it any hotbed of radicalism. Still, it exposed Wheelis, who was older than most of his classmates, to a view of life not commonly held by the farm folk of Mart. Upon graduation, he decided that the life of a farmer was not for him.

Putting his college education to use, Wheelis became a county farm agent in Canadian, Texas, a small town in the Panhandle. He remained there until he was drafted into the army in November 1943. Once he completed his basic training, he was sent to Europe as an enlisted man. In January 1945, and probably because of his college education, Wheelis was promoted to the rank of second lieutenant. At the time he was assigned to the 6850th Internal Security Detachment, he was still a second lieutenant. Wheelis possessed no special talents for guarding the Nazi prisoners but was selected for the job because he was a member of the 26th Infantry, First Infantry Division, the unit from which most of the guard personnel were drawn, and was not scheduled for early release from the army. Nothing else in his background accounted for the decision to bring the Texas lieutenant into proximity with the German Reichsmarschall—and much could have argued against it.

One of the first persons I found who remembered Jack Wheelis from Nuremberg was Nadine Finley, a former secretary at the trials. Mrs. Finley recalled that Wheelis was "a rather flamboyant character," and it was her opinion that anyone who had known Wheelis was not apt to forget him. She was, I found, quite correct.

Emma Haynes, who was in charge of the rooms in which Goering and the others conferred with their lawyers, thought that Wheelis was "an outgoing, likable person." Genelle Salles, whose husband was also from Texas, had many "fond memories" of both Wheelis and his wife.

Wheelis and her husband, she said, were "tall, good-looking, 'good-ol'-boy' Texans." She remembered Wheelis as being well liked. "He was an easygoing guy who made friends everywhere. The old cliché 'he would give you the shirt off his back' fitted Tex perfectly, and he *would* have given you the shirt off his back if he thought you needed it—or even wanted it." The Salleses and Wheelises spent much time together on vacation tours, and Mrs. Salles particularly remembered that Wheelis had "a thing" about wanting to swim in every major body of water in the world. Once, when Wheelis and his wife accompanied the Salleses on a trip from Nice to Paris, he first swam in the Mediterranean and then insisted that the four make a "special trip" so that he might swim in the Adriatic. Mrs. Salles recalled another of Wheelis's personal peculiarities: he recognized no social distinctions at all in choosing his friends. Her husband, Mrs. Salles said, was an excellent example. James Salles was a sergeant, and though Wheelis was perfectly aware that army custom discourages social fraternization between officers and enlisted personnel, "it made not the slightest difference in their relationship."

Wheelis also had friends who were officers. One of them was Brig. Gen. Eugene Phillips, who was a major at the time of the trials. He told me that "Jack Wheelis remains one of the most colorful figures I recall from the Nuremberg Trials." After I asked General Phillips if he would write a character sketch of his old friend for me, he responded:

> Tall, brawny, and muscular, with a rugged, chiseled face, Jack Wheelis would have been the perfect model for a Marlboro cigarette commercial. His appearance commanded attention, his friendly and outgoing manner drew people to him. Handsome in his army uniform, he was a striking figure. His speech evoked the broad expanse of his native Texas and fell pleasantly upon the ear in an environment characterized by the babble of many tongues, a slim majority of which were indigenous to the United States of America.

By nature, Wheelis was "gregarious and a skilled raconteur." Whether in the Palace of Justice mess hall or at his table in the ballroom of the Grand Hotel, the meeting place for off-duty officers, Wheelis was always surrounded by an eager coterie of friends anxious to hear his stories—whether of his military experiences, his contacts with Hermann Goering, or amusing regional anecdotes. Impressionable young secretaries, newly arrived from the States, Phillips noted, "flocked to him as bees to pollen-laden blossoms." But, the general was quick to add, "Insofar as I observed, Tex Wheelis's conduct was always exemplary in public, though one could easily see that he set female hearts to throbbing."

Concluding his comments to me, General Phillips wished me well in my research and adjured me to be fair in reaching a conclusion on Jack Wheelis. "His numerous old friends from the Nuremberg Trials days will be grateful," he said.

One of Wheelis's "numerous old friends" was Col. Bud Jones, who was a freshly promoted lieutenant at the time of their meeting at Nuremberg. His friendship with Wheelis came about because he (Jones) was a relative latecomer to the 6850th Internal Security Detachment. "It was a lonely life for a newly assigned regular army second lieutenant who had 'come up through the ranks,' " recalled Colonel Jones. He believes that Wheelis sensed this loneliness and befriended him because he was not a member of any established clique. While the other officers had little to do with Jones, Wheelis readily accepted him and would often join him for a drink and give him advice. "I valued his friendship and easygoing manner," Colonel Jones told me.

Because Jones and Wheelis belonged to different sections of the 6850th Internal Security Detachment, the two met most frequently during off-duty hours spent in the 6850th's officers' club, near the Nuremberg zoo, or at the "Snake Pit," as the bar at the Grand Hotel was called. Colonel Jones remembered several incidents involving Wheelis that took place during the nightly sessions of drinking and conversation. Shortly after arriving in Nuremberg, Jones was invited by the officers at his table to participate in the drinking game of 'Cardinal Puff,' an elaborate ritual that required the player to perfectly repeat certain phrases and at the same time perform complicated hand movements. If the player were able to do so, he became a "cardinal." Jones succeeded on his first attempt, and this prompted a major, who was sitting at the same table, to say that if a lowly second lieutenant could become a "cardinal," then he could too. When the major tried but failed, he became somewhat abusive, making several remarks about Jones. "Since he was the senior officer present, no one spoke up to him—except Tex Wheelis, who told him in effect to leave me alone." Accepting the reprimand with poor grace, the major rose from his chair and stomped out of the bar. When Wheelis noticed the look of consternation on Jones's face, he just smiled and waved his hand in a gesture of dismissal, obviously not worried by the encounter with the higher-ranking officer. Jones was grateful to his new friend.

On another occasion when Jones and Wheelis were sitting at a bar, a lieutenant colonel, unknown to them, came up and joined the two. After a few minutes, the colonel turned his back on Jones and directed his conversation toward Wheelis. After they talked for ten or fifteen minutes, the colonel excused himself and left the bar. When he returned, he was carrying two beautiful hunting rifles in leather cases. He gave these to Wheelis without explanation and left the bar. "I asked Tex what it was all about," Jones said, "and Tex said that he didn't know." Jones gave the matter little thought at the time "because Tex seemed to be the type of person that people just liked to do things like that for." However, Jones was a bit envious of Wheelis's ability to charm those with whom he came into contact, and his admiration of his friend grew.

A third incident that Jones recalled also involved a gift given to Wheelis—the wristwatch from Hermann Goering. New to the trials, Jones told Wheelis that he would like to have a souvenir of Goering or one of the other top Nazis. Wheelis told him that it was "almost impossible" to obtain personal souvenirs but then showed Jones the wristwatch he was wearing. "It was a large silver watch," Jones recalled, "about the size of a pocket watch. It was slim, and its face had several dials on it." Turning the watch over, Wheelis showed Jones Goering's name on the back. "Tex told me simply that Goering had given it to him—and I believed him, as I still do today," Jones told me.

I was surprised by what I had learned. Wheelis hardly sounded like the type of person who would have taken a bribe from Goering in return for the poison. How, then, did this story originate?

Dr. Bross evidently was not the first person to suspect Jack Wheelis of giving the poison to Goering. When I visited Wheelis's widow, she showed me a German newspaper article about her former husband. As I recall, the article dated from the late 1940s and was entitled something like "Did This Man Give Goering the Poison?" Accompanying the story was a picture of Wheelis and Goering standing together. As Mrs. Wheelis showed me the article, she said with an embarrassed smile, "They claimed that my husband gave Goering the poison." She did not elaborate on who "they" were nor why they thought her husband guilty, and I was not, at the time, interested enough in the subject to ask her. Later to my regret, I did not even bother to read the article she showed me. As I had not yet come into possession of the report of the board, I dismissed the idea as absurd; it had been "proven" long ago, I believed, that no one had aided Goering in his suicide. When I finally became interested in the article, it was too late. Mrs. Wheelis, her second husband told me, had died the year before, and the newspaper clipping had disappeared.

I knew that Mrs. Wheelis had donated some of her husband's Nuremberg-related books and other material to the Barker Texas History Center at Austin, so I wrote to the director, asking if the newspaper clipping was included in the donation. I was informed that no clipping could be found, but folded inside one of Jack Wheelis's books was a magazine cover from 1950. When a copy of the *Weltbild* cover was sent to me, I saw that the picture used on the front was the same one that I remembered seeing with the lost newspaper article. The tantalizing caption under the picture read: "Goering smiles mysteriously as Captain Williams [sic], the adjutant of the Prison Commandant, hands him a book. After Goering's suicide, this officer was suspected of passing him the deadly poison." Unfortunately, the magazine article referred to by the cover, like the newspaper clipping, was not among Jack Wheelis's souvenirs at the history center.

The picture itself, and the fact that Wheelis saved it, intrigued me, and I was therefore determined to find back issues of *Weltbild*, a now-defunct magazine. It was no easy matter to do so; even the Library of Congress had no copies. Finally, through the assistance of Dr. Eberhard Jäckel, a German historian, I received photocopies of the magazine article. Despite the caption under the picture, there was *no* mention of Wheelis (or "Williams") in the article itself. Goering's smile remained as mysterious as ever.

The magazine and newspaper leads came to nothing. Nevertheless, they reinforced what I already knew: for some reason and by someone, Wheelis had been suspected of giving the poison to Goering. Despite the paucity of evidence at this point, I was convinced that I was on the right track.

I continued my research on Jack Wheelis, writing and telephoning those who had been at Nuremberg at the same time as he. As the number of my contacts increased, it became obvious to me that not all of those who had known the Texan held the same high opinion of him as did his "numerous old friends." Coming to light was a side of Wheelis that Mrs. Salles, General Phillips, and Colonel Jones evidently had never seen. It was as though Jack Wheelis, much like Hermann Goering, had a split personality.

I questioned Dr. Roska about Wheelis, and it was obvious that he did not think too highly of him. He characterized Wheelis's personality as "perverse" and told me that he "had the mind of a juvenile delinquent." Roska was aware of the rumors concerning Wheelis and Goering, and he volunteered his opinion that "if anyone gave the poison to Goering, it was Wheelis!" Britt Bailey, a translator at the trials, told me that he knew Wheelis "as well as anyone did." After I sent him a summary of my conclusions and the evidence upon which they were based, Bailey wrote, "I have thought at length about Tex Wheelis, and I am now inclined to agree with you. I believe that you are right in pointing at him as the most likely channel for the poison. He was the most unscrupulous person who had the capacity, and the one with the most unprincipled friendship with Goering, and also the only man who could have remained absolutely cool after he had done such a thing."

Others reacted to my forwarded summary much as Bailey did. Mrs. Haynes recalled for me her experiences with Wheelis and Goering: "It is true that Lieutenant Wheelis enjoyed talking with Hermann

Goering. Both were ardent hunters and would engage in long conversations about the joys of hunting. As you may know, I was in charge
of the rooms in which the defendants met with their lawyers. Lieutenant Wheelis would often use this occasion to converse with Goering
before Goering's defense counsel arrived."

However, Mrs. Haynes had great difficulty in accepting the idea
that Wheelis had given the poison to Goering; the thought troubled
her tremendously. But, she admitted, "I am old enough to know that
stranger things have happened." The problem was, Mrs. Haynes wrote
me, "that someone in my position could not possibly have given the
poison to Goering, and perhaps that is why I am trying to conclude
that Jack Wheelis could not either." Acknowledging that Wheelis was
a "very unconventional character," Mrs. Haynes finally concluded,
"At least, it is fairly obvious that if an American officer gave Goering
the poison, then Wheelis would be the first one suspected of having
done it."

Britt Bailey and Mrs. Haynes were joined by others in concluding
that Wheelis probably was the one who had aided Goering. Arnold
Joseph, who knew Wheelis, wrote that "the personalities involved fit
very well into the scenario which you have constructed." Professor
Telford Taylor, former chief of counsel for war crimes, told me that
he, too, remembered Wheelis and thought my thesis both "fascinating
and plausible." Former Lt. Jean Paul Willis, a contemporary of Wheelis at Nuremberg, discussed the Texan at length with me one night at
the Dallas–Ft. Worth airport. He described Wheelis as "young, tall,
arrogant, and an opportunist." When I asked Willis if he thought
Wheelis capable of giving the poison to Goering, he immediately
replied, "I would believe him capable of *anything* he thought he could
get away with." Willis smiled and added, "It looks like he did get away
with it, didn't he?"

I agreed with Willis. My research convinced me that the 1946
investigation into Goering's suicide was flawed, and I was strongly
leaning toward the conclusion that Jack Wheelis was the one who had
helped Goering escape the gallows. But the proof for that conclusion
still eluded me. I had not yet contacted anyone, who was in a position

to know, who had flatly said, "Yes, Wheelis did it!" But I was soon to find that person.

A former Nuremberg officer advised me to contact Col. Gerald R. Wilson, previously the commanding officer of Company L of the 26th Infantry and a close friend of Major Teich. According to my informant, Colonel Wilson knew "the truth" about Goering's death. Rather than waste time with a letter, I telephoned Colonel Wilson at his home.

Wilson's response to my introduction was very friendly, and he seemed genuinely interested in the subject of Goering's suicide. I did not immediately tell him the thrust of my research but asked if he would be surprised to learn that an American officer had given the poison to Goering. "No, that's right," he said without hesitation. "He lived right down the street from me."

For a moment, I was nonplussed, thinking that Wilson meant the officer was a neighbor of his here in the States. "No," I protested, "the man I am thinking of came from Texas."

"That's right," Colonel Wilson again said. "You mean Tex Wheelis. He gave the poison to Goering. He lived right down the street from me in Nuremberg."

Wilson and I went on to discuss Wheelis at length. The colonel remembered Wheelis as an "opportunist" who first made a good impression on those who met him but disappointed those who got to know him well. After Goering killed himself, there was much talk among the Nuremberg officers about Wheelis's close relationship with the former Reichsmarschall. The talk intensified after Wheelis was "suddenly gone" from the Nuremberg scene. "I didn't see him again for a month," Colonel Wilson said. No one knew where Wheelis had gone nor the reason for his sudden departure, but his absence added fuel to the fire of controversy that surrounded him.

Colonel Wilson later attempted to discuss Wheelis and Goering with Major Teich, with whom he was on very good terms. Much to Wilson's surprise, Teich cut him short, saying, "Jerry, let's don't talk about that. That's better left alone. There are some things that I just can't discuss with you." As far as Wilson could observe, the subject of Jack Wheelis and Goering's suicide was "dead, dead, dead." It simply "was not discussed in the ISD anymore." Despite this silence—or perhaps because of it—Wilson was convinced from that time on that the story circulating among certain of the prison officers was true: Jack Wheelis had given the poison to Hermann Goering.

Quite some time after I spoke with Colonel Wilson, I found additional evidence that Wheelis was suspect among the members of the 6850th Internal Security Detachment. After a lengthy search, I found one of the key witnesses to the events of October 15–16 and the time that followed. This former officer, who responded warily to my questions by telephone one night, did not answer my follow-up letters nor did he accept my repeated invitations to meet for personal discussions. In view of his demonstrated "I don't want to get involved" attitude, I do not feel at liberty to use his name. Suffice it to say, he had a position of authority in the Nuremberg jail and knew Wheelis well.

I telephoned this individual at his home one evening, telling him that he had been extremely difficult for me to locate; none of the other former prison personnel I had contacted had any idea where he had subsequently settled. He replied that he had not maintained contact with any of the prison personnel over the years, as this was a time he preferred to forget. I asked if the Goering suicide was one of the reasons he wished to forget this period of his life, and he admitted it was. I then told him it was my opinion that the 6850th Internal Security Detachment, of which he had been a member, had suffered a "bad rap" as a consequence of Goering's suicide and that the suicide had not been the result of any negligence on the part of that unit. I went on to say my research had convinced me the board's explanation of how Goering retained and concealed the poison was "so full of holes" that I found it impossible to accept. He said nothing to this, but laughed, giving me the distinct impression he already knew the story was an improbable one. After we discussed several aspects of the case, he asked me, "How do you think Goering got the poison?" When I told him I thought one of the prison officers furnished Goering with the poison, he instantly responded: "No, I can't accept that. There were too many others who had an opportunity to do it. I just can't accept that." When I persisted, telling him that the man I suspected had not only opportunity but means and motive as well, he blurted out, "Do you mean Tex Wheelis?" I said that I did.

Almost as fast as he had volunteered the name of Wheelis, the former prison officer began to backtrack. "No," he said, "I can't believe that even Wheelis would do that." Then he asked, as if the thought was not entirely unacceptable to him, "Did he ever say he did it?" Rather than answer the question directly, I invited the gentleman to meet with me in order to review all the evidence I had collected. He replied he would be "very busy" in the next few weeks, but he would get back in touch with me. Despite my follow-up letters, he never did.

Still, the matter was not a complete loss. During our brief conversation, I learned there had been conflict between Colonel Andrus and Wheelis and that the Texan had been "almost insubordinate" while under the colonel's command. I also learned that Wheelis, shortly after Goering's suicide, had been "run out" of the 6850th Internal Security Detachment, ostensibly because of "poor fitness reports." Most important, I had additional confirmation that if Goering had an accomplice, Wheelis was the most obvious suspect. Despite the former prison officer's refusal to believe Wheelis guilty, nothing could erase the fact that Wheelis's name was the first that came to his mind after I said an American officer had given the poison to Goering. I do not think the thought was new to him.

Colonel Wilson and the former prison official confirmed my suspicion that it was Jack Wheelis who had helped Goering escape the gallows, but I had yet to discover *how* and *why* he had done it. As I was to learn, few truly understood Wheelis's motives for giving Goering the means to escape hanging. Most believed that Wheelis had been bribed by Goering to furnish the poison. Wheelis's open display of the valuable gifts given to him naturally led to this conclusion. Colonel Wilson recalled the wristwatch that Wheelis wore and showed with pride to all who would look, and he even remembered that Wheelis had once shown him Goering's name on the back of it. He also remembered the gold pen bearing Goering's facsimile signature.

Rumors of a "bribed guard" quickly spread throughout the Nuremberg press corps. Walter Cronkite wrote me he had "always assumed, by the process of elimination, that the poison had to be slipped to Goering by an American officer." DANA's William Stricker said, "I've also heard rumors that it was an American who supplied Goering with the poison." Both believed that bribery was the most likely motive for the act. Victor Bernstein, correspondent for *PM*, told me, "I did nothing but report rumors, labeling them as such. Among the rumors was, of course, that an American guard might have been bribed." The rumor of a bribed guard was so persistent that Major Teich was forced to make an official denial to the press. According to one reporter, "one theory that Teich sought to explode was that one of the prison guards had traded Goering the poison" in return for some jewelry. In scotching this rumor, Teich assured reporters that all of Goering's jewelry was locked in the prison strongbox. Presumably, Wheelis was wearing Goering's wristwatch and carrying the gold pen and cigarette case at the time of Teich's statement, though he was probably far from Nuremberg.

It is easy for some to condemn Jack Wheelis. Whitney Harris, author of *Tyranny on Trial*, found it shocking that an American officer would have furnished Goering with the means to commit suicide. "Why would anyone do this, even for a bribe???" he asked. Fred Brand, a former intelligence officer, was outraged at the thought. "I can't believe that it was done this way," he wrote. "I find it only slightly credible that a trusted and loyal officer of the guard detail used his position to supply Goering with the poison, accepted some minor favors in return, and even found it prudent to brag about this piece of treason to Goering's lawyer! What a crook he must have been to nullify the judgment of the most important international tribunal ever for a few pieces of jewelry! What a low thing to do!"

If Wheelis actually helped Goering commit suicide in return for "a few pieces of jewelry," his motive certainly would be reprehensible. However, I found it difficult to believe that personal gain on the part of Wheelis was the actual motive. His gesture toward the wristwatch when discussing the matter with Dr. Bross is subject to interpretation. It is clear that Wheelis meant to imply that he was the one who had given the poison to Goering, but he did not necessarily mean that the wristwatch was the *reason* he had done so. I came to believe that Wheelis acted from motives entirely different from bribery.

In the words of Mrs. Wheelis, "My husband liked Goering. They became friends." When I visited with her, she still had a large photograph that Goering had signed for her husband. The photograph showed a smiling Goering, appearing diminutive beside the towering Wheelis, holding out a book for the officer's inspection. It was the same picture that appeared on the cover of *Weltbild* and in the newspaper article that had disappeared. Goering had signed the front of the picture, and on the back was a warm inscription to "the great hunter from Texas." In addition to another signature, Goering had scrawled his former title of Reich hunting master. Another Goering autograph appeared in a book that Wheelis had saved. On September 28, with little over a few weeks to live, Goering wrote: "In sincere appreciation of your human kindness and best wishes for the future."

Bailey had already told me of Wheelis's "unprincipled friendship" with Goering, and I found out that others recalled the extraordinary relationship between the American lieutenant and the German Reichsmarschall. According to Dr. Roska, the friendship between the two was so obvious that it was the subject of many jokes, and much negative comment, among Wheelis's fellow officers. Wheelis, Roska confirmed, openly wore the Goering wristwatch and "liked to act as if he was 'thick' with him." General Phillips remembered that Wheelis made no secret of his liking for Goering, though "not many Americans at that time had any inclination to hobnob or even to sympathize with Hitler's lieutenants." But Phillips did not find it surprising that Goering and Wheelis became friends: "Both the number two Nazi, Fat Hermann, and Tex Wheelis were hail-fellow-well-met and, according to Tex, hit it off famously." Phillips characterized the relationship as a "personal affinity." Goering took a liking to Wheelis, Phillips said, "perhaps because of some chemistry between them. They were both bon vivants in the true sense." It was obvious, the general recalled, that Goering and Wheelis liked each other, "but this is not to say that Wheelis entertained any admiration for Goering's evil record as Reichsmarschall and commander of the Luftwaffe."

After I informed some of Wheelis's "numerous old friends" of the information that indicated he had given the poison to Goering, their reaction was somewhat curious. Initially they showed disbelief but later accepted the possibility that Wheelis had done so; but they still completely rejected the thought that Goering had bribed their old friend. Mrs. Salles wrote me:

> You asked me what Tex and Goering might have had in common, and I actually know of at least one common bond between them. It was hunting. Tex said that they often talked about hunting, and evidently they were both avid hunters. Your theory that Tex might have given the poison to Goering came as a shock to me. My first reaction, as you know, was complete disbelief. I've lain in bed many nights wondering about this, and I've asked myself why he would do it, *if* he did it. If Tex had anything to do with it, I'm sure his act would have had nothing to do with ideologies but would have been a gesture of "giving the shirt off his back" to help a friend.

Even the faithful Bud Jones had to admit to the possibility that his old friend had given Goering the poison. He wrote, "I can see where Tex may have made the poison available to Goering, but *not* through gain or to injure others, or to discredit the tribunal." It was Jones's opinion that Wheelis, if he actually gave the poison to Goering, did so in keeping with his habit of championing the underdog.

However, Jones inadvertently suggested another clue to Wheelis's possible motives, one that might explain why the Texan was perceived so differently by those who knew him. Jones told me that the 6850th Internal Security Detachment "was an elite unit, and, in every case I know of, the members were handpicked." That was true, as far as Jones's statement went. But what Jones did not know is that there was not a vast reservoir of officers from which Colonel Andrus could draw. In writing his memoirs, Andrus complained long and bitterly about the lack of qualified officer material. "To be blunt, and without criticizing some really fine soldiers I had under my command," he wrote, "I was getting the cast-offs; and I was getting some very mediocre officers." In a letter to his superior, Colonel Andrus reminded him that he had requested West Point graduates for his prison staff, but none had been sent to him. Rather, the officers who had been sent were below standard in "both education and military training." One must keep in mind that Colonel Andrus, when writing his memoirs, naturally emphasized conditions that may have contributed to Goering's suicide. Yet there *was* among some of the prison staff the real feeling that they were not getting the caliber of officers they needed and wanted.

After he was selected for the 6850th Internal Security Detachment, Bud Jones was frankly told that a young West Pointer had been wanted, "but since none was available, then I would just have to do." It was not a very gracious welcome to the unit, and Jones, until befriended by Jack Wheelis, was ostracized by most of the other officers. "A West Pointer, or even a VMI [Virginia Military Institute] grad, would readily be accepted, while an officer from the ranks would not." Though Andrus himself was not a West Point graduate, many of the more permanent officers of the 6850th ISD were, and their exclusiveness grated on Jones. Even today, nearly four decades after the fact, one can sense Jones's deep resentment of the treatment he received from many of the officers in Colonel Andrus's unit.

If Jones was made to feel unwelcome and an outcast in the 6850th Internal Security Detachment, would Wheelis, who also came up through the ranks, have fared any better? Wheelis had a further handicap because he looked, acted, and spoke in the manner generally associated with the stereotypical image of a Texan. Whereas Wheelis's friends may have found his "good-ol'-boy" personality engaging and likable, Colonel Jones admitted that the Texan's "slow, easygoing manner and drawl did seem to grate upon some of his associates." Col. Tommy Cook, a lieutenant during the trials, still remembers Wheelis as "a BS'er, always bragging, a slow-talking Texan." Dr. Roska recalled with obvious disdain that Wheelis "always played the Texas bit to the hilt." It may well be that Wheelis, with his intense desire to be liked, found more acceptance from Hermann Goering than he did from many of the officers of his own unit. If so, resentment of the cavalier attitude shown toward him by some of his fellow officers might have played some part in his decision to aid Goering.

Support for my theories came to me from a totally unexpected source: Jack Wheelis's son. Judge James Wheelis telephoned me one night at my home, saying he had learned I was making inquiries into the relationship between his father and Hermann Goering. "Why?" he asked. I frankly told him that I was convinced his father had given Goering the poison he used to kill himself. After a long pause and much to my surprise and relief, Judge Wheelis replied: "Mr. Swearingen, if you write that, you will have no problem from me. I have always believed that, too."

Judge Wheelis volunteered so much information about his father and Goering that the notes I was taking were all but illegible because of the speed with which I was forced to write. I asked him if he would be willing to put his comments into writing, and he readily agreed. Impatiently, I awaited his letter.

Finally, his typed, two-page letter arrived. Judge Wheelis felt it necessary to preface his remarks by saying that he and his father "did not get along; however gregarious he was to others, he was not a very good father." It was not, Judge Wheelis said, "very pleasant being his son." The judge explained that his father had "the usual reverse aspect of an extrovert's personality where his more intimate relationships were concerned; he was somewhat irritable, with little time for his family." Judge Wheelis remembers his father's habit of being "short and curt" to him and only rarely making a few halfhearted efforts to assume the traditional role of a father. Calling young Jim aside one day, his father asked if there was anything he needed to know about sex. When Jim replied, "No, I guess I know all about it," an obvious look of relief came over his father's face. "Thank God," exclaimed Jack Wheelis, "then we don't need to go into that." A few hunting and fishing trips, as well as going to football games, did little to bring father and son together. Jim Wheelis was a scholarly boy whose interests were not in line with his father's, and Jack Wheelis did not know how to cope with this. The result was that he largely ignored his son. To this day, Judge Wheelis, who is an avid reader, has never liked Ernest Hemingway's books, "because they remind me too much of my father, with their emphasis on 'macho' accomplishments."

To the important question of whether his father gave the poison to Goering, Judge Wheelis replied, "My father never discussed the executions of the major war criminals, even though he was apparently present. But I recall once, when we were looking through a drawer holding pictures, watches, a fountain pen, and other memorabilia, I saw the German publication accusing him of helping Goering kill himself. I asked whether this was true, but he refused to answer." Despite his father's refusal to answer the question, Judge Wheelis believes that his giving the poison to Goering "would not be inconsistent" with the memories he has of his father.

But Judge Wheelis adamantly denied the suggestion that his father had given the poison to Goering in return for a bribe. As he pointed out, a carton of American cigarettes in postwar Germany would have been payment enough for a dozen wristwatches of the type that Goering gave to his father. He further commented, "I would not find his aiding Goering inconsistent with what I remember about him, but I am sure that whatever he might have done would not have been because of a bribe. He simply was not financially motivated. He was content to drift along on an army salary, and he made no attempt, ever, to earn very much. He made no personal profit from the gifts that Goering gave him. Indeed, he wore the watch from Goering just as an ordinary watch. Certainly, he did not ever mention the value of the various gifts from Nuremberg, even in reference to a future sale."

The judge, too, maintained that his father sincerely liked Goering. "It does not astonish me," Judge Wheelis wrote, "that my father befriended Goering, even in view of Goering's participation in the savage excesses of his government. My father was a true extrovert whose main enjoyments were hunting, drinking, and talking with friends. He would cross the street to talk to the village idiot in our hometown, when everyone else would cross to avoid that. It would have been difficult for him to hold against anyone presented to him, as Goering was, what he had done to others in the past."

Judge Wheelis said that his father was "indiscriminate" in forming friendships. "He certainly had no trouble in doing so, and from what I have heard of Goering, it would be natural for them to like each other. But my father was somewhat naive, and he would certainly have been out of his depth with someone like Goering." Whenever Jack Wheelis spoke of Goering, his son recalled, "he smiled, referring to him as one would a friend who had died and whose death has been accepted."

The judge also remembered that his father had been the type of person who could accept another as a friend even if they held widely divergent philosophies. "I quite vividly remember him being the only adult around when I was a child who was not a racist, though he had some rather bitter ones as friends. It was the only topic on which I saw him argue in a serious manner."

Despite this objection to racism, Wheelis was able to feel sympathy for some of the greatest racists of modern history. "I know that he felt a certain compassion for the German prisoners," Judge Wheelis wrote, "telling me in rather vague terms that they had been bad but never telling me about the Nazi regime in strongly opprobrious language."

When I asked Judge Wheelis if he believed that resentment against some of his fellow officers might have played a part in his father's decision to help Goering escape the gallows, thus putting the "West Point clique" in an extremely embarrassing position, the judge replied, "Yes, that may have played a part." He remembered that the "West Point type," with their artificial barriers, "grated" on his father. "He was defensive and did not think that barriers drawn up by other people should apply to him. He was a 'people watcher,' who wanted to be liked and wanted to please."

While Judge Wheelis conceded that resentment on the part of his father may have played a part in his decision to give Goering the poison, he still believed that he was chiefly motivated "because he pitied his friend Goering, who accepted that he was to be executed but did not wish to hang."

Judge Wheelis ended his long letter, saying, "If I knew more, I would tell you, since I think it is a pity that the story did not come directly from my father."

From Judge Wheelis I now had solid support for my theories concerning who had given Goering the poison and why. All that was left was to discover *how* it was done.

I still suspected that the poison had been in the prison baggage room. I believed the capsule had remained there until shortly before Goering's death. It was obvious to me that Wheelis had access to the baggage room, but could he enter the depository at will and unobserved at the end of the trial? A few more telephone calls, and another piece of the puzzle fell into place: Jack Wheelis had become property officer in charge of the baggage room during the last weeks of Goering's life! Tom Modisett, a former prison officer and "old drinking buddy" of Wheelis, first told me that his friend had been placed in charge of the area in which Goering's belongings were stored. This was later confirmed by Britt Bailey, who told me, "I know that Tex was property officer toward the end of the trial. I was assistant to him."

Did Wheelis, then, remove the poison from the baggage room and give it to Goering, as I suspected? Yes, but not in the manner I had at first thought.

The enigmatic Dr. Pfluecker, who later became "convinced" that the poison came from the baggage room, emphasized the fact that Goering and the others, when they went into that room, were *always* escorted by an American officer. In direct contradiction to the sworn statements signed by Wheelis and nine other prison officers, Pfluecker wrote: "To my certain knowledge, Goering had access to his luggage only a few days before the executions." What was he insinuating? The combination of Pfluecker's belated conviction that the poison had come from the baggage room and his insistence that Goering had been taken into that room by an American officer only shortly before his suicide persuades one that the doctor, without coming right out and saying it, was trying to impart the information that this officer was responsible for Goering's death!

The American officer who most likely would have escorted Goering to the baggage room in those last days was the prison property officer: Jack Wheelis. All he had to do, once they were in the room, was look the other way while Goering retrieved the poison for himself. There was little doubt in my mind that this was exactly what Wheelis had done—*if* he was actually in the prison just prior to the executions.

This posed another question: Was Wheelis in the prison at the time of the executions? There was no evidence in the report to indicate that he was in personal contact with Goering during those last days. It seemed odd to me that Wheelis, even if he was off duty, did not pay a last visit to the man he had befriended. If Wheelis was not in the prison during Goering's last days, that fact would punch a large hole in my theory that he was responsible for Goering's suicide.

I combed the dozens of letters that I had received from those who had known Wheelis, looking for evidence that he was present at the time of the executions. Judge Wheelis had said that his father "was apparently present" at the time, but that was only a general impression that he had retained. Better information came from Bud Jones, who vividly remembered Wheelis telling him how "gory" the hangings were. General Phillips went even further in one of his letters to me, writing that he was sure that Wheelis "was in touch with the number two Nazi during his last days in prison." He recalled that Wheelis "mentioned that Goering appeared to have no apprehension about his sentence, appearing even jolly on the eve of his date with the hangman."

With this last piece of evidence falling into place, I understood why Goering showed no apprehension about "his date with the hangman." He knew that, thanks to his American friend, he was not to keep it.

My research on Jack Wheelis was finished. I was satisfied that I had established that he was the one person in the Nuremberg prison who possessed means, motive, and opportunity to permit Goering to commit suicide.

There remained one more important question to be answered. If I was able to pinpoint Wheelis thirty-five years later, why was the Board of Officers unable to do so in 1946?

15

Whitewash

It is almost impossible to believe that Wheelis's extraordinary relationship with Goering did not come to the attention of the board. His open flaunting of and bragging about the wristwatch and other gifts he received from Goering, if nothing else, should have aroused some suspicions. Colonel Wilson told me when I asked him if no one thought it strange at the time that an American officer was in possession of such gifts. "I always wondered about that," he said. "He was only a first lieutenant, and here he was bragging about his presents from Goering. I wondered why someone did not take him aside and tell him that this sort of thing was not done. We were not supposed to accept presents of any kind from these people who were criminals."

In particular, I wondered why Colonel Andrus did not do something about Wheelis and his gifts from Goering. He was not the type of man to have allowed one of his officers to accept gifts from the prisoners. John Pearsall, who served under Andrus, never forgot the prison commandant. "I guess the outstanding memory of him was that he was GI all the way. You never knew where or when he was going to make a spot check, and you had better be prepared at all times." However, Sergeant Raabe suggested to me that Colonel Andrus might never have been aware of the situation with Wheelis. "You see," Raabe explained, "Andrus was RA [regular army], a career officer, and he never got close to his officers."

Still, the members of the board should have learned about Wheelis, if they did not already know. While Colonel Hurless was new to the Nuremberg prison and probably knew none of its officers, Colonel Tweedy and Major Rosenthal were both members of the same military unit as Wheelis, Colonel Andrus's 6850th Internal Security Detachment. Britt Bailey told me that Rosenthal knew Wheelis well, "although he was not as close to Tex as Fred Teich was." Rosenthal was the major Wheelis angered on the occasion Bud Jones became a "cardinal." In all likelihood, a lieutenant would not feel free to reprove a major and then think so little of it unless the two knew each other fairly well.

Yet neither Teich nor Rosenthal ever mentioned Wheelis during the course of the investigation. The only indication that Wheelis came to the attention of the board at all was through his submission of a signed statement that he had in his possession "the key to the baggage room of the Prison during the period 1 October 1946 to 15 October 1946 and can state positively that Goering received nothing from, nor had access to, the baggage room during this period." Nine other officers submitted identical statements.

Despite the fact that there was enough rumor and hard evidence in 1946, the board displayed no interest in the possibility that an American could have given the poison to Goering. It is possible, of course, that the board, in its eagerness to settle the controversy surrounding Goering's death, did a hasty and slipshod job of questioning witnesses and evaluating testimony. Though the report states that during the night of October 15–16, "guards and prison personnel who had contact with Goering were interrogated," this is a misleading statement. It is true that during the night, affidavits from thirty-four individuals were taken, but there is no evidence that these witnesses were "interrogated." It is not clear from the report how these affidavits were procured, but it is likely that they were given to Major Rosenthal alone. One gathers the impression that Rosenthal called all the witnesses together, asked them to write brief statements, and later witnessed the signing of each. All of the depositions bear at the top of the page the date of October 16, but most were sworn and subscribed to before Rosenthal at later dates. His signature alone appears at the bottom of each affidavit. It is clear from the choppy and incomplete sentences of Chaplain Gerecke, for example, that these affidavits were not given verbally but were written in haste. Therefore, no specific questions were asked of any of these thirty-four witnesses, nor were any of these witnesses later called before the board for clarification or amplification of their written testimony. There was, therefore, no "interrogation."

The only witnesses actually to appear before the board were Andrus, Teich, Roska, Starnes, and Dr. Pfluecker. Despite their frequently conflicting testimony, none was recalled for further comment or questioning. Other prison personnel, such as Dr. Martin and Lieutenant Croner, were not questioned at all, nor did they submit written statements.

It is possible that the officers of the board were misled, though they denied it, by Goering himself in that they placed too much faith in his letter to Colonel Andrus. Rather than seriously investigating the possibility that someone gave the poison to Goering, the board might have spent too much time trying to establish a credible answer to where the poison was hidden. If it accepted Goering's letter as factual, the board might have forced together ill-fitting pieces of the puzzle hoping that the result would be a semblance of what it believed the true picture to have been. Desperately searching for the answer that would solve its dilemma, the board might have seized upon Goering's letter and then blindly followed the misleading signposts down the path of least resistance. Perhaps this was the reason the board did not investigate alternate possibilities.

Some do not accept this possibility but believe that the board deliberately withheld the information to which it was privy, issuing instead a report that it knew to be at variance with the facts. DANA's William Stricker, who followed the army's press releases every day after Goering's suicide, said that "the investigation . . . had all the aspects of a whitewash." Dr. Bross observed, "The Americans apparently long knew who gave Goering the capsule. Their investigating commission was extremely lax in its work." And according to Desmond

Zwar, even Colonel Andrus believed that the investigation left many
questions unanswered and "complained darkly about 'carrying the can'
for Goering's suicide."

If the board deliberately issued a report that it knew was at variance
with the truth, it is almost a certainty that it was acting under orders.
Even to protect the prestige of the United States and the army, the
members of the board—even if they could agree among themselves to
do so—would never have dared to issue a false report on their own.
If orders were given for the board to find that no one was involved in
Goering's suicide, such a directive would not have been committed
to writing but would have been given verbally to the officers. While
it is impossible to prove that such orders were given, there is inferential
evidence that such was the case.

The report states that the board, in the early hours of October 16,
decided "to take" the various items of physical evidence (the brass
capsule, Goering's pipe, etc.) "to the 27th C. I. D. Laboratory, Frankfurt, for analysis." The morning reports of the 6850th ISD reveal that
Colonel Tweedy and Major Rosenthal did leave for Frankfurt on October 17 and returned to Nuremberg on October 19. Because Colonel
Hurless was not a member of Andrus's unit, his name does not appear
in the morning reports, though it may be reasonably assumed that he
accompanied Tweedy and Rosenthal.

Why was it necessary for all three officers of the board, so early in
the investigation and at such a crucial time, to personally take the
items of evidence to Frankfurt? Could not the items have more easily
been entrusted to someone else, thus leaving the board free to consider
more important matters? If the evidence was considered so essential
to the investigation, why did the board return two days before the CID
agents completed their report.

Perhaps the board officers traveled to Frankfurt not so much to
deliver the items for analysis but to consult with higher authority at
Headquarters, U.S. Forces, European Theatre, that was under the
command of General McNarney. If not this, then what else did the
board do in Frankfurt for two days?

Once the board returned to Nuremberg, an immediate search was made of the vanity kit in the prison baggage room to find the poison capsule referred to in Goering's letter to Colonel Andrus. After the poison was found just where it was supposed to be, the board appeared to accept the remainder of Goering's letter as factual, carefully structuring the investigation to coincide with Goering's assertion that no one was to blame for his suicide. The subsequent investigation so blatantly ignored all that stood in the way of this finding that one is persuaded the board was acting under orders to do so. If this is what happened, then the omissions of the board and its faulty conclusions are made understandable.

Was there an actual whitewash by the board? Among the persons who could authoritatively answer this question are Colonel Tweedy and Major Rosenthal, the two surviving members of the board. My efforts to locate Rosenthal came to nothing. However, the Retired Activities Division of the Department of the Army advised me that their records showed that Colonel Tweedy retired from the army in 1960, and while they were not allowed to give me his current address, they would forward a letter to him.

I wrote to Colonel Tweedy, requesting that he answer some specific questions and generally comment on my research. In a terse letter, he informed me: "Regarding the several requests contained in your letter, please be advised that: (1) I have no evidence that is not contained in the official records, and (2) I decline to discuss or to comment on hearsay or opinion or any other matter not previously established as evidence under United States rules."

Colonel Tweedy further wrote, "In view of the foregoing, my address is intentionally omitted for the reason that further correspondence would serve no useful purpose." Evidently unaware that the board's report is now available to anyone who requests a copy, Tweedy indicated concern that I had learned his identity and role in the investigation through "official sources" and said that he was sending a copy of my letter and his answer to the Department of the Army.

For a long time, I made no further attempt to contact Colonel Tweedy. Finally, in February 1983, after I had completed most of my research, I again addressed a letter to the colonel. I explained that "elementary fairness" to him and the other members of the board demanded that I make at least one more attempt to obtain his comments on my findings. Without going into great detail, I told him that I was more convinced than ever that Jack Wheelis had given the poison to Goering and that I believed the board was in error to conclude otherwise. I conceded the possibility that I could be wrong and said that I was still open to reason. I emphasized to the colonel that I was "perfectly willing at this point to junk five years' work if I am convinced my conclusions are incorrect." Again, I asked him to get in touch with me. I never heard from him.

Unless Colonel Tweedy or someone else decides to tell, it may never be established what really motivated the board to come to the conclusions it did. The continued silence only adds to the suspicion that the board, suspecting (although not knowing) an American was involved, might have seized on any other available explanation, no matter how unlikely, and thus whitewashed the Goering suicide.

In addition to the board, the members of the Quadripartite Commission must have had information on the circumstances of Goering's suicide. But the commission's reaction to those facts might have been similar to the board's. Other than its endorsement of the board's findings, the commission placed nothing in the report.

There was, however, in that endorsement, a reference to a "Special Working Party" that "conducted their own further inquiries." This reference greatly interested me because I had found evidence that there had been another and independent investigation carried on apart from that of the board. Jean Paul Willis told me that at least one of the witnesses questioned by the board, Private Johnson, was "questioned repeatedly" by another group of officers. Johnson was of special interest to them because he had been the guard on Goering's cell when the suicide occurred. According to Willis, "This young kid was *really* nervous, and he was interrogated, and I mean really strongly, about three or four times." Willis said that Johnson even had to take a lie-detector test. "He asked me what to do, and I told him, 'Well, you didn't give the capsule to Goering, so don't tell them anything but the truth.'" Since there was no indication in the report that the board had "repeatedly" questioned Johnson and certainly no hint that he or anyone else had been subjected to a lie-detector test, I thought that perhaps this had been the work of the Special Working Party referred to in the report. I had hopes that there would be more records to be examined.

I wrote to Brig. Gen. James L. Collins, chief of military history, Department of the Army, asking if he knew where the pertinent records of the Special Working Party might be. General Collins replied that they should be in the Nuremberg War Crimes Trials Records at the National Archives. I sent a letter to that agency, and a few weeks later came the reply: "We examined the records . . . but were unable to locate references to members of the Special Working Party. As far as can be determined, the working papers of the Special Working Party were not included as part of the file and were subsequently disposed of." In other words, if the records ever existed, they could no longer be found.

It was impossible for me to determine with accuracy just what the Quadripartite Commission did or did not know. The only hint of its knowledge of the affair came from a press conference held by Brigadier Paton-Walsh to announce the findings of the board. Richard Stokes, correspondent for the *St. Louis Post-Dispatch*, reported on the conference.

According to Stokes, only Brigadier Paton-Walsh and French Gen. Pierre Morel were present at the gathering. The Russian member of the commission, General Malkov, had been called to Berlin several days previously and had not seen the statement drafted by the commission. "It was declared, however, that he was informed of the general content, which met with his entire approval, and that rumors of a break on the part of the Soviet commissioner were unfounded." The reason for the absence of General Rickard was not given.

General Morel limited his comments to "a special word of praise for the jail commandant, Col. Burton C. Andrus," leaving Brigadier Paton-Walsh to announce the board's findings and answer questions. After reading the findings of the board to the correspondents, Paton-Walsh told them that the names of "the three officers from the Third

Army who served as an investigating board for the commission would not be revealed and that their report will be withheld." No reason was given for the need for such secrecy.

Paton-Walsh then told the members of the press that the letters written by Goering would also be withheld. "The senior surviving Nazi," explained Paton-Walsh, "was a clever and astute man. He wrote each note with a purpose. Why should we abet him in this plan?" The brigadier admitted that Goering's letter to Andrus "did have some relation to the commission's findings" and that Goering specifically exonerated his American guards. Commenting on the contents of the letter, Paton-Walsh said, "We drew our own conclusions regarding its veracity." Paton-Walsh told the correspondents "that between 8 and 9 o'clock on Tuesday night of last week, Goering was observed writing at the table in his cell." From this information, Stokes and the other correspondents came to the "reasonable assumption" that it was during this time that Goering was working on the three letters.

Paton-Walsh then recounted for the press his version of Goering's activities after he had finished writing the letters. According to the brigadier, Goering undressed at 9:00 P.M. and lay down on his cot, "assuming a reposeful attitude." For a long time his hands, according to the regulations, were outside the blanket. "When he was found dying, however, both arms were under the covers with one hand hanging down from beneath it." When asked why the guard did not interfere on seeing this breach of the regulations, Paton-Walsh countered, "What is one to do if a man apparently sound asleep happens to move his arms? It's a perfectly natural thing."

Paton-Walsh confirmed that Goering had died by cyanide poisoning, saying of the device, "This was standard equipment for Nazi leaders." When asked if any autopsy had been performed, Paton-Walsh "parried with the remark that laboratory tests had been made involving certain parts of the body." He added it would be fair to say that "Goering's body was cremated intact."

The theory that Goering had hidden the poison under a scar or in some sort of "kangaroo pouch" in his skin was denied by Paton-Walsh.

If there had been any evidence of this, he declared, it would have been mentioned in the commission's report. The brigadier then said, without explaining further, that the investigation confirmed a statement he had made some days previously to reporters. "He said then that the essential clue to the mystery was available to anyone who saw Goering's body but that it could have been detected only by a trained eye. Walsh [sic] is by profession a policeman." On this note, the press conference ended.

I was astounded when I read Stokes's report of Paton-Walsh's comments. Much of what the brigadier had told reporters was in direct contradiction to what was stated in the report. Unless Paton-Walsh had not read the report (and this is too farfetched to believe), there must have been another reason for him to have strayed so far from what the board had determined.

He had led reporters to believe that all three of the officers of the board were disinterested investigators from Third Army Headquarters, whereas Tweedy and Rosenthal were actually officers of Colonel Andrus's unit. He had allowed them to believe that Goering's letter to Colonel Andrus was written on the night of the suicide, though the letter was dated October 11 and there was no evidence Goering wrote any letters between 8:00 and 9:00 on the night of his death. Paton-Walsh told the reporters that Goering had placed both arms under the blankets, though the report itself denied this. He told reporters that "certain parts" of Goering's body had been subjected to laboratory tests, though this could be true only in the broadest sense. Finally, he told the members of the press that the "essential clue" to the mystery of Goering's death was apparent to anyone who had seen the body. If anyone had seen such an "essential clue," there was no mention of it in the report, nor anywhere else that I could find.

As incredible as it seemed, upon reading Paton-Walsh's comments, I was forced to conclude that not only had the Quadripartite Commission gone along with the board's findings but had buttressed them with what could only be termed misleading statements of its own. I simply could not understand this.

I learned from the British Ministry of Defence that Brigadier Paton-

Walsh was still alive, and I wrote him, asking why he had made the statements he did. His wife answered my letter, saying, "He asks me to write and say that he is, at present, very ill, having suffered a severe stroke some weeks ago and he is not able to help you." I then wrote Mrs. Paton-Walsh, asking if she had learned anything of Goering's suicide from discussions with her husband. She replied, "I regret that I am unable to help you. My husband never discussed matters concerning his professional duties."

Six months later, I again wrote to Brigadier Paton-Walsh, asking only that he confirm or deny my suspicion that the board and the commission had withheld information on Goering's suicide. Mrs. Paton-Walsh again answered my letter to her husband. "My husband is still too ill to respond, and I am sorry to say that he is not likely to improve. His speech is totally impaired." Mrs. Paton-Walsh told me that she had been in touch with the Ministry of Defence, "who have suggested that, if you wish to pursue the matter from this end, you should contact Mr. John F. Smith."

I wrote to Mr. Smith, who was responsible for the Ministry of Defence Archives, told him of my research, and asked if he could help me. He suggested that I write to the Public Record Office at Kew. I did so and received a letter from Dr. M. J. Jubb of that office. Dr. Jubb wrote, "I am afraid that I have been unable to trace in the public records any papers relating to the investigation into Goering's suicide." He explained that the records for the Allied Control Commission for Germany, "in whose records I should expect such papers to survive," had not yet been transferred to the Public Record Office. It was his opinion that the records would be transferred "in the next few years."

Because my correspondence with Brigadier Paton-Walsh's wife and the British Ministry of Defence was begun in November 1980 and Dr. Jubb's letter was not received until October 1981, I did not wish to wait another "few years" to receive an answer to my questions. I again wrote to Mr. Smith, detailing for him exactly what conclusions I had reached, and asked for his comment. He responded, "On your recent inquiry, I have no reason to believe that the Allied Control Commission's decision was not based on the evidence available at the time."

It became obvious to me that my efforts to learn anything from the British authorities were futile, so I abandoned the attempt.

With no more leads to follow and the research complete, I decided that it was time to see what U.S. Army authorities had to say about my findings. I addressed another letter to General Collins, telling him of my own conclusions and how they differed from those of the board in 1946, and asked for an official response to my speculations. I received no answer, so I wrote again some months later, telling General Collins I did not wish to read anything into his silence but preferred an answer to my questions. In May 1983 I received an answer from the office of Brig. Gen. Douglas Kinnard, who evidently had replaced General Collins as chief of military history. Col. Glen D. Thornton, writing for General Kinnard, told me, "Although your conclusions are quite plausible, we are unable to corroborate your findings." Colonel Thornton said he was unaware of any other "official investigatory source on this matter," other than the report that I had already consulted.

I was disappointed of course that the army could not, or would not, specifically reply to my conclusions, but I was gratified and a bit surprised that Colonel Thornton did not reject them out of hand but considered them "quite plausible." This, I believed, would be about as close as I was going to come to an "official response" from the army.

However, even if my speculations were correct, there was still one thing about them that troubled me greatly: Why did Colonel Andrus—whose career was blighted by Goering's suicide and the inference of negligence drawn from it—never repudiate the findings of the board? If Andrus knew the board made an error concluding that Goering had always had the poison, why did he acquiesce in the board's damning findings? He might have been under orders to do so in 1946, but why did he not later speak out in an effort to set the record straight? Why did he not "tell all" in his book?

The answers to those questions, I long believed, went to the grave with Andrus in 1977. But I was wrong.

16

The Andrus Papers

On the morning of October 15, 1984, the thirty-eighth anniversary of Hermann Goering's suicide, I said good-bye to Colonel Burton C. Andrus, Jr., the son of the Nuremberg prison commandant. Three days of conversation with the colonel, coupled with a complete examination of his father's official and personal papers, had convinced me that I had arrived in Colorado with certain misconceptions about his father and the role he had played at Nuremberg. I now considered it my duty to correct these misconceptions not only for the sake of historical truth but for the sake of righting a wrong done to Colonel Andrus, Sr., long ago.

A few weeks before my visit with Burt Andrus, a retired air force officer, I had sent him a detailed summary of my research. Some days later, he telephoned me at my home, saying that he was intrigued by what I had learned of Goering's suicide. He invited me to Colorado Springs to examine his father's papers and to talk. I was, he told me, the first person to whom he had granted this privilege. Previously, the subject of Goering's suicide had been so distressing to him that he preferred to ignore it completely.

My son and I flew to Denver, where we were met by Colonel Andrus, a tall, gray-haired, distinguished-looking man. Though he was dressed in casual civilian clothes, everything about him gave one the impression of an officer and a gentleman of the old school. I had

189

the immediate feeling that we were going to get along and that I could ask the most probing questions without fear of his taking umbrage.

Once we were at the colonel's mountain home, he took me to the lower floor, where there was a large metal filing cabinet. "All of my father's papers," he said, "are in here." My excitement turned to dismay as he began to open the drawers. I saw that three drawers were literally crammed with loose papers and documents, innumerable bound folders, tape recordings, magazine and newspaper articles, and all the other items that his father had saved from Nuremberg and during the years that followed. No attempt at organization had been made after the papers came into the possession of Burt Andrus; everything was piled together in a confusing jumble. Later Andrus told me, "I have not studied these papers. Until I heard from you, I considered Goering's suicide to be a very unpleasant chapter in the life of our family. I thought that I would someday examine the papers, but I also thought that nothing would be revealed in the papers that would alter what I had perceived: that it was the judgment of the time that my father was completely responsible and that, whether or not he was negligent, he was faulted for being so. I preferred to just forget the whole matter."

Now that the colonel had changed his mind, he began taking the papers out of the cabinet by the armload. After a large cardboard box was filled to overflowing, he drove me to my motel, where I began the process of making order out of chaos. I had the distinct feeling that I was looking for the proverbial needle in a haystack. But as I searched through the papers for the next few days and nights, reading pertinent documents aloud into a tape recorder, I had the good fortune to find several "needles."

By sheer coincidence, one of the first documents I examined offered proof that the army had ordered a cover-up of an earlier suicide in Nuremberg prison. On October 6, 1945, Dr. Leonardo Conti, former Reich minister for health, hanged himself from the window of his cell. However, the matter did not become public until January 1946, when *Stars and Stripes*, acting on information supplied by an unnamed source, reported the full story.

On January 14, 1946, Colonel Andrus wrote a memorandum to

the commanding general, Headquarters, International Military Tribunal, in which he reported he had told inquiring correspondents that they had to address their questions to the source from which the information was obtained, "as we have no information to give out." Andrus told the general that, "as far as the office of Internal Security is concerned, its records show Conti as transferred to the hospital. At the time of Conti's death," Andrus admitted, "my office was ordered to classify the matter as 'Secret.' " Andrus further admitted, "All of the information at the time was furnished to the Interrogation Division of Mr. Justice Jackson's office, and pertinent records were forwarded to Third Army and to USFET [United States Forces European Theater], including the investigation of cause of death." It was Andrus's opinion that only two persons, neither of whom were still under his command, knew enough of Conti's death to have discussed the suicide with the correspondent who had written the story.

Thus, I found documentary proof that high-ranking army officials had ordered a cover-up of the suicide of a relatively unknown Nazi functionary. Now I began to comb Andrus's papers for evidence pertaining to Goering's suicide and Wheelis's involvement. Every piece of paper on which Wheelis's name appeared, I set to one side. I learned that Wheelis was not, as I had previously thought, a relative newcomer to the Nuremberg prison. According to a roster of officers I found, Wheelis arrived at the prison, as a second lieutenant, on November 26, 1945, almost a full year before Goering's death. That he was personally known to Colonel Andrus is a certainty. Evidence for this is found in a letter, dated June 20, 1946, that Andrus wrote to his daughter. The commandant wrote, "Dottie, my friend Tex Wheelis suggests that you and Bill had better go to Siebold's and eat a steak dinner for us since we are not 'right in the heart of Texas.' " Wheelis is again mentioned in "Special Orders, No. 45," July 4, 1946, when he was appointed, by Colonel Andrus, to the position of assistant operations officer for the prison.

There is also evidence among Andrus's papers that Wheelis was not always above reproach and that he was suspected of being the cause of some problems. One document indicated that there had been a leak to the press about an alert that had been called in the prison and the Palace of Justice. It was determined that the offending correspondent received the information from a prison officer when the two discussed the matter in the bar of the Grand Hotel. Attached to the report of the CIC agent is a certification addressed to Colonel Andrus: "I, Jack G. Wheelis, Second Lieutenant, Infantry, certify that, to the best of my knowledge, I did not enter into a conversation with George Tucker, correspondent, on Monday night, February 4, 1946." Another letter, from Dr. Hans Laternser (defense attorney for the General Staff and High Command of the Wehrmacht) to the secretary of the International Military Tribunal, requested that a gold cigarette case, taken from General von Gersdorff, be returned. Dr. Laternser's request was referred to Colonel Andrus, and among his files is a letter written by Wheelis, who processed von Gersdorff into the prison, disclaiming any knowledge of a gold cigarette case. "A thorough investigation," wrote Wheelis, "revealed no record of such article having been surrendered." The last reference I found to Wheelis was in a letter Andrus wrote to the minister of justice, Luxemburg, on November 5, 1946. The letter expressed Andrus's profound disturbance and embarrassment "over the carelessness of my Lt. Wheelis and the two pilots." It is not clear from the letter what "carelessness" had taken place, but the colonel promised that, if the matter was not resolved, he planned to "take the strongest disciplinary actions against all those concerned."

Therefore, it is evident that Colonel Andrus knew Wheelis, and apparently quite well. But I found nothing in Andrus's official papers that linked Wheelis to Goering's suicide.

The personal letters written by Colonel Andrus after the suicide of Goering are not numerous, but they are extremely important. They contain some curious misstatements of fact that are to be found nowhere in the report prepared by the board.

On October 22, 1946, Andrus wrote to a friend in England who had invited him to a social gathering on October 19. Andrus expressed his regret that he had not been able to attend, explaining that "the suicide of that horrible criminal created so many complications that it was absolutely impossible for me to get away." He went on to say that the investigation of the board and the Quadripartite Commission, "to determine whether or not I was at fault," had demanded his presence in Nuremberg. Two days later, Andrus wrote to a former prison staff member, "Authorities are meeting to determine the exact cause of the suicide of Convict Goering and to affix the responsibility." He explained that the investigation was taking so long "because our security regulations were so extensive that it actually takes a long time for an outsider [presumably Colonel Hurless] to become familiar with them." In an attempt to salvage something from the disaster of Goering's suicide, Andrus wrote that he would have been "very much upset had this suicide occurred before the conclusion of the trials, and thus prevented a verdict and sentencing." Andrus expressed his opinion that he very much disagreed with "the view so frequently expressed that [Goering] has cheated justice or cheated the gallows. Even a plant fights for life, and to take one's own life is far more ignominious than to meet death in any other way."

As soon as the Quadripartite Commission released the summary of the board's report, Colonel Andrus wrote to Dr. Kempner. In a letter dated October 28, 1946, the colonel said, "The Quadripartite Commission had just completed its study of the Board's proceedings in the investigation of Goering's death. That man had the poison all the time." Curiously, and in direct contradiction to what the board had actually determined, Andrus wrote, "His navel had been subjected to an operation of some kind and readily provided a repository big enough for the cartridge case." He correctly reported that there was evidence that the case was at one time in Goering's rectum. But in what probably was a deliberate distortion of fact intended to hinder the rise of a Goering legend, Andrus concluded: "So, in his horrible self-destruction, he was mouthing his own dung."

One day after he wrote to Dr. Kempner, Colonel Andrus addressed a letter to a former staff member, telling his correspondent that he did not feel "the least bit embarrassed over not guessing what Goering had in mind. Because we took all reasonable precautions, as established by the board, or rather the Quadripartite Commission." He repeated the erroneous assertion that "Goering had an operation of some sort on his navel which permitted the concealing of this cartridge which contained the poison in a recess there." In what is apparently a reference to the debris found around Goering's navel by Lieutenant Roska— and later called by Dr. Lattimer "the dirt that accumulates in the umbilicus of unwashed fat persons"—Andrus incorrectly stated that "residue found in the recess indicated that the cartridge had been kept there." The colonel went on to say that the case had also been in Goering's rectum, again adding the misleading phrase that Goering had died "mouthing his own dung."

Andrus wrote another letter on October 29, this time to a prison officer who had returned to the United States. Only a few days before Goering's suicide, this officer had written a letter of praise to Andrus, his former commanding officer. Andrus answered:

> I am afraid that your high praise was a little premature because, in spite of all our carefully laid plans, one of the prisoners committed suicide at the last minute. I still feel very thankful that nothing like that occurred until after the conviction and sentences had been approved by the Quadripartite Commission and the judgment was absolutely final. What happened then is of less importance. But, unfortunately, a lot of people voiced the sentiment that Goering cheated the hangman. I do not feel that suicide is a better death than one meted out by another man. I think that being destroyed by a shark is less disgraceful and ignominious than suicide; added to that, we have the revolting condition that this suicide concealed the container for his poison in his rectum, which was proven by laboratory tests of matter still clinging to the container when it was found in his possession after death. So we have the horrible condition of a human being mouthing his own dung.

In his own defense, Andrus maintained that, in spite of being accused by an article in *Time* of a lack of imagination, "it is not in the least embarrassing to me that I had not the imagination to visualize such a thing as that."

Nowhere in his personal letters did Andrus express disagreement with the findings of the board, nor did he attempt to blame anyone else for the failure of his mission. Though he believed that he had been maliciously misrepresented by the press, Andrus dutifully shoul-

dered the blame for Goering's suicide. On November 1, 1946, he
wrote to his family:

> I knew, and I think that I told you when I started this job, that it was
> one where it was impossible to win. In fact, I was told when I was
> appointed, "This is so important a job that we wanted to put a brigadier
> general on it, but we could not find a brigadier general available to take
> it." Those last three words reveal to me that they had offered the job to
> several brigadier generals who did not wish to take it. I said that I was
> not afraid to take it. I also told them that I knew what it meant: that I
> would be like the man trying to cross Niagara Falls on a tightwire. If I
> slipped, it would be my neck that got broken, and if I got across, the
> gate receipts would go to the stockholders.

Denying that he had reason for self-reproach, Andrus concluded that
he had "put on a good performance until the trials were over."

After reading Andrus's letters, I was convinced that he had left
Nuremberg completely accepting what he believed to be the findings
of the board. However, doubts may have crept into his mind during
the years that followed.

Among the cache of papers that Colonel Andrus had preserved
were the typewritten drafts of his book. Information contained in these
drafts, much of which was never used in the book, reveal that Andrus
was no longer so sure of the "facts" of Goering's suicide as he had
been in 1946. When reading the drafts, one gains the impression that
Andrus had done some serious thinking over the years and that, though
he was unable to suggest an alternative to what had been concluded
in 1946, he had experienced some disquieting thoughts about what
he had been told at that time. There are several examples of doubt
and indecision that appear in his notes but not in the book itself.

At one point, when Andrus referred to the poison, he wrote, "He
concealed this (I believe . . . I know . . ?) sometimes in his rectum
and sometimes in his navel." In another place, he said, "I have no
doubt (?) that Goering hid this vial on his body and that, when he
committed suicide, he had removed it from the orifice in his body."
Andrus still maintained that Goering had had an operation on his
navel, but there was now an element of doubt even on this point. He

wrote, "He had an operation on his navel and he could have concealed it there. It could not have been concealed completely though, so it could not have been concealed there when the searches or baths were going on. I was told by a member of the Quadripartite Commission that it could not have been completely concealed there. They had apparently measured this orifice."

When Andrus's book was published, there was no mention whatsoever of Goering's having had an operation on his navel.

When preparing his initial draft, Colonel Andrus expressed doubt that the toilet in Goering's cell could have been used as a longtime place of concealment for the poison. He wrote that on October 25, 1946, that the Quadripartite Commission went through the prison on an inspection tour "to test the hiding places for the vial." After making a "detailed inspection" of the toilet, the commission told Andrus that the poison could have been hidden there "but not for a long time, because it would not have been practical." Andrus's own conclusion was that "it might have remained there part of the time. But it could not have remained there when the toilet was flushed, or in his anus when he was actually passing stools. I doubt that he would ever risk leaving it in the toilet, even though none of my personnel was a plumber, and the searches were so thorough that I feel certain he would never have left it there when he was absent from his cell." This doubt, too, never appeared in Andrus's book.

Despite the probability that Andrus later questioned the conclusions reached by the board in 1946, he still had nothing to offer as an alternative. Though the board's conclusions saddled him with the implication of negligence, he was once again, when preparing his book, forced to dutifully accept responsibility for Goering's death. But in so doing, bitterness surfaced in the drafts, if not in the book. Again using the analogy of the tightwire walker, Andrus followed it with this complaint: "It was true: 'box office' got all the credit. I happen to be the only person who served at Nuremberg or 'Ashcan' who did not get a very considerable reward or advancement. Even the minor Nuremberg lawyers got high honors like President of the U.S. Bar Association, Chief Justice of Britain [sic] and Lord Chancellor of Britain."

By the time I finished reading all the papers that Burt Andrus had entrusted to me, I had radically changed my opinion of his father and the role he played at Nuremberg. Whereas I had previously believed that Andrus must have at least suspected that Wheelis had given the poison to Goering, I was now convinced that the thought had never entered the colonel's mind. I had believed that Andrus had to know that the findings of the board were flawed, but I was now convinced that he had completely accepted the findings as factual. I now strongly suspected that Andrus accepted the findings without question because of "misinformation" he had received from someone in 1946 and that he later began to have doubts about what he had been told. I was further convinced that Colonel Andrus, even if there were some doubts in his mind about what actually happened, was never able to free himself from the nagging belief that he was responsible for Goering's suicide and that feelings of guilt plagued him for the rest of his life.

With all these thoughts in mind and armed with the documents that had inspired them, I began talking with Burt Andrus, who had been reading my manuscript for the past few days. The table piled high with documents and photographs and a tape recorder between us, we spoke of the event that had influenced both our lives for so many years.

Before we discussed Goering's suicide, I told Andrus that it had been a surprise to me to find among his father's files evidence that he had been well liked and respected by so many of his subordinates. I confessed I had previously believed his father was disliked by his officers and men and hated by many members of the press. It was not a trivial point, because I had suspected that such dislike of Andrus might have played some part in Wheelis's decision to assist Goering in killing himself.

Burt Andrus looked perplexed for a moment. It was obvious that the thought of his father being disliked by his officers was new to him. He was not comfortable with it. "I would think," he said, "that a more accurate description might be that, because he was of the old, rigid school, he was perceived by some to be unreasonable and too much of a disciplinarian." Many of his father's officers, Andrus said, "had come in during the war, were not regular army, and they were not used to being treated in the formal, old-style manner." In support of his contention that his father had always lived by "some very, very rigid traditional military ways of thinking," Andrus related an anecdote from his father's youth. Andrus Senior's father, a West Point graduate, loved a good cigar. It was his habit, when Burton Andrus, Sr., was a young man and still living at home, to offer him a cigar from time to time. But as soon as Andrus turned eighteen, his father told him that he could no longer give him the cigars that had been obtained from the army commissary: "You are not getting any more of my cigars, because you are not entitled to them. You are a civilian." Laughingly, Burt Andrus said, "That is the way my father was brought up, and he accepted it as correct." It was this total acceptance of the "formal old-style manner," Andrus suggested, that caused some of his father's subordinates to have a negative opinion of him.

However, the press was another matter. "I think that this was a completely different relationship. I know that my father had a very hostile attitude toward the press." Andrus said that his father considered the press to have been "an irresponsible group who only made his job more difficult." Andrus believed that the press had considered his father to be arrogant because "he did have a certain arrogant streak in him, which he did not hesitate to display if he felt it was necessary to accomplish his mission." Andrus concluded that his father "cordially disliked the press" but never let them influence the performance of his duty. However, he had to admit that it was the press reports of the time, more than anything else, that had injured his father's reputation. "They had the last say."

We then turned our attention to other matters. I asked the colonel if his father had ever indicated to him that he thought Goering's suicide might have been the result of an "inside job." Without hesitation, Andrus answered, "Absolutely not! Between the time of the trials and his death, we saw each other frequently and regularly, and our relationship was ideal. He confided in me on many other things, but there was never any possible suggestion to me that he suspected any of his subordinates, nor even the German employees. Nor did he at any time point the finger at anyone else. I never heard my father suggest that anyone had assisted Goering in any way. I am satisfied," concluded Andrus, "that my father went to his grave believing that he had been hoodwinked by Goering and that this was just a fact of life."

Before reading my manuscript, Burt Andrus had never heard of Jack Wheelis. However, he said that his sister, who had been at Nuremberg at the time of the trials, remembered the Texan well. Andrus recounted a recent telephone conversation with her: "I am not sure what term she used in reference to Wheelis, but it was a denigrating term. It was 'squirrelly' or something like that. She said that he was a loudmouthed show-off, irresponsible and unreliable." Andrus explained that his sister was always included in the social activities at Nuremberg and had dated some of the officers. "So she had a pretty good idea who the 'good guys' were and who the 'bad guys' were. Wheelis was a 'bad guy' as far as she was concerned."

Burt Andrus had read my chapter on Jack Wheelis, and I asked him his assessment of Wheelis's character and personality. He hesitated for some time before answering, obviously trying to remain objective. Finally he said, "I would have to say that he was not unlike many who came up through the ranks—and I am not belittling that. But to go from enlisted status to officer status changes one's social structure. And if Wheelis was, by nature, an outspoken and flaky person, then I could see how he, with his personality, would be pleased to brag about 'My friend, the Reichsmarschall' and display the souvenirs he had of him."

"Why didn't your father do something about Wheelis?" I asked. "Here he was, a lieutenant, wearing Goering's wristwatch and bragging about what great friends they were. Why wasn't something done about this before it was too late?"

Perplexed, Andrus answered, "I really don't understand that. Knowing my father the way I did, I would bet my right arm that had he known, he would have taken some very strong action." He suggested that his father simply had not known what Wheelis was doing and saying, and "none of my father's subordinates saw fit to bring this to his attention." Explaining his father's lack of personal knowledge of an officer on his own staff, Andrus said, "Again, we have to go back to the classical mode of the 'Old Army,' and though this was after World War II, my father had not changed his modi operandi. And a colonel just did not socialize with a lieutenant. So I would assume that he had no firsthand knowledge of what Wheelis was doing."

Andrus did not appear completely satisfied with this explanation, and he sat silent for a moment. "I don't know at what period of time this officer was showing off the wristwatch," he said, "but I assume that it was fairly late in the game. And I think that it is very important, in any analysis of my father's behavior, to remember the impact of my mother's illness, which was discovered within weeks of the executions. She had been a smoker, and a spot was found on her lung. They expected to find cancer. So that was a tremendous preoccupation that certainly would have interfered with any of my father's normal reactions up to the time of Goering's suicide."

We then discussed the supposed hiding places for the poison, and I asked Andrus what he thought of the board's finding that the cartridge had been hidden in Goering's navel. Shaking his head before I had finished the question, Andrus answered, "I read the doctor's report, and I believe that there was not the remotest possibility of its being there. The medical testimony rules that out. And even though my father seemed to think that was the case, I can't agree with that one at all."

Andrus could not account for his father's apparent belief that Goering had had an operation on his navel. He could not recall his father ever mentioning this to him.

Andrus also rejected the idea that Goering could have swallowed the cartridge. "No, I do not believe that," he said, "based on the fact that the cartridge was almost two inches long, a piece of rigid metal that had no flex." And even granting that Goering could have swallowed the capsule before he came into the Nuremberg prison, Andrus found it impossible to believe he would then have had the good fortune to both retrieve the capsule and find a secure hiding place for it in his toilet where it would remain undetected for over fifteen months. However, Andrus did not entirely rule out the cell toilet as a hiding place for the poison. "I don't feel strongly that the toilet could not have housed it for a short period of time," he said. "Even though the testimony from the guards indicated that they did inspect the toilets, I would think that, unless a man was very diligent, it would have made a possible hiding place." But like his father, Burt Andrus was forced to conclude, "I seriously doubt, due to the frequency of the inspections, that Goering left it in his toilet for any length of time." He agreed that if the poison could not be left in the toilet when it was flushed— as his father had maintained—then "the toilet *certainly* could not have been the hiding spot for any length of time."

The colonel accepted the board's conclusion that the cartridge was at one time concealed in Goering's rectum. "I think there is evidence that was medically corroborated that there was excrement on the capsule, and I could see that this would have been a very logical place to hide the poison. But not for any length of time." It would have been impossible, he believed, for Goering, with only a pan of water for washing himself, to have continually removed the cartridge during the passing of stools and then, without detection by the cell guard, replaced it in his anus. "No," Andrus said, "if Goering had the cartridge in his rectum, it had to be during the last days before the executions."

Among the pile of books and documents lying on the table between the colonel and me was a copy of the letter that Goering had written to Andrus's father on October 11, 1946. I handed it to Andrus and asked him to read it carefully. When he finished, I asked him if he believed that Goering, if his sole purpose was to state that he had always had the poison, would have written such a dangerous document four days in advance of his suicide. "No," answered Andrus, "because, had it been discovered, it would have tipped his hand. That makes no sense at all."

Picking the letter up from the table, Andrus reread it and said, "I now see a facet to the letter I had not formerly seen. Previously, I had thought that the purpose of the letter was to say, 'I got away and I outsmarted you.' Now I can see that it could very well have been structured to provide cover for someone who helped him." Replacing the letter, Andrus commented, "In fact, I would have to say that the most likely objective of this letter was to protect the man who made Goering's suicide possible for him."

Tapping the date at the top of the letter with his fingers, Andrus remarked that "another, completely new thought" had crossed his mind. "If, in fact," he asked, "the letter was written to protect someone, why would Goering *not* have written it early to show to that person, in order to ensure that all bases were covered?" (Perhaps Andrus forgot that this thought had already occurred to me and that I had mentioned this in my manuscript.)

Andrus appeared to accept my theory that one of his father's own officers had betrayed the mission assigned them, and I asked him why this idea had never occurred to his father. "I would have to say," he replied, "that it was the utter confidence he had in his officers. My father adhered to the classic code that an officer always told the truth, that duty came before everything else, and that one's loyalty was to one's organizations. Even though the records show that he made numerous efforts to improve the quality of his staff, I can see nothing that indicated that he lacked confidence in his officers' loyalty. The thought of one of them being treacherous or hostile to the mission was impossible for him to conceive." Then Andrus added, sadly, "He covered all the bases except one: an attack from the rear. It never occurred to him that his rear echelon was not covered. The soft spot was right in his officer staff."

I asked Andrus to comment on the board's makeup, in particular the fact that two members of this investigative body were members of the 6850th Internal Security Detachment, the very unit that had the responsibility for delivering Goering to the gallows. He replied, "As a military man, I have to assess this as being a *most* unusual procedure. It was a completely atypical thing to do. Any experience I have had— and I was inspector general at one time—the very basic rule is that one brings in people who are completely objective and have no association with the incident or the organization associated with the incident. This was a *very* unusual structure, and I can't understand it."

Andrus was particularly disturbed by the thought of two subordinates sitting in judgment of their commanding officer. This was, he said, "*very* unusual, *completely* unusual, because it would put them in an awkward position and my father in an awkward position." Andrus said that he knew of "no other experience in my many, many years of military service where this kind of thing happened."

The colonel criticized other aspects of the board's investigation. "It's hard for me to imagine," he said, "that an incident as serious as this, which attracted worldwide attention, was disposed of in such a short period of time." It was not the norm, he observed, that the board was "taking affidavits from key witnesses without any cross-examination or extensive interrogation." It appeared to Andrus that the investigation was done "in a very cursory and perfunctory manner, and it could very well have been guided by some instructions to do just that, to get the matter over with, to blunt the thrust of Soviet criticism and that of the press."

I asked Andrus if he meant to insinuate that there had been a cover-up by the board. Andrus was unwilling to say that there had been an actual cover-up, if this meant that the board had knowledge of Wheelis's complicity in Goering's death and then concealed this information. Instead, he said that he could "very easily see a scenario, particularly if the Soviets were alleging a plot originating in Washington, where there could have been a telephone call from the chief of staff in Washington to General McNarney's headquarters, saying, 'For God's sake, get this thing cleaned up and disposed of.' And particularly since these three members of the board proceeded to Frankfurt early in the investigation and spent some days there, only to deliver some of the evidence. I keep asking myself: What else did they do there?"

After a few moments, Andrus answered his own question by expressing his belief that "the trip to Frankfurt was to prepare the officers for the job they had to do." He said that it would have been "very easy in the military system to have closeted the members of the board with a senior officer who said, 'We want you to get this thing done, and we want you to get Washington off the hook and the press off our backs.' " He reminded me that "this was still the 'Old Army,' and it was not unheard of for a person, like the chief of staff, to say, 'Gentlemen, we want to get Washington in control of this thing, and we want to get it cleaned up. Do it as you best see fit.' "

If this had actually happened, I asked, would his father have been informed of the orders issued to the board? "Absolutely not!" he answered. "My father would have been the last man they would have told. He would not have acceded to this method of running the investigation, because his career and reputation were at stake." Andrus also said that it would be illogical "to have issued what amounted to covert orders to a group of officers and then allowed anyone who was to be involved to be privy to these orders."

Andrus was very suspicious of the reaction of the board member I had contacted a few years earlier. He thought this officer's reaction to my letter very strange.

"It sounds like, at least, an overreaction, particularly with the intervening time period," he pointed out. "All constraints should have lapsed by that time. Normally, people feel that constraints last only for a few years and have no impact whatsoever once one has left the service. So I am surprised that the man was so reactive, refusing to answer any of your questions, refusing to reveal his whereabouts, and showing considerable agitation that you had access to the report. That the man was still upset over being confronted tells me there was something he wanted to conceal," Andrus concluded. It also seemed to Andrus that the Western members of the Quadripartite Commission "had received some sort of guidance similar to that given to the board, or they had some sort of sympathetic reason for wanting to make the whole affair very fuzzy." The conclusions reached by the commission, Andrus said, were "very spooky, about as spooky as those reached by the board; all the more reason, the more I think of it, to believe that there is something not said, and this could easily be attributed to the desire to get the thing over and done with. I don't like the word 'whitewash' because it has some other connotations, but I can see a scenario where a very senior officer might have said, 'There is nothing to be gained by digging up dirt, throwing mud, and pointing fingers. The prisoners have been executed, and one committed suicide. All we need to do is quiet the press and get the Soviets off our backs.' "

Andrus thought it very significant that General Malkov, the Soviet member of the Quadripartite Commission, was not present when the findings of the board were released to the press.

Even though Andrus now accepted my own conclusions that Wheelis had given Goering the poison and that the board was in error in its finding, he emphasized that his father never felt "he had been 'framed,' if that is the word. He felt that Goering's suicide was his responsibility as a commander. *Nothing* I ever heard from him indicated that he thought the responsibility should be shouldered by anyone else."

I asked Andrus what effect Goering's suicide had upon his father's life. "I think that it haunted him his entire life," Andrus replied. "In his very last hours he was still anguishing over what happened." Andrus continued talking about his father's last days: "In January of 1977 he became ill. It was discovered that he had myologinous leukemia. In the advanced stages of the disease, there was a serious infection of the interior of his mouth, and he had a great deal of difficulty speaking. It was late in the evening that he woke up for the last time, and he was hallucinating. He motioned me over to his hospital bed, and speaking with difficulty, he said, 'Goering has committed suicide. I must report it to the Quadripartite Commission.' I told him that it was the middle of the night and it could wait until morning. Then I left the room to get the doctor, who was right across the hall. When I returned, Dad had managed to reach over to the dresser where his clothing was, and he had succeeded in getting his trousers on over his pajamas. Finally, we got him back into bed. Four hours later my father died."

For almost a full minute the tape recorder picked up nothing but silence. Finally, attempting to break the tension both Burt Andrus and I sensed, I asked him how he now felt about the event that had haunted his father to the moment of his death. Andrus's face registered relief as he answered, "I would have to say that I am now much more comfortable than ever before in thinking about the whole experience and the torment that it put my father through. I am hopeful that your book will leave my father's image less tarnished than most of the other books which have been written."

Then Andrus said, "I only wish that my father . . ." Andrus could not finish the sentence, but I knew what he wanted to say. I was wishing the same thing.

17

Conclusions

My research into Goering's suicide had changed me from an uncritical proponent to a complete skeptic of the story that Goering had brought poison into the prison and hidden it in his cell toilet. My change of mind was not deliberate but one that built slowly and was reinforced the longer I studied the case. Each time I released a belief that had become untenable, I checked and double-checked to make sure there was no way I could be mistaken. Some answers still eluded me, but I found enough to give me an almost complete picture and understanding of how Goering managed to kill himself while under constant observation.

In my opinion, the poison container remained in the prison baggage room hidden among Goering's personal possessions. Despite Colonel Andrus's careful inventory of these items, the suitcases and their contents had never been properly searched. Otherwise, the poison container hidden in the jar of face cream would have been found before Goering's death. If one poison capsule escaped detection, it is also quite possible another did so as well. Dr. Pfluecker's belated conviction that the poison had been hidden in the baggage room was probably based on more than merely his deductive reasoning.

As late as October 7, Goering told his wife he had no poison. There was no reason for him to lie to her. It is nonsense to think that Frau Goering, even if surprised, would have betrayed this secret. In asking him her question, she was prepared for an affirmative answer—

206

certainly she hoped for it. If Goering actually had the poison at the time of his last meeting with his wife, why would he have denied it, knowing he would be subjecting her to many days of needless anguish?

Goering's insistence that he would not hang and his possible "hint" of this to his wife indicate he was reasonably sure the poison would be passed to him. Charles Bewley, the only author with whom Frau Goering fully discussed the matter, made a point of saying Goering received the poison on the very night of his suicide.

It was probably not until Goering learned his petition to be shot had been rejected that he attempted to procure the vial of cyanide; on that day, October 11, he wrote to Colonel Andrus, stating his intention to kill himself.

Goering's letter to Colonel Andrus was, I think, only a sham to protect the person who was to furnish him with the poison. Goering never intended to resolve the mystery of the hiding place for the capsule; he never specifically revealed the place of concealment in his cell because he was *unable* to suggest a single spot that had not, time and again, been carefully searched. I strongly suspect the letter was written well in advance of the actual procurement of the poison and was reintroduced into his cell on the day of the executions. Goering wrote the letter on October 11, not during his last hours, because on October 11 he became certain that were he to escape the gallows, he would need help from someone, who, in return, would demand evidence of good faith and protection.

The internal structure of Goering's letter is evidence of his frame of mind and true intent at the time he wrote it. It reveals above all that he wanted to make people believe he had always had the poison and no U.S. military personnel helped him. Only parenthetically and in a postscript did he mention his reason for electing to kill himself. This is in marked contrast to the farewell letter he left for his wife. There he went into great detail concerning *why* he was going to commit suicide, only mentioning the supposed retention of the poison in a vague sentence. Clearly Goering's letter to Andrus was not the sort he would have written had he *not* had an ulterior purpose—to protect a U.S. Army accomplice.

Despite the board's conclusion that no American "would leave a stone unturned" to ensure Goering met his punishment, the evidence shows he had tried to ingratiate himself with the young Americans guarding him. It is certain his efforts were successful in some instances. It is almost equally certain that at least two members of the board should have known this to be a fact. Perhaps the officers deliberately avoided investigating this area because they feared it would show some Americans had succumbed to the Goering charm, of whom Lt. Jack G. Wheelis is a prime example.

Judge Wheelis told me he thought it was a shame "the whole story did not come from my father himself." I agreed with the judge, but I felt my own research had given me enough background to piece together the details of the strange relationship that developed between the German Reichsmarschall and the Texas lieutenant.

From the time Goering surrendered to American forces, he had concentrated on charming his captors. At first there may have been no ulterior motives; Goering was genuinely convinced that he enjoyed a certain popularity with the Americans, and his initial contacts with high-ranking army officers did nothing to dispel this belief. Only after Eisenhower's order did Goering experience less than cordial treatment and begin to worry about his future. By the time he was committed to Colonel Andrus's supervision, he was under no illusions. He knew he was scheduled to be tried as a war criminal. He was also under no illusions about the probable outcome of such a trial. While he fleetingly entertained the idea of a court-imposed exile to some remote island, subsequent events convinced him that he would be condemned to death. The prescribed manner of execution was also known to him—hanging.

Goering came to Nuremberg with at least two poison vials hidden in his luggage; one was hidden in the vanity case, while the other with which he killed himself was hidden in another piece of luggage. Throughout the trial, he worried and fretted over the possibility of being separated from his luggage. His concern was so obvious that it was remembered by the surviving defendants, though they misinterpreted his cause for concern.

Having brought the poison into the prison, Goering had to devise a plan to secure the capsule when it was needed. From the first day of the trial, he began the antics that were to characterize his behavior throughout the following year. He was aware that all eyes were on him and was determined to take full advantage of this fact in order to impress and dominate others. Goering was so successful in dominating his fellow defendants that he was separated from them during meals. For the remainder of the trial, he was forced to eat alone in a small room.

For all practical purposes, Goering's influence over the other defendants had ended. However, he not only imposed his personality upon his comrades in the dock; Goering also greatly impressed and influenced many of those who had so recently been his mortal enemies, particularly the young American guards selected to staff the jail and courtroom.

These guards were no different from others who had been conditioned by wartime propaganda to regard Goering as a cross between a fat clown and a thug, the embodiment of the evils of Nazism. However, Goering refused to fit this mold. He showed no Nazi arrogance in his day-to-day contact with his guards. He always had a joke or a quip to exchange with those who escorted him to the courtroom, stood watch after he arrived, or spent countless hours peering into his cell. Young, impressionable, and undoubtedly awed by their close, friendly contact with the man who had been Hitler's chief lieutenant, the American guards began to succumb to Goering's charm. His behavior throughout the trial and his skillful, courageous conduct on the witness stand increased his popularity—and not only with the younger members of the guard. It was generally conceded that Goering was "quite a guy." He was equally at home discussing literature and art with Lieutenant Roska and the Bible with Chaplain Eggers. But he was in his favorite element when discussing guns and hunting with Tex Wheelis.

It was natural that Wheelis and Goering would be drawn together; each served a need in the other. Of all the American prison officers, Wheelis was probably the most vulnerable to Goering's calculated amiability. Early in his life, the Texan had learned that those in less fortunate positions—the underdogs of the world—accepted him. The incarcerated Goering was no exception. While many of Wheelis's peers kept him at a distance and considered him to be a joke, Goering welcomed his friendship and treated him with respect. Additionally, Wheelis's close relationship with Goering gave the attention-seeking Texan a wealth of stories to enthrall the junior officers and young secretaries and an opportunity to breezily display to all newcomers the wristwatch that had once belonged to Adolf Hitler's second-in-command. With his ability to overlook faults in those who accepted him as a friend, Wheelis saw nothing wrong or strange in his relationship with the Nazi Reichsmarschall. At the Nuremberg prison, Wheelis's lack of discrimination in forming friendships was no different from what he was to display later by going out of his way to talk to the village idiot.

Considering the relationship that had developed between Goering and Wheelis, it is not difficult to imagine how Goering succeeded in persuading the lieutenant to help him. After learning that his petition to be shot had been rejected, Goering may well have said to Wheelis, "*Herr Leutnant,* I know I have to die. That I accept. But I don't want to hang. Think of my wife and child. Help me." Wheelis would have asked how he could help, and Goering would have confided there was poison in the baggage room. Wheelis would probably protest that such a plan would be risky and suspicion would surely fall on him, but Goering assured him he had already thought of that possibility and showed him the note exonerating all American personnel. At this point, Wheelis agreed to help and took the note with him.

Shortly before the executions were scheduled to begin, Wheelis took Goering into the baggage room on one pretext or another. There was no need for Wheelis actually to hand the poison to Goering but merely to turn away as the luggage was gone through. Goering himself brought the poison into his cell.

I believe Wheelis agreed to help Goering not in return for a bribe but because he felt more personal loyalty to the man who had accepted his friendship than he did to his peers, whose responsibility it was to see that Goering was delivered to the gallows. Mrs. Salles said that

Wheelis was the type of person who would give a friend "the shirt off his back." This may well have been true, but it seems equally true that Wheelis, to aid a friend, was quite capable of giving the shirts off the backs of others.

Once the poison was in the cell, there was no reason for Goering to go to exotic lengths to hide it. The rents in his mattress discovered on the night of the suicide would have served the purpose since the prisoners were not allowed sheets; only loose blankets covered the cots. If the poison were hidden in one of these rents, Goering would not have had to leave his bed in order to retrieve it. The poison could also have been in the glasses case to which Goering paid so much attention before he went to bed. There was no cell inspection on the night of October 15, and either place would have escaped detection.

However, the most logical place for the poison to have been hidden was in Goering's rectum. Because Goering could not be sure he would remain in the same cell, it was essential for him to have the capsule somewhere on his person. The presence of excretal material on the brass capsule is evidence that he did indeed place it in his rectum.

Although the poison could be introduced into the cell anytime before the start of the hangings, the letter presented another problem. It was too dangerous for it to remain in the cell. Moreover, Wheelis wanted to make sure the letter was found after Goering's death. Perhaps it was agreed that Wheelis should take the letter for his own protection and that it could be smuggled back into the cell that last day. If someone were needed to bring the letter back to the cell, perhaps Dr. Ludwig Pfluecker, who was in and out of Goering's cell several times on October 15 and who later found the letter (which had been undetected by all others), was such a man. If so, many of the remaining pieces of the jigsaw puzzle fall neatly into place, and the result is a much more complete picture than the board was able to draw.

The roles played by the Board of Officers and the Quadripartite Commission can only be speculated upon. Colonel Tweedy is unwilling to answer for the board. Brigadier Paton-Walsh, because of ill health, is unable to speak for the commission. Colonel Hurless and General Rickard are both dead, and nothing came of my efforts to trace Major Rosenthal and General Morel. I made no effort to contact General Malkov. Thus I am forced to draw my own conclusions on the qualifications of the board and the commission to objectively evaluate and render an opinion on the evidence presented to them.

At one point in my research, I was inclined to believe the board actually knew Wheelis had given Goering the poison and deliberately withheld this information. I was even more convinced when I found evidence in Colonel Andrus's files that the army had ordered a cover-up in the suicide of Dr. Conti and that the colonel had abetted this cover-up. However, by the time I read through the Andrus papers, I was convinced such was *not* the case with Goering's suicide. I found no evidence that either the board or Colonel Andrus knew anyone on the prison staff was involved in Goering's escape from the gallows. However, I am equally convinced that the manner in which the investigation was conducted precluded the board from discovering the truth about Goering's suicide.

I accept the conclusion of Burton Andrus, Jr., that the board's mission was not to delve deeply into Goering's suicide but to settle the matter as quickly and conveniently as possible to blunt the Soviet charges and quiet the hostile press. The board accomplished these objectives through its investigation; but the evidence upon which it based its findings was so obviously specious that the official records had to be withheld and all personnel connected with the investigation had to be required to maintain silence on what they knew of the affair. In short, the board did not actually withhold evidence that might have involved a member of the prison staff, but it did at least whitewash the Goering suicide by not conducting a thorough investigation.

Was the board acting under orders to conduct the investigation in such a desultory manner? Though I was unable to discover any hard evidence for this possibility, I have to agree once again with Burton Andrus, Jr., that this most likely was the case. I share his suspicion that the board's quite unnecessary and oddly timed trip to Frankfurt, ostensibly to deliver items of evidence for analysis, might have had another purpose—to receive "guidance" on how to conduct the investigation. Only if this were the case would the board's method of conducting the investigation and the conclusions it reached make sense. Even for the most altruistic of reasons, the board, alone and on its own initiative, would never have dared to issue as incomplete and misleading a report on Goering's death as it did. But if the three officers were acting under orders and had been assured of support from superiors, I do not doubt they would have obeyed these orders, just as Colonel Andrus did in the case of Dr. Conti's suicide. If this actually happened, I find no fault with the officers of the board. What they did was the proper thing to have done at the time.

The endorsement of the board's findings by the Quadripartite Commission is as open to questions as the report itself. It appears that Brigadier Paton-Walsh, by his statements at the press conference, demonstrated his bias in favor of the conclusion that the United States Army was not responsible for Goering's suicide, and indeed he had done so long before there was evidence for his contention and even after there was evidence to the contrary.

It is in my opinion likely that Paton-Walsh was one of the two Allied generals who, only days after Goering's death, predicted the "sensational" solution that would absolve the army from blame. His statements at the press conference, over which he presided when the board's findings were released, offer hard evidence that at least two members of the Quadripartite Commission—he and General Morel—apparently were willing to aid and abet the board in the whitewash of Goering's suicide.

It can be safely assumed that General Rickard was hardly a disinterested party to the board's workings but had a vested interest in the outcome of the investigation. Thus he would put no stumbling blocks in the way of the board. General Morel, the distinctly junior member of the commission, probably acceded to his colleagues in accepting the report without question in order for them to present a united front against Russian charges of conspiracy and to preserve the honor of his wartime ally.

Despite the denials of Paton-Walsh, it is probable that General Malkov broke with the commission over the board's report and wished to have nothing to do with the commission's endorsement of the board's conclusions. If Malkov did not actually reject the findings of the board, it is possible that the Western members of the commission took advantage of the Russian's absence in timing the release of the endorsement. In this manner, the probable Soviet objection to the report was avoided. In effect, Malkov was neutralized by the actions of the other members of the commission.

With the release of the commission's endorsement of the board's findings, criticism of the army and interest in Goering's suicide ceased. Goering's death was no longer news, and those who had been suddenly thrust into unwelcome controversy welcomed the end of the attention that Goering's suicide had focused on them. Colonel Andrus left Nuremberg shortly afterwards, giving rise to the rumor that he had been sacked. He never achieved higher rank but retired from the army a bitter man convinced that he had been forced to "carry the can" for Goering's death. He died in Tacoma, Washington, on February 1, 1977. Emmy Goering and her daughter moved to Munich, where they sought to escape the public eye and begin a new life. Frau Goering died in 1973, but Edda Goering still is in Munich, shunning all publicity and refusing to answer any questions, including mine, about her father's death. Dr. Pfluecker retired to a small village in Germany, only surfacing again shortly before his death to write his memoirs for a local newspaper. Jack Wheelis remained in the army but was never to rise in rank higher than captain. He served in Korea and was eventually transferred to a small school as an ROTC instructor. He died of a heart attack at Ft. Hood, Texas, on May 13, 1954, taking with him the definitive answer to the riddle of Goering's suicide. But he left behind him a tantalizing trail of clues for one curious enough to follow.

18

Farewell to Jack Wheelis

With my research completed and the manuscript almost in final form, there was just one more thing that I wanted to do. To satisfy my own curiosity, I wanted to visit Mart, Texas, the hometown of Jack Wheelis.

Late in 1984 my son, Stephen, and I drove to Mart, which the map showed to be not far from Waco. By today's standards, with improved roads and efficient means of transportation, it really is not far. But as my son and I left the main highway and drove along the back roads leading to Mart, it was impressed upon me what an extremely isolated and insulated life Wheelis must have led as a young man. Once we left the highway, we saw little besides a few scattered farms, flatlands, and woods.

Presently, we saw the cutoff to Mart. As we drove in, I noticed that the few blocks of the business section, located on Texas Avenue, constituted the major part of the town. Though it was not yet 4:00 P.M., most of the businesses were either closed or about to close for Saturday evening. There were few people on the streets. After parking the car, Stephen and I sat in the shade on the raised curb, drinking a Coke. As I looked up and down the main street, I reflected that the town probably had not changed much from the days when Wheelis had walked its streets.

Our sodas finished, my son and I drove along the residential streets. I saw two ladies sitting on the porch of a house, and I stopped to ask

215

them the site of the old Wheelis farm. They were not sure. The ladies appeared to be longtime residents of Mart, and I asked if they had known the Wheelis family. Yes, they had, they told me. When I mentioned Jack Wheelis, one of them volunteered, "He is buried here, you know." I did not know.

Following directions, Stephen and I drove to the local cemetery, which was only a short distance from the main street. In a few minutes, we saw the iron gate to the burial ground. A sign indicated that the cemetery had been in use since the 1880s, a fact amply attested to by the great number of markers and headstones that loomed before us. How to find the grave of Jack Wheelis was the problem.

Strangely—and it could only have been blind luck—we located the Wheelis family plot within minutes of driving through the gate. We stepped from the car and approached the low concrete border that surrounded the area. Though there were numerous markers in the plot, Jack Wheelis's immediately caught my attention. Beside the marker—and probably placed there on the Fourth of July by the local veterans group—was a small faded American flag on a stick. The flag was listing precariously, and I instinctively righted it before walking to the front of the marker.

A very unsettling feeling came over me as I stood before Jack Wheelis's final resting place. Beneath the ground lay the mortal remains of the man I had pursued for so many years, and now, literally, to the grave. It was one thing to write dispassionately about a man I had never met, but standing in front of his grave—surrounded by the graves of his mother, father, sister, and brothers—the matter had become more personal. As I read the simple, yet proud, inscription on his gray marble marker—"Capt. Jack G. Wheelis"—and saw the crossed rifles, the insignia of the U.S. Army Infantry, carved into the stone, I began to have regrets about the probable effect of my book upon the memory of this veteran of World War II and the Korean War. Turning this thought over in my mind, I stood at the grave site much longer than was necessary for the eye to take in all before it and the mind to commit it to memory.

"Well, we've seen it. Let's go," said my son, with the impatience of youth, undisturbed by the thoughts I was having.

As I turned away from Jack Wheelis's grave and walked to my car, I suddenly remembered something that his son had once told me, something that greatly put my mind at ease. "I believe," said Jim Wheelis, "that my father thoroughly enjoyed the cloud of mystery which swirled about him as a result of all the rumors." I hoped that this was so. And I hoped that the shade of Jack Wheelis would appreciate the attention that may now accrue to him as the man who helped Hermann Goering make good his prediction "They will not hang me!"

ACKNOWLEDGMENTS

Due to the nature of my research, it was necessary for me to speak to and correspond with many people, some of them off the record. However, there were many others who helped without this restriction, and it is to them that I would like to express my thanks and appreciation.

Among those to whom I am indebted are Col. Burton C. Andrus, Jr., Britt Bailey, Victor Bernstein, Fred Brand, Dr. Werner Bross, Col. Thomas Cook, Walter Cronkite, Ray D'Addario, Chaplain Carl Eggers, Nadine Finley, William J. Foley, Col. Henry H. Gerecke, William Glenney, Whitney Harris, Emma S. Haynes, G. K. Hodenfield, Dr. Eberhard Jäckel, Lt. Col. Thomas M. Johnson, Col. Bud Jones, Arnold Joseph, Lt. Col. Robert L. Keeler, Dr. Robert Kempner, Joseph Kingsbury-Smith, Dr. John K. Lattimer, James LeMay, Dr. Clint L. Miller, Peter Misko, Tom Modisett, Rex S. Morgan, Col. Richard Nalle, John Pearsall, Gen. Eugene Phillips, Richard Raabe, Rudolf Raith, Fred Rodell, Dr. Charles J. Roska, Genelle Salles, Henriette von Schirach, Dana Adams Schmidt, Albert Speer, Don Spencer, Gen. Robert I. Stack, William Stricker, Professor Telford Taylor, Rolf Wartenberg, Judge James Wheelis, K. Robert Wilheim, Gen. Samuel T. Williams, Jean Paul Willis, Col. Gerald R. Wilson, Dr. Richard Worthington, and Desmond Zwar.

I am particularly grateful to John Toland, who took time from his busy schedule to read my manuscript, offer suggestions, and write comments about my book. His help and encouragement over the years have been much appreciated.

In addition, there is one person without whom this book could not have been written: my longtime friend Edward A. Schaefer. More than anyone else, Ed has helped me in every possible way, from much-needed moral support to thoughtful and honest criticism of the various stages of my manuscript. Together, we considered every aspect of Goering's suicide for years, and I am sure that Ed is as glad as I am to finally lay the subject to rest. For all his help and for just being a good friend, I would like to express to him my sincere thanks and appreciation.

NOTES

All references are listed in abbreviated form. For full information on published works, please see the Bibliography.

Preface
xiii to kill himself—I collect the more rare and unusual souvenirs of World War II.
xv a Dr. Kramer—von Lang, p. 365.
xv suicide of Goering—German Documents Section of the United States Archives, Washington, D.C.

1. *Visits with a Dead Man*
   2 a short time—Goering, p. 300.
   3 he can talk—Ibid.
   3 Do they tickle—Mosley, p. 347.
   4 up all hope—Goering, pp. 301–2.
   4 sentenced to hang—Col. Bud Jones was in the courtroom when Goering was sentenced to hang. He described the drama: "Goering was the first defendant to emerge from the elevator, followed by two guards. I handed him the headset so that he might hear his sentence. The judge started to read the sentence. Goering said nothing but raised both hands in a gesture of despair. At first, I did not know what was wrong, but then Goering put his hands to the headset and shook his head. It was obvious that he could hear nothing. I took the headset from him and put it to my ear. There was no sound. When I attempted to adjust the control knob, I succeeded only in breaking the wire. The judge had stopped reading the sentence and was waiting. I spotted Captain Valentine, the court communications officer, sitting near the dock. All it took was a look from me, and Captain Valentine vaulted over the dock and quickly replaced the headset. There was no further problem, and Goering reacted well to the minor mishap. He stood motionless with a calm expression on his face." With the replacement headset, Goering heard the words he had expected all along: "Death by hanging." Personal communication to the author, as are all quotes from Colonel Jones.
   4 miracle will happen—Goering, p. 302.
   4 us up there—Ibid., pp. 304–5.
   5 her once more—Pfluecker, October 20, 1952.

5 in my hand—Goering, p. 303.
6 and our child—Goering, pp. 303–7.

2. *The Road to Nuremberg*

7 post in Haiti—Gritzbach, p. 311. Gritzbach, Goering's Nazi biographer, insinuated that it was Franziska Goering's love of the German fatherland that prompted her to return home for the birth of her child. The more prosaic truth is that she did not wish to entrust herself to the primitive medical facilities then available in Haiti. Much of Gritzbach's book is suspect, since it was written to present Goering to the German people as he wished to be seen and since it accords with the sentiments of the time in which it was written. Still, it is the main source for information on Goering's early life.
7 in his infancy—Frischauer, p. 7.
7 of fifty-six—Retirement was forced on Heinrich Goering. His liberal views made him suspect in the eyes of his superiors, some of whom thought him to be a Socialist. Mosley, p. 4.
8 become a general—Gritzbach, p. 224.
8 young Hermann Goering—Ibid., p. 225.
8 thick and thin—Mosley, p. 8.
8 would burn down—Gritzbach, p. 313.
8 become a soldier—Ibid., p. 227.
8 was a Jew—The proof for this assertion, which has been argued by various authors, is the inclusion of von Epenstein's name in the *Semi-Gotha*, the book in which titled families of Jewish descent were listed. It was this book that the headmaster at Ansbach showed to young Goering when the latter protested his godfather was a Catholic. Mosley, p. 8.
9 take a risk—Ibid., p. 9.
9 name of Goering—Manvell and Fraenkel, p. 27.
9 he would win—Ibid., p. 28.
10 Pour le Mérite—Goering's final tally of downed planes was twenty-two.
10 little as possible—Mosley, p. 44.
11 my own soul—Ibid., p. 64.
12 the ideological stuff—Gilbert, *Nuremberg Diary*, p. 67.
12 even unto death—Andrus Papers. Among the papers of Colonel Burton C. Andrus were copies of the interrogations of Goering at Augsburg in 1945.
13 told the sisters—Frischauer, p. 39.
13 white as snow—von Wilamowitz-Moellendorff, p. 75.
14 this Jew Republic—Ibid., p. 93.
14 Fascist awaiting orders—The quote is taken from a collection of letters

written by Goering to an Italian friend between 1924 and 1925. These letters, which I discovered in Munich in 1973, give vivid new insight into Goering's life during his exile in Italy. Among other things, they prove that Goering did not meet Mussolini in 1924—contrary to what other biographers have written, often with great embellishment.

14 basic moral courage—Mosley, p. 103.

15 are old enough—Ibid., p. 112.

15 *vice* to anyone—Ibid., p. 135.

16 them into effect—Though Goering was merciless in stamping out political opposition, he showed great compassion for animals. In a radio speech, he said, "I have forbidden vivisection in Prussia with immediate effect and have put it under punishment for the time being until the law itself puts it under severe penalties, under the punishment of being thrown into a concentration camp." Kelly, pp. 62–63.

16 fanatic for justice–Bewley, p. 21.

16 my head pronto—Mosley, p. 164.

17 the carnage ended—Some estimates run to over one thousand dead. The truth will never be known.

17 the high treason—Mosley, p. 195.

17 beamed at Emmy—Goering, p. 35.

18 no Jewish grandmothers—Oechsner, p. 28.

19 from future performances—Mosley, pp. ix–x. There is no credible evidence that Goering ever engaged in homosexual practices. Stories that he painted his nails, used rouge, etc., are equally without foundation.

19 uniforms and medals—How many medals did Goering possess? It is impossible to say, but his American captors showed him an eight-page list of the foreign decorations bestowed upon him, calling them "the greatest collection of medals in the world." Goering protested that the crown prince of Germany had more medals than he and that he had accepted the foreign medals only because Hitler would not. "As for the foreign medals," Goering explained, "I never wore them more than two or three times, only when the Ministers of foreign countries came." Andrus Papers.

When Goering was entertained by high-ranking American officers shortly after his surrender, he chose to wear only five of his medals: the Grand Cross of the Iron Cross, the Pour le Mérite, the Golden Flyer's Badge with Diamonds, an Iron Cross First Class, and the 1939 award to those who already possessed the latter award from World War I. All these decorations subsequently disappeared and are probably in the possession of the family of some American officer.

20 the Nazi party—Though he loved decorations, Goering rarely wore the

coveted Golden Party Badge to which he was entitled as an "Old Fighter" of the Nazi party.

20 of his Führer—Bewley, p. 156.

20 character and genius—Ibid., p. 155.

20 frame for it—This massive frame, sans eagle and swastika, is now in my collection. It was auctioned along with other of Goering's personal belongings by the Bavarian state government some years ago. Much to the surprise and embarrassment of German officials, the Goering relics fetched extremely high prices.

20 do the same—Andrus Papers.

20 them leave Germany—Ibid.

21 helped, even . . . Jews—Ibid.

21 Himmler after me—Frischauer, p. 129.

21 Fuehrer against me—Mosley, p. 229.

22 be quite ruthless—Manvell and Fraenkel, p. 159.

22 mercy on us—Schmidt, p. 158.

23 of the lid—Shirer, p. 456. The collar insignia—presumably designed by Hitler, who paid great attention to such things—was not to Goering's liking; it consisted of an eagle and swastika on one collar tab and crossed batons on the other. Goering changed this combination to crossed batons on both tabs. The shoulder boards—massive eagles perched on crossed batons—were left unchanged.

23 as Germany's Reichsmarschall—This baton, which had an intrinsic value of thirty-five thousand dollars in 1945, is now displayed in the West Point Museum.

23 not being bombed—Goering, p. 192.

24 and militarily mistaken—Mosley, p. 275.

24 front saved England—Andrus Papers.

25 recalled was pitiable—Frischauer, p. 196.

25 all of Germany—Much has been written about Goering's "dope addiction." According to Dr. Kelley, the prison psychiatrist who broke Goering of his dependence on the drug, "these tiny tablets each contained only a small amount of paracodeine, and a hundred of them, Goering's average daily dose, are the equivalent of between three and four grains of morphine. This is not an unusually large dose. It was not enough to have affected his mental processes at any time." Dr. Kelley likened Goering's pill habit to those "many people who have the cigarette habit. Just as smokers are careful to have a supply of cigarettes and tobacco on their desks each morning, so Goering would place on his desk a bottle containing a hundred of his little pills." Then, during the day, Goering would consume the tablets. Kelley stated that Goering's dependence on

these tablets "was not very severe. If it had been, I could never have taken him off the drug in the manner I did . . . cutting down the dosage each day until no more drug was allowed." pp. 57–58.

26 and Hitler's successor—When asked by the Americans why he did not resign as head of the Luftwaffe, Goering replied he was afraid he would consequently lose his place as Hitler's successor and would be replaced by Martin Bormann, whom he hated. At another time, Goering said his fear of what might happen to his family, should such action be interpreted by the Fuehrer as a lack of faith in his leadership and ultimate victory, kept him from offering his resignation. Andrus Papers.

26 is no escape—Goebbels, p. 266.

26 eventual Final Solution—According to Dieter Wisliceny, Adolf Eichmann told him in 1942 that Himmler had ordered the physical destruction of the Jews. When Wisliceny asked to be shown the order, Eichmann showed him a secret document, signed by Himmler, that stated, "The Fuehrer has decided that the final solution of the Jewish question is to start immediately." Eichmann told Wisliceny that the words "final solution" meant the biological extermination of the Jews. Office of United States Chief of Counsel, *Nazi Conspiracy and Aggression*, Vol. 8, p. 607.

In issuing this order to Himmler, Hitler circumvented Goering.

26 the extermination camps—Goering's protestations of ignorance of the facts are not very convincing. "I have heard such stories before," he told his American captors, "for example, that a large load of Jews left Poland during the winter, where some of the people froze to death in their vehicles. When I made inquiries, I was told that such things would not happen again—it was claimed that the trains were sent on the wrong route." He had heard, he said, "that there were many diseased people in these camps and that many died of pestilence." The SS troops who staffed these camps, Goering claimed to have believed, were responsible for "bringing the corpses to a crematorium where they would be burned." Goering vehemently denied he had anything further to do with the concentration camps once he had turned them over to Himmler in 1934. Insisting he had never visited any of the camps—and there is no evidence that he did—Goering claimed he always thought "that they were places where people were employed for some useful work." Shown pictures of the liberated camps, Goering said Himmler was to blame: "Himmler must have gotten a fiendish pleasure out of such things." Andrus Papers.

27 loyal to him—Goering, p. 255.

27 Commander-in-Chief—Andrus Papers.

28 his true situation—In a private conversation, a retired general told me

of Goering's reaction to the prospect of this interview. After donning his dress uniform for the occasion, Goering peered through a window at reporters waiting for him on the lawn. Spotting a woman he had known in Germany before the war, Goering said to the general, "See that woman? She was often at my home before the war and we were very friendly. Now she will attack me worst of all." Goering's prediction, said the general, came true.

28 cannot imagine why—Heydecker and Leeb, p. 24.

28 a foregone conclusion—Goering was exonerated on many of the specific charges brought against him. The judges found that the so-called terror bombings of Warsaw, Rotterdam, and Coventry were militarily justified, a rather remarkable decision in light of wartime propaganda. It was further decided that the evidence was not sufficient to convict Goering of responsibility for the murder of Allied fliers who had escaped from Sagan, a prisoner-of-war camp. Conot, pp. 485–86.

Still, Goering was convicted on all four counts of the indictment brought against him. In an all-encompassing finding, the judges concluded: "There is nothing to be said in mitigation. For Goering was often, indeed almost always, the moving force, second only to his leader. He was the leading war aggressor, both as political and as military leader; he was the director of the slave-labor program and the creator of the oppressive program against the Jews and other races, at home and abroad. All of these crimes he has frankly admitted. On some specific cases there may be conflict of testimony but in terms of the broad outline, his own admissions are more than sufficiently wide to be conclusive of his guilt. His guilt is unique in its enormity. The record discloses no excuses for this man." Office of United States Chief of Counsel, *Nazi Conspiracy and Aggression, Opinion and Judgment*, p. 110.

28 a dramatic gesture—Gilbert, *Nuremberg Diary*, p. 435.

3. Nuremberg

30 freedom of movement—Goering, p. 259. In a telephone conversation with me, General Stack denied telling Goering that Eisenhower had agreed to meet with him. In answer to a follow-up letter containing the Emmy Goering quote, General Stack further said that it was untrue that Eisenhower had guaranteed Goering freedom of movement. "This should clear up what happened," he wrote. "I remember it very clearly." Still, Goering must have had some reason to believe that Eisenhower had at least agreed to his freedom of movement. In a letter to Eisenhower, written at Mondorf, Goering complained, "What hurts the most is that I believed firmly to have had a safe conduct and thereupon to return to

my family to attend there to the most essential things." Andrus, p. 46.

31 to accompany me—Frischauer, p. 228.

31 or necessary clothing—Johnson, p. 255.

32 of utter dejection—Frischauer, p. 228.

32 pants off me—Mosley, p. 321.

32 discussing the war—Frischauer, p. 229.

32 still has it—Personal communication to author.

33 from his prisoner—Frischauer, pp. 229–30.

33 disappoint his audience—Andrus Papers.

34 specially built rack—Personal communication to author, as are all quotes from Wilheim.

34 piecing history together—Personal communication to author, as are all quotes from Raabe.

36 in my life—Andrus, p. 30.

36 happens to him—Andrus Papers.

36 man of him—Mosley, p. 326.

37 nothing but fear—Andrus, pp. 34–35.

37 of heart attacks—Andrus Papers. Although Goering had been having palpitations, his heart problems are here called heart attacks.

37 plausible to him—Ibid.

38 see of it—Andrus, p. 64.

39 in solitary confinement—Davidson, p. 21.

41 twice a week—"Report of Board of Proceedings in Case of Hermann Goering (Suicide) October 1946," henceforth referred to as Board Report.

42 of toilet paper—Personal communication to author.

42 Hess were clean—Andrus, pp. 125–26.

4. Death in Cell #5

43 about to happen—Personal communication to the author, as are all quotes from Willis.

45 was very proud—Pfluecker, October 11, 1952.

45 the most dignity—*St. Louis Post-Dispatch*, October 8, 1946.

46 were in there—Board Report, as are all quotes in this chapter, unless otherwise indicated.

46 on his cot—*St. Louis Post-Dispatch*, October 17, 1946.

48 scheduled to begin—October 18, 1946.

48 nothing about it—*St. Louis Post-Dispatch*, October 17, 1946.

52 between his teeth—Pfluecker, October 24, 1952.

53 consider the idea—Personal communication to the author.

54 having a fit—Although Pfluecker states that Gerecke was already in the

cell, Andrus may have thought Gerecke had just arrived. The sequence of events that night was unclear.

54 for the happening—Andrus, pp. 191–92.

54 hanging the corpse—First reported to me by a source who wishes to remain anonymous; but the information was later confirmed by Jean Paul Willis. The Americans were not the only ones who wished to hang Goering's corpse. Wilhelm Hoegner, the president of Bavaria, upon viewing Goering's body, said, "The scoundrel—even dead he should be hanged." Hearing this remark, a British reporter replied, "Only Germans hate so—and then only one another." Fritzsche, p. 320.

54 treated so brutally—Andrus, pp. 196–97. A major disturbance during the hangings was created by Julius Streicher, former *Gauleiter* of Nuremberg and editor of *Der Stuermer*, the most viciously anti-Semitic newspaper in Nazi Germany. Father Sixtus O'Connor, the Catholic chaplain and a witness to the executions, recalled that Streicher, when called upon to identify himself after he entered the execution chamber, refused to do so. Instead, he spat out, "You know damn well who I am." When he refused a second time to state his name, the officer in charge yelled at him. The tension was growing unbearable for Father O'Connor, and he begged Streicher in German, "Julius, for the love of God, tell them your name and get it over with!" Finally Streicher gave his name and was maneuvered toward the gallows. Standing on the trap, Streicher repeated his prediction that all those present would some day be hanged by the Communists. "Adele, my dear wife," he was heard to utter just before he fell to his death. Powers.

55 before he died—Maser, p. 255.

55 2:54—carcass delivered—The original sheet of paper on which Colonel Andrus recorded the times of the hangings is in the possession of Desmond Zwar, who kindly made a copy available to me.

56 into the water—*Stars and Stripes*, March 20, 1947. Today there is a sign posted at the site, warning without explanation that no one is allowed to enter the area. Parents are warned that they will be held responsible for children who trespass.

57 had committed suicide—All communications between the outside world and the prison had been cut off during the night of October 15–16, with one exception. The 1946 World Series baseball games were going on, and arrangements had been made between those in the prison and an officer on the outside to telephone the score at the end of each inning. Father Sixtus O'Connor, an avid Dodger fan, had "two five spots" bet with the Protestant chaplain, and they both waited in the prison office for the officer's telephone call. As they waited, a guard came running

in to say that "Goering is having a little fit." Reluctant to leave the office, Father O'Connor said to Chaplain Gerecke, "That's your man— not mine." It was only after a junior officer came back and "began yelling for the colonel" that O'Connor abandoned his position by the telephone. It was days later before Father O'Connor thought to ask what happened after the eighth inning. Powers.

57 and his person—*St. Louis Post-Dispatch*, October 16, 1946.

57 who suicided cyanidewise—Personal communication to the author.

57 in the hallways—Personal communication to the author, as are all quotes from Hodenfield.

58 and the executions—Colonel Andrus must have realized that his military career was near an end. Shortly after Goering's suicide, Lt. Bud Jones encountered Andrus eating alone in the mess hall. Contrary to the colonel's usual reserve with junior officers, Andrus was friendly toward Jones, asking him to come to his office as soon as he finished breakfast. There, Andrus gave Jones his highly polished riding boots, the pride of every cavalry officer, telling him to give the boots to a deserving officer. Though Andrus did not appear despondent, Jones realized "that he would never have given away his riding boots if he expected to remain on duty." Personal communication to the author, as are all quotes from Jones.

58 the outside world—Fritzsche, p. 72.

58 of the proceedings—Ibid., p. 120.

59 of the Tribunal—*St. Louis Post-Dispatch*, October 16, 1946.

59 show international ramifications—The *New York Times* (December 8, 1946) reported that Colonel Andrus's job as Commandant of the Nuremberg Prison ended in December of 1946, when he was removed from this position by Army authorities. Though the report mentioned that Andrus had returned to the United States to be with his hospitalized wife, it gave more importance to the real reasons for his dismissal: the need for newer "streamlined" security regulations in the prison during the subsequent trials of twenty-three Nazi doctors and Andrus's own "elaborate precautions" that had allowed Goering to cheat the gallows by swallowing a "long-hidden" vial of poison.

5. Why Suicide?

60 to the gallows—Board Report.

60 fourteen years old—Gilbert, *Psychology of Dictatorship*, p. 87.

60 most people achieve—Gilbert, *Nuremberg Diary*, p. 172.

60 I handle myself—Pfluecker, October 21, 1952.

61 on the Allies—*St. Louis Post-Dispatch*, October 8, 1946.

61 at any point—Andrus, p. 169.

61 go out fighting—Ibid., p. 96.
61 face the enemy—Kelley, p. 75.
61 and war crimes—Ibid., p. 70.
61 lost the war—Personal communication to the author.
62 dispatch me now—Mosley, p. 350.
62 for a while—Gilbert, *Nuremberg Diary*, pp. 431–33.
63 to Nikitchenko's demands—Smith, p. 172.
63 can't shoot straight—*PM*, October 19, 1946.
63 *would kill himself*—Andrus, p. 184.
64 the German people—Board Report.
64 execution to shooting—Ibid.
64 cannot be allowed—*Washington Star*, February 21, 1978. This letter
     was one of three found in Goering's cell after his death. The second was
     to Colonel Andrus, while the third was supposedly a proclamation to
     the German people. The third letter has never been released for pub-
     lication, and its whereabouts are unknown. The Berlin Document Cen-
     ter, which sent me a copy of the letter from Goering to Andrus, denied
     knowledge of the third one in a letter to me, dated July 7, 1981: "The
     'Proclamation to the German People' is unknown to us and in any event
     is not on file in the center."
64 and deep conviction—*New York Times*, October 17, 1946.
64 want to hang—Ibid.
65 own past actions—Guderian, p. 374.
65 a different death—*PM*, October 18, 1946.
65 no task unfulfilled—Bewley, pp. 502–3.

6. The Investigation
66 convicted war criminal—Board Report, as are all quotes used in this
     chapter.
72 the past year—Almost all of the prison staff to whom I spoke agree this
     was "the big mistake" that allowed Goering to kill himself. Actually, it
     made no difference at all.
73 degree of certainty—I asked Dr. John K. Lattimer, who was a medical
     officer at the Nuremberg Trials, to describe the effects of the poison
     Goering used to kill himself. Dr. Lattimer replied: "Cyanide (hydro-
     cyanic acid) is very volatile and very quickly absorbed. It poisons all the
     protoplasm in the body, preventing each cell from taking up oxygen.
     Thus every cell dies of suffocation individually and abruptly after large,
     lethal doses such as Goering took. The brain goes dead in less than ten
     seconds, sometimes after a few convulsive twitches. There may be a
     blowing respiratory effort, occasionally causing a single loud cry (even

though the level of consciousness has already faded), using the last bit of air in the lungs. Breathing then ceases, and the heart stops beating in two to five minutes."

78 to mean that—Joseph Kingsbury-Smith, one of the eight reporters, agreed with Starnes. "I believe that the commotion caused by our visit may have served to tip off Goering . . . that the hour of doom was about to strike." The likelihood is great that Goering's advance knowledge of the "hour of doom" had nothing to do with the visit of the reporters.

80 been *pure accident*—Though not included in the Board Report, Goering's letter to his wife seemed to confirm this statement. To his wife, Goering wrote, "I take it as a sign from God that he allowed me to keep the means to free myself from all earthly things, through all the months of captivity, and that it was not discovered." *Washington Star*, February 21, 1978. Both letters are misleading.

7. The Board's Findings
82 of a third—Board Report, as are all quotes used in this chapter.

8. The Press versus the Army
88 prisoner of war—Andrus, pp. 48–49.
89 The Mondorf Monster—Ibid., p. 50.
89 world within minutes—Ibid., p. 128.
89 I couldn't win—Ibid., p. 143.
90 to be so—Maser, pp. 228–29.
90 the visiting correspondents—December 4, 1945.
91 be improved upon—*St. Louis Post-Dispatch*, October 8, 1946.
91 for various reasons—Baillie, pp. 229–30.
91 to the executions—October 15, 1946.
91 due to suicide—Personal communication to the author.
92 a hempen noose—*Washington Post*, October 15, 1946.
92 within the prison—*Times* (London), October 18, 1946
92 was doubly serious—Andrus, p. 88.
92 the Nuremberg jail—October 17, 1946.
93 pretty clever things—*PM*, October 17, 1946.
93 proceedings against them—*New York Times*, October 17, 1946.
93 from certain shoulders—October 16, 1946.
93 preceded its announcement—*St. Louis Post-Dispatch*, October 16, 1946.
94 speed and accuracy—October 17, 1946.
95 of painstaking work—October 28, 1946.
96 Hermann after all—October 28, 1946.
96 unrepentant German nationalists—October 17, 1946.

96 him the poison—Maser, p. 251.
98 was to blame—November 4, 1946.

9. *The Donovan Connection*
99 United States government—According to Willi Frischauer, it has been
   hinted that "an American diplomat" arranged for Goering to get the
   poison. p. 251.
100 *Lick my arse*—Gilbert, *Nuremberg Diary*, p. 113.
100 vanquished the accused—Ibid., p. 4.
101 court of peers—Ibid., p. 193.
101 that it needed—An author who contrasted the trial of the German war
   criminals with that of their Japanese counterparts described the latter as
   "a curiously subdued affair," because it "lacked anyone of the color of
   Goering."
101 my wife today—Gilbert, *Nuremberg Diary*, pp. 12–13.
102 felt he deserved—The conversation between Donovan and Goering is
   quoted in a 1950 edition (exact date unknown) of *Weltbild*, published
   in Munich. The month was either September or October.
104 gently, then forcefully—Brown, p. 744.
104 a good bet—Gilbert, *Nuremberg Diary*, p. 59.

10. *The Hiding Spot*
105 Nuremberg jail himself—Mosley, p. 356. On the same page, Mosley
   quoted Albert Speer: "I had a tube of toothpaste with poison in it all the
   time I was in Nuremberg, and took it on with me to Spandau jail."
   However, Speer denied to me he ever had any poison.
107 the prison doctor—Andrus, p. 29.
112 have concealed another—*PM*, October 17, 1946.
112 pipe is baseless—This "poison-in-the-pipe" theory surfaced again in Robert E. Conot's *Justice at Nuremberg*. Rejecting the board's findings,
   Conot thought it "more logical" to believe the poison was in the pipe.
   p. 504.

   After I contacted Conot, he told me had taken the story from Baldur
   von Schirach's *Ich glaubte an Hitler*. Referring to my own theory, Conot
   wrote, "As far as Goering's suicide is concerned, I have little doubt that
   you are correct." He said that when he was working in Washington,
   D.C., "the papers to which you refer [the report of the board] had been
   removed from the files, and I was told they were untraceable, so I was
   not privy to the information you obtained."
112 in that pipe—Heydecker and Leeb, p. 381.
113 around the navel—October 18, 1946. A curious variation of this "poison

under the skin" theory is first reported by Frischauer, who wrote, "Rumors of a surgical operation which he was supposed to have undergone to bury the capsule in his flesh were discounted. As often happens in death, the scar of his war wound had broken open." p. 250.

Manvell and Fraenkel report this strange story in their book, too, undoubtedly taking it from Frischauer. p. 426.

The truth is, of course, there was no reopening of Goering's scars whatsoever.

114 never properly searched—Sergeant Raabe told me the vanity set was never searched. "We never had anything to do with it, and I myself (it was not my job) never went around sticking my finger into it, because it all looked innocent."

114 about this possibility—Fishman, p. 79.

114 to his cell—Pfluecker, October 25, 1952.

115 and traveling clocks—Kelley, p. 68.

11. Sympathies: German and American

119 wishes and encouragements—Speer, p. 508.

119 highly precarious position—Maser, p. 250.

119 administered the poison—October 28, 1946.

119 for the Nazis—Andrus, p. 34.

120 than another doctor—Pfluecker, October 4, 1952.

121 the bad times—Ibid., October 7, 1952.

121 of their status—Ibid., October 10, 1952.

121 we said goodbye—Ibid., October 21, 1952.

122 speaking with them—Dr. Roska was at first reluctant to talk to me. He confirmed that all those questioned by the board were required to swear they would never discuss what they knew of Goering's suicide. The oath was so emphasized, Dr. Roska said, "that for years I discussed the matter with no one. I was afraid I could be prosecuted." Roska's eventual decision to talk with me may have been prompted by the publication of Die Kapsel, which hinted that he might have given the poison to Goering. Roska denied that he had done so, and I found no evidence whatsoever that he was involved in Goering's suicide.

122 hour of dawn—If Goering knew the executions were to begin at midnight, his information was more precise than that of most of the prison officers. Col. Bud Jones told me, "Even I did not know the exact time the executions were scheduled to take place, and I was in charge of an exterior gate to the prison grounds." Usually there were no officers assigned to the exterior gates, "but because of rumors of a demonstra-

tion by German nationals, the guards at the gate were increased and put under the command of an officer." Jones did not learn the executions had taken place until he went off duty at 8:00 A.M. on October 16.

122 the Wednesday bug—*PM*, October 19, 1946.

123 him anything definite—Pfluecker, October 24, 1952.

123 executions were imminent—Ibid., October 23, 1952.

124 use of gesture—Mosley, pp. 342–43.

125 countless glittering medals—Kahn, p. 84.

125 brave bastard too—Neave, p. 257.

125 away with it—Ibid., p. 314.

125 to the hangman—Kahn, p. 145.

125 the Allied powers—Kelley, pp. 76–77.

125 to win over—Gilbert, *Psychology of Dictatorship*, p. 107. Only Fred Rodell, an interrogator, told me of difficulty with Goering. Rodell, twenty-four at the time, was questioning Goering when the lunch bell rang. Goering refused to answer any more questions, saying he was going to lunch. Rodell told him he could go only when he, Rodell, dismissed him. Huffily Goering again said he would answer no more questions, to which Rodell replied, "I can go to lunch any time. You cannot." With matters at an impasse, Rodell lit a cigarette and sat silently with Goering. Rodell later ate lunch. Goering did not. Rodell had no further problems with Goering.

126 with the Americans—Personal communication to the author. According to Col. Bud Jones, the German lawyers were selling autograph collections to help support the defendants' families. "The value of a set of autographs (less any from Hess, who never signed, to my knowledge) was about two hundred dollars at the time."

126 in his hands—Frischauer, p. 234.

127 good-natured charmer—Personal communication to the author. In fact, Goering scored third highest on the IQ test Dr. Gilbert administered. Hjalmar Schacht scored highest (the result was favorably weighted because of his age), and Arthur Seyss-Inquart was second. Gilbert, *Nuremberg Diary*, p. 31.

127 into that business—Powers.

127 a fat clown—Personal communication to the author, as are all quotes from Mrs. Haynes.

128 Goering didn't hang—Personal communication to the author.

128 rid of him—*Memoirs*, p. 551.

128 I still do—The individual quoted has not been mentioned by name anywhere in this book.

12. *The Letter to Colonel Andrus*
130 and recovered it—*St. Louis Post-Dispatch*, October 17, 1946.
130 entered the cell—*Saturday Evening Post*, September 1, 1951.
131 the German people—Andrus, p. 200.
131 his flabby navel—Ibid., p. 184.
132 three penciled notes—*Times* (London), October 17, 1946.
133 a white envelope—October 17, 1946.
133 with the rule—Kelley, p. 10.
133 snatches of sleep—*Memoirs*, p. 549.
133 the frigid cell—*New York Times*, October 16, 1946.
133 of the executions—*Times* (London), October 16, 1946.
134 its own conclusions—*New York Times*, October 22, 1946.
137 even a comb—Andrus, p. 46.
137 and other impedimenta—Kelley, p. 10.
137 much too thorough—Frischauer, p. 250.
137 took his life—Fishman, p. 78.
139 and open it—Personal communication to the author.
139 thoughts on earth—Andrus, p. 200.
140 they have done—Ibid., p. 173.

13. *Conspiracy: Yes or No?*
141 list of suspects—Frischauer, p. 250.
142 with his wife—*Washington Post*, October 17, 1946.
142 the visitor's side—*Saturday Evening Post*, September 1, 1951.
143 it got stuck—von Schirach, p. 85. Hans Fritzsche, another of the defendants, insisted that all contact between visitors and prisoners was "impossible, and the passing of the smallest object, even a cigarette, was out of the question. If it is considered with later events, that perhaps a poison capsule was passed during these visits, that is to miss the point." Fritzsche, p. 310.
143 before his death—*Weltbild*, September 10, 1950.
143 to see him—*PM*, October 17, 1946.
143 thick wire netting–Ibid.
143 of a crime—Frischauer, p. 250.
144 during their visits—*Washington Post*, October 17, 1946.
144 suspicious of all—Andrus, p. 125.
144 anything with him—Letter in possession of an American collector.
144 him the poison—*PM*, October 18, 1946.
144 considerable legal skill—Neave, p. 255.
145 know any lawyers—Ibid., p. 72.
145 their nation's misfortune—Smith, p. 82.

145 have been impossible—*PM*, October 19, 1946.

145 all the attorneys—Ibid.

145 and by whom—Ibid.

147 anything against ourselves—*St. Louis Post-Dispatch*, October 17, 1946.

148 as he did—*New York Times*, October 17, 1946.

148 considered him suspect—After writing this, I learned from Col. Henry H. Gerecke, son of Chaplain Gerecke, that this was perhaps not true. Colonel Gerecke told me, "Dad was under investigation for two weeks after Goering's suicide and was under house arrest." It was the Russians, Colonel Gerecke said, who insisted the chaplain had given the poison to Goering. "Dad was a German and a Lutheran, and Goering was a German and a nominal Lutheran, and this was enough for the Russians." The colonel further told me the army was completely satisfied that his father had nothing to do with Goering's suicide, promoting him to major on the very day the investigation came to an end.

148 of his cell—October 18, 1946.

149 of GI soap—April 16, 1951.

149 poison changed hands—Heydecker and Leeb, p. 384.

150 whole goddam setup—Gilbert, *Nuremberg Diary*, p. 114.

151 got the comb—Maser, p. 252.

151 island like Napoleon—von Schirach, p. 87.

151 out in surprise—*Washington Post*, October 19, 1946.

152 not hang me—Goering, p. 306.

152 *eine Kugel geben*—Ibid., p. 305.

152 I am ready—Kelley, p. 71.

152 died that way—*PM*, October 19, 1946.

153 not hang me—Goering, p. 308.

153 God any more—Frischauer, p. 250.

153 who did it—*PM*, October 17, 1946.

153 with the poison—Ibid.

153 to her husband—p. 426.

153 in his cell—Maser, p. 252.

153 capsule at Nuremberg—Böddecker and Winter, p. 176.

154 him at Nuremberg—Ibid., p. 175.

154 poison to him—Ibid., p. 176.

154 in its procuration—Bewley, p. 502. Frau Goering was familiar with Bewley's book and praised it highly in her own book, citing its objectivity and truthfulness. She took no issue with Bewley's assertion that her husband received the poison from a "non-German in the prison."

154 solved for me—Böddecker and Winter, p. 182. In naming Wheelis, it is significant that Dr. Bross thought the American officer was still alive

(one can say anything about a dead person without fear of a libel suit). Dr. Bross wrote me, "I did not know he had died in the meantime. He was a big, healthy, young officer. What happened to him?"

14. The Lieutenant from Texas

157 by the Japanese—Böddecker and Winter, p. 181.
157 some years later—Personal communication from Judge James Wheelis, as are all quotes from Judge Wheelis.
160 in their relationship—Personal communication to the author, as are all quotes from Mrs. Salles.
166 discuss with you—Personal communication to the author, as are all quotes from Colonel Wilson.
169 the prison strongbox—*St. Louis Post-Dispatch*, October 17, 1946.
169 for a bribe—Personal communication to the author.
169 thing to do—Personal communication to the author.
170 with Hitler's lieutenants—Wheelis relished his close association with even the most odious of "Hitler's lieutenants." One of the most revealing photographs in his personal collection of souvenirs shows him with Walter Schellenberg, a former SS and Gestapo general. The impression one gets from the photograph is that the American lieutenant was proudly posing with his favorite movie star. On the back of the picture, Wheelis wrote admiringly that "Walter," as he called him, had become a general in his early thirties. Wheelis was obviously impressed.
171 very mediocre officers—Andrus, p. 68.
172 and military training—Ibid., p. 155.
174 a future sale—There is evidence that Wheelis might have received gifts from other prisoners and their families. "One could smuggle much into the cells," Henriette von Schirach told me, and she recounted several harmless instances in her book. In order for this to have been done, the assistance of an American prison guard would have been necessary. Therefore, it may be of some significance that the one item Mrs. Wheelis did not wish to sell was an antique pocket watch that she had given to her second husband. The original owner, she told me, was Baldur von Schirach. Retained among Jack Wheelis's personal collection of Nuremberg souvenirs were several autographs of von Schirach. A page in a trial-related booklet was signed by the former Hitler Youth leader, "In memory of the many conversations in Cell 29." Another page, signed on January 18, 1946, bore the heading "Three cheers to [sic] Texas!" and the dedication "In memory of the evening conversations as we in Nuremberg met with our lawyers and you told us about Texas."
176 before the executions—Pfluecker, October 25, 1952.

15. Whitewash

180 of a whitewash—Personal communication to the author.

180 in its work—Böddecker and Winter, p. 180.

181 for Goering's suicide—Personal communication to the author.

186 profession a policeman—St. Louis Post-Dispatch, October 27, 1946.

16. The Andrus Papers

192 gold cigarette case—I remembered the gold cigarette case I had purchased from Wheelis's widow. Though she had told me it had belonged to Goering, I was now convinced that it was von Gersdorff's. It seemed unlikely that Dr. Goebbels would have given Goering a cigarette case inscribed only with his name; a more laudatory dedication would have been mandatory.

194 thing as that—But it must have been so! Among the letters received by Andrus after Goering's death were several that suggested Goering's rectum as the hiding place for the poison. Typical was a letter from a woman in Ponca City, Oklahoma, who wrote, "I am only a housewife, but my hunches have always been good. May I suggest that it was hidden in his rectum?" If a housewife in Ponca City had the imagination to suggest the supposed correct hiding place for Goering's poison, it must have been galling to Colonel Andrus to think he had overlooked such an obvious spot.

194 of his mission—Though Colonel Andrus did not attempt to evade the ultimate responsibility for Goering's suicide, I found evidence that he believed Dr. Gilbert, the prison psychologist, had precipitated the suicide by telling Goering the executions were to begin on the night of October 15. "In my heart," wrote Colonel Andrus in the draft of his book, "I believe that this fellow told them they were to be executed right after he went to see them." Contrary to Dr. Gilbert's statement to the board that he last saw Goering on October 13, Andrus mistakenly believed "it was just after his visit with Goering that Goering suddenly opened this little capsule and gulped the poison." It obviously never occurred to Colonel Andrus that Dr. Pfluecker, and not Dr. Gilbert, had told Goering when the hangings were to begin.

196 measured this orifice—According to the draft of Andrus's book, the prisoners were bathed twice a week, "and when they went to the baths, they went by, nude, before the doctor who gave them an examination." A partially concealed poison capsule in Goering's navel would not have escaped detection.

200 this to him—Shortly after I returned from my visit with Burton Andrus, Jr., I wrote to Dr. Roska, asking him to comment on the story that

Goering had had an operation on his navel that allowed him to conceal the poison there. Dr. Roska telephoned me on November 18, 1984, and laughingly dismissed the story as a piece of nonsense. "Someone," he told me, "must have had a rather simplistic view of anatomy to have come up with that."

201 October 11, 1946—Despite my earlier suspicion that Colonel Andrus knew as early as the time of the board's investigation the contents of Goering's letter to him, I could find no evidence for this among his papers. In the draft of his book, Colonel Andrus wrote, "I have never found out to this day what was on this paper. The Quadripartite Commission did not see fit to inform me." Burton Andrus, Jr., assured me that his father, until he received the translation of the letter while writing his book, never knew its contents. "He did discuss the letter with me, and I am confident he did not know nor much care what Goering had written." Perhaps Andrus's indifference to finding the letter, as Zwar described to me, was the result of the colonel's belief that it would, in the long run, make no difference in his presumed responsibility for Goering's suicide.

203 best see fit—The information I found on Dr. Conti's suicide is proof that the "Old Army" was capable of ordering a cover-up of facts embarrassing to it.

17. Conclusions

211 such a man—It is difficult for me to assign an exact role to Dr. Pfluecker in Goering's suicide. But I am sure of one thing: if he collaborated in any way, his role was secondary. I think it is likely that Pfluecker was responsible for planting the letter to Colonel Andrus in Goering's cell, either before or after the suicide. I believe that Pfluecker informed Goering the executions were to begin at midnight October 15, rather than at the traditional hour of dawn. Of all the defendants, only Goering seemed to have this information. I am suspicious of Pfluecker's motives in giving Goering less than the normal dosage of sleeping pills on the night of October 15. His explanation to the board that he did so because he did not wish Goering to be awakened one-half hour later and "maybe get excited" makes little sense. In my opinion, it is more likely that Pfluecker did not wish to dull Goering's mind and reflexes during the last hours. I believe that Pfluecker, at the very least, knew Goering was going to kill himself with poison. If he did know this, I do not believe the doctor would have lifted a finger to prevent it from happening. Indeed, after he was summoned to the cell on the night of October 15, Dr. Pfluecker simply informed the guard that Goering was dying and

nothing could be done. All he did was take Goering's pulse. This was in marked contrast to his frantic efforts to revive the moribund Dr. Ley a year before. Then Dr. Pfluecker had given Ley "two injections, one cc. of Cardiazol and one cc. of Lobulin, and tried artificial respiration." Heydecker and Leeb, p. 86.

BIBLIOGRAPHY

BOOKS

Andrus, Burton C. *I Was the Nuremberg Jailer*. New York: Coward-McCann, 1969.

Baillie, Hugh. *High Tension*. New York: Harper Brothers, 1959.

Bewley, Charles. *Hermann Goering and the Third Reich*. New York: Devin-Adair Co., 1962.

Brown, Anthony C. *The Last Hero: Wild Bill Donovan*. New York: Times Books, 1982.

Böddecker, Guenter, and Ruediger Winter. *Die Kapsel*. Düsseldorf: Econ-Verlag, 1979.

Conot, Robert E. *Justice at Nuremberg*. New York: Harper and Row, Publishers, 1983.

Davidson, Eugene. *The Trial of the Germans*. New York: Macmillan, 1966.

Fishman, Jack. *The Seven Men of Spandau*. New York: Rinehart and Co., 1954.

Frischauer, Willi. *The Rise and Fall of Hermann Goering*. New York: Ballantine Books, 1951.

Fritzsche, Hildegard. *Vor dem Tribunal der Sieger*. Preussisch Oldendorf: K. W. Schuetz, Verlag, 1981.

Gilbert, Gustave M. *Nuremberg Diary*. New York: Farrar, Straus and Co., 1947.

—— *The Psychology of Dictatorship*. New York: Ronald Press Co., 1950.

Goebbels, Joseph. *The Goebbels Diaries 1942–1943*. Edited and translated by Louis P. Lochner. Garden City, N.Y.: Doubleday and Co., 1948.

Goering, Emmy. *An der Seites meines Mannes*. Preussisch Oldendorf: K. W. Schuetz, Verlag, 1972.

Gritzbach, Erich. *Hermann Goering, Werk und Mensch*. Munich: Zentral Verlag der NSDAP, 1938.

Guderian, Heinz. *Panzer Leader*. New York: Ballantine Books, 1965.

Heydecker, Joe J., and Johannes Leeb. *The Nuremberg Trial*. Cleveland: World Publishing Co., 1962.

Johnson, Thomas M. *Collecting the Edged Weapons of the Third Reich*. Vol. 2. Columbia, S.C.: R. L. Bryan Co., 1976.

Kahn, Leo. *Nuremberg Trials*. New York: Ballantine Books, 1972.

Kelley, Douglas M. *22 Cells in Nuremberg*. New York: Greenberg, 1947.

Lang, Jochen von. *The Secretary: Martin Bormann, the Man Who Manipulated Hitler*. New York: Random House, 1979.

Manvell, Roger, and Heinrich Fraenkel. *Goering*. New York: Simon and Schuster, 1962.

Maser, Werner. *Nuremberg: A Nation on Trial*. New York: Charles Scribner's Sons, 1979.

241

Mosley, Leonard. *The Reich Marshal*. Garden City, N.Y.: Doubleday and Co., 1974.
Neave, Airey, *On Trial at Nuremberg*. Boston: Little, Brown and Co., 1978.
Oechsner, Frederick. *This is the Enemy*. Boston: Little, Brown and Co., 1942.
Papen, Franz von. *Memoirs*. New York: E. P. Dutton and Co., 1953.
Schirach, Henriette von. *The Price of Glory*. London: Frederick Muller, 1960.
Schmidt, Paul. *Hitler's Interpreter*. London: William Heinemann, 1951.
Shirer, William L. *Berlin Diary*. New York: Alfred A. Knopf, 1941.
Smith, Bradley F. *Reaching Judgment at Nuremberg*. New York: Basic Books, 1977.
Speer, Albert. *Inside the Third Reich*. New York: Macmillan, 1970.
Wilamowitz-Moellendorff, Fanny Graefin von. *Carin Goering*. Berlin: Verlag von Martin Warneck, 1934.

PERIODICALS

Gerecke, Henry F. "I Walked to the Gallows with the Nazi Chiefs." *Saturday Evening Post*, September 1, 1951.
Pfluecker, Ludwig. "Als Gefängnisarzt in Nürnberg." *Waldeckische Landeszeitung*, in serial from October 4 to October 29, 1952.
Powers, Jimmy. "The Powerhouse." *Washington Times-Herald*, April 21, 1947.
"Das wussten Sie nicht von Nürnberg." *Weltbild*, in serial from September to October 1950, exact dates unknown.
"Dawn without Tears." *Time*, October 28, 1946.
"How Goering Died." *Time*, April 16, 1951.
"Nuremberg: Last Laugh." *Newsweek*, October 28, 1946.
"P.S. to Nuremberg." *Newsweek*, November 4, 1946.

NEWSPAPERS

Almost every major newspaper gave front-page coverage to Goering's suicide and its aftermath. Newspapers used in preparing this work include
Daily Mail (London)
Daily Worker
New York Daily News
The New York Times
PM
St. Louis Post-Dispatch
Times (London)
Washington Post
Washington Star

MISCELLANEOUS

Personal and official papers of Col. Burton C. Andrus, commandant of Nuremberg prison. Access to these papers, which include transcripts of Goering's interrogations before he came under the supervision of Colonel Andrus, were made available to me by Col. Burton C. Andrus, Jr.
The Goering-Negrelli letters. A large collection of letters written by Hermann Goering

to Dr. Leo Negrelli between 1924 and 1925. These letters were discovered by me in Munich in 1973.

National Archives. German Documents Section. "Report of Board of Proceedings in Case of Hermann Goering (Suicide) October 1946."

Nazi Conspiracy and Aggression. Vol. 8. Office of United States Chief of Counsel for Prosecution of Axis Criminality. Washington: United States Government Printing Office, 1946.

Nazi Conspiracy and Aggression, Opinion and Judgment. Office of United States Chief of Counsel for Prosecution of Axis Criminality. Washington: United States Government Printing Office, 1947.

INDEX